# Wake Up Call

"Tom Rapsas's *Wake Up Call* is well written. You'll enjoy it. And, from a "regular guy," it gives you imaginative yet practical guidance for finding your way in life. The spiritual traditions all invite us to wake up because unconsciousness is our biggest problem. This book will stir you."

—Thomas Moore, author of *Care of the Soul* and *The Eloquence of Silence*

"If you consider yourself a spiritual seeker but feel lost and alone in your searching, you will discover companionship and guidance in *Wake Up Call: Daily Insights for the Spiritually Curious*. In his thoughtfully detailed commentary on the words of those he has found helpful in his own journey, Tom Rapsas assures us that there are many voices, his own included, that can point the way to the Mystery that beckons us onward in the quest for the fulfillment of our souls longing."

—Tom Stella, author of *Finding God Beyond Religion*

"*Wake Up Call* is a jolt for the soul, a thunderbolt of profound insight, awareness and growth. In this collection of his favorite teachers and writings culled from his columns, Tom Rapsas writes from a place of such deep authenticity and curiosity, one can't help but want to join him on the journey to self-discovery. Together we become attuned to our soul's intention and awaken to our glorious nature."

—Karen Brailsford, author of *Sacred Landscapes of the Soul*

"For the spiritually curious, *Wake Up Call* is contemplative joy. Tom Rapsas questions the universe as a master, exploring the meaning of everyday happenings and providing insight he's found in his journey. His 'regular guy' humility is refreshing and provides a beautiful voice to walk us through these deep contemplations. A wonderful read!!"

—Dana Drake, author of *The Benevolent Universe: The Story of Your Unique Genius*

"Tom Rapsas provides a gallery of spiritual lessons for spiritual seekers to ponder and reflect on. In his book *Wake Up Call*, you'll find a delightful combination of practical and spiritual lessons learned, a recipe for personal happiness and contentment."

—Eiman Al Zaabi, author of *The Art of Surrender* and *Finding Grace*

"*Wake Up Call: Daily Insights for the Spiritually Curious* is well written and well named. The author invites people to look deeper than the demands of the everyday to explore questions ranging from the "silence of God," to questions to ask before death, to ways to meditate, to getting old and more. Calling his work a kind of *Reader's Digest* of spiritual texts proves quite accurate. He invokes scholars and saints and people in between, Christians, Buddhists and more. The author's own curiosity pays off, the reader is introduced to a number of questions, practices and reliable religious guides for deeper spiritual journeying. Bon Voyage!"

—Matthew Fox, author of *Creation Spirituality*

"Tom Rapsas calls on us to wake up to the spiritual treasures within us and around us, and every page of his eminently practical book rings out with insight, inspiration, and instruction. Whatever path you're on, whatever your soul yearns for, you're sure to find spiritual sustenance in this banquet of offerings."

—Philip Goldberg, author of *American Veda* and *Spiritual Practice for Crazy Times*

# Tom Rapsas

# WAKE
# UP
# CALL

 Wildhouse
Publications

Published by Wildhouse Publications, an imprint of Wildhouse
Publishing (www.wildhousepublishing.com). No part of this book may
be reproduced in any manner without the written permission from
the publisher, except in brief quotations embodied in critical articles
or reviews. Contact info@wildhousepublishing.com.

Design by Melody Stanford Martin

Printed in the USA

All Rights Reserved

ISBN 978-1-961741-04-1

*For Laney and Jade*

# Contents

WEEK ONE . . . . . . . . . . . . . . . . . . . . . . . . . . . . . 1

WEEK TWO. . . . . . . . . . . . . . . . . . . . . . . . . . . 25

WEEK THREE . . . . . . . . . . . . . . . . . . . . . . . . 47

WEEK FOUR . . . . . . . . . . . . . . . . . . . . . . . 71

WEEK FIVE . . . . . . . . . . . . . . . . . . . . . . . 91

WEEK SIX. . . . . . . . . . . . . . . . . . . . . . . 109

WEEK SEVEN . . . . . . . . . . . . . . . . . . . . . 131

WEEK EIGHT . . . . . . . . . . . . . . . . . . . . . 151

WEEK NINE. . . . . . . . . . . . . . . . . . . . . . 171

WEEK TEN. . . . . . . . . . . . . . . . . . . . . . 193

WEEK ELEVEN. . . . . . . . . . . . . . . . . . . 213

WEEK TWELVE . . . . . . . . . . . . . . . . . . 235

WEEK THIRTEEN . . . . . . . . . . . . . . . . 255

WEEK FOURTEEN. . . . . . . . . . . . . . . . 275

WEEK FIFTEEN . . . . . . . . . . . . . . . . . 297

WEEK SIXTEEN . . . . . . . . . . . . . . . . . 319

# WAKE UP CALL
## Daily Insights for the Spiritually Curious

———

### Week One

Day 1: Inspiration

Day 2: Awareness

Day 3: Character

Day 4: Calling

Day 5: Practice

Day 6: Inner Work

Day 7: Contemplation

### Weeks Two to Sixteen

*Repeat*

# Introduction

I'm what you might call a "regular guy." For virtually all my adult life, I've worked a nine-to-five job in an office. My wife and I have been married for more than twenty-five years, we have a house in the suburbs, and our daughter is in college. I cherish our family vacations and my morning runs along the Jersey Shore, as well as a hot cup of coffee in the morning and a pint of cold craft beer at night.

Yet, like many of you, I'm deeply curious about all things spiritual. My spiritual quest started in my twenties and has continued throughout my life. Raised Roman Catholic and force-fed religion during my youth, I had abandoned all religious or spiritual pursuits by the time I graduated high school. But all that changed when, a few years into my career in advertising, I began to wonder if there might be more to life than the daily cycle of work-home-sleep-repeat.

As I grappled with the mystery that is life, I didn't quit my job and jump on a plane to India, join a cult, or sequester myself in a monastery. My nine-to-five routine continued. But beneath the surface, a shift began to take place beneath my "regular guy" persona. I began to read voraciously, everything from books on Buddhism, Hinduism, and the Jesus teachings I grew up on, to the latest spirituality bestsellers, self-help columns and human-interest stories in my local newspaper.

Some things I read failed to strike a chord, but a lot of what I learned resonated deeply within me. I eventually came to a realization: true wisdom, or what you might call "words to live by," couldn't be found in a single magical book or a particular religion or one enlightened spiritual teacher. True wisdom is found in many places and comes from many sources.

I started writing about my spiritual explorations in 2010, penning stories for the online publications *Elephant Journal* and *Contemplative Journal*. In 2012, I began writing the weekly *Wake Up Call* column at Patheos.com, specifically addressing topics related to spirituality in everyday life. The book you're now holding includes many of my top stories.

Some of these stories stirred controversy among my diverse group of readers, as I wandered outside the lines and challenged some traditional religious beliefs. But many of my columns seemed to meet a real need for my fellow wisdom-seekers, resulting in scores of positive comments and social media shares. Gathered here in book form are 112 of these stories, which include fan favorites, several that were controversial, and many that are especially important or meaningful to me. Each one holds a message that I believe is worth repeating.

As I compiled and reviewed the hundreds of stories I've written over the years, one thing stood out. While every column falls loosely under the umbrella of "spirituality," they cover a lot of ground. The reason? To me, there's more to spirituality than matters of the spirit and soul—although these are vital aspects. If your spirituality is genuine, you're not just concerned with your own personal development. You care about the impact you have on those around you, including your family, friends, and community. A person committed to the spiritual path takes a full-circle view of life, knowing that it's not just about their own inner well-being, but also the values and character they bring to the world.

Like me, you may find yourself troubled by news reports of misbehaving yogi masters exploiting their students, the abhorrent behavior of clergy covered up by religious institutions, and the selfishness and greed that seem so widespread among many who claim to be "of the cloth." But instead of walking away from spirituality and the quest to find meaning in life, people like you and me can simply step up and carve out our own path. We are our own best gurus. And there's no better classroom than the world around us.

On a personal note, for many years one of my best classrooms has been a bus. On a daily basis, at least until the COVID-19 pandemic hit the US in March 2020, I commuted in and out of New York City for a couple of decades, spending four hours a day on public transit. During that time, I read a lot. And I do mean *a lot.* A NJ Transit bus was the backdrop for most of the stories you're about to read, as I took what I learned from each book, article and occasional podcast, and attempted to distill its essence into a single, short, filler-free story. This may be why my *Wake Up Call* column at Patheos.com has been called "a spiritual *Reader's Digest.*"

You'll find there are some authors I lean on heavily for wisdom and guidance. Life philosopher and philanthropist John Templeton is one of my favorites, especially when it come to matters of character. So is my go-to expert on all matters related to the soul, Thomas Moore. Then, there's Richard Rohr, who has given me a fresh perspective on what it means to be a Christian. And no one has done more to broaden my view of religion than the interspiritual writer Mirabai Starr.

But I also find inspiration in other places. It might come from a newspaper article or a documentary film, a church sermon or advice from a friend. Like John Gray, an 89-year-old American living in France. He was a regular reader who responded to my stories frequently and in doing so passed along much wise advice to me in his final years. Wisdom often comes to me when I least expect it, like when I wrote a story about a love manifesto scrawled in magic marker on an abandoned phone booth in midtown Manhattan.

I've also had a couple of personal experiences that transcended ordinary life, where it was revealed to me that there was more to the world than what can be seen with the naked eye or interpreted by the brain. They are experiences that took mere seconds to unfold but left indelible marks on the way I view the world.

We've all had times when we sensed a greater presence both within us and around us, a feeling of awe and wonder that made us believe there was a powerful life force in our midst. Some of these moments almost sound cliché, that is, until you experience them for yourself. It can happen when you're holding a newborn baby or witnessing an otherworldly sunset or getting a lifechanging medical diagnosis. Life is full of windows that give us a glimpse of this greater power.

Then, there are experiences that defy logical explanation and seem to indicate the real presence of the Divine in our lives. It's a sense that something greater than ourselves might be pulling the strings. You may have experienced this feeling through an uncanny coincidence or a synchronicity that put you on a new life path or reaffirmed the course you're already on. These wake-up calls of life give us the ability to see the world in new ways.

While I have had my fair share of synchronicities, there are two specific events in my life that took me beyond my normal range of reason into the realm of the unexplainable. They are moments where I believe this life force, one that I recognize as God, interceded in my life.

The first moment happened in 1993 when I heard the voice of God, or at least I believed it was his/her voice. (I see God as gender neutral.) I was living in Houston and had just completed a 6-mile run in Memorial Park. The weather was overcast and misty. As I walked slowly to cool off, everything around me went quiet. A voice came into my head, one I swear to you was not my own. It gave me a set of explicit instructions that would lead me to move halfway across the country and reconnect with the woman I would later marry.

If you had told me the day before that I would take the steps necessary to make this happen, I would have told you "never in a million years." Aside from being just plain weird, it involved moving to New York City, near my childhood home, a place I swore I would never live again. But the voice was so clear and commanding, I felt I had to listen to it. I was certain it had my best interests in mind.

Ever since that day, I thought the voice might return with further guidance, but I have not heard it again—well, at least not that clearly and distinctly. I sometimes wonder why, but perhaps it was only to give me a needed course correction in life, through a message I could not ignore. It put me on a very different life path than the one I was on, and I have continued on that path to this day.

There is another even more bizarre story where I believe God revealed himself/herself to me. I have rarely shared this story because it is so unusual and haunting. The event it recounts rattled me so deeply that I told no one about it for many years after it happened, not even to those closest to me. It goes like this:

I was living in a small town on the Jersey Shore where I ran a 4-mile course on a regular basis. My 5-year-old daughter had just learned to ride her bike, on which she would sometimes accompany me on my morning jog. Since she was new to bicycling and was still learning the rules of the road, I kept a close eye on her, warning her when to stop and steering her well out of the way of any oncoming traffic. Then, one morning she got away from me.

We were coming up a short hill at the top of which we would make a left turn onto what passed for the main street in our hometown. There's a wide shoulder there, so normally we had plenty of room to make the left and be clear of any oncoming traffic. Only on this day, there was a large moving truck parked where we were about to turn.

Coming up the hill, my daughter had a sudden burst of energy and raced ahead of me. Even though I yelled for her to stop, she pedaled onward—making the left turn as she usually did until she was out of sight behind the truck. A split-second later a car driven by an elderly man zoomed by in the very lane of traffic my daughter had just entered.

I sprinted to see beyond the parked truck, terrified of what I would find, my heart jumping out of my chest. I could not imagine how she could have avoided being hit by the speeding car. But there she was, sitting on her bike, a few feet onto the road, her head turned toward me. She was fine. How had the car missed her?

I might have accepted this as an error of perception, but what happened next shook me to my core. She turned to me and asked, "Am I dead, Daddy?" I gave her a hug, told her no, and we headed home. I was so shaken by this "near miss" that I told no one, not even my wife. I didn't sleep a wink that night, replaying the event over and over in my head. Had my little girl somehow found a sliver of space between the moving truck and oncoming car? Had the old man swerved to miss her? Still, even if that had been the case, it did not explain her question to me, "Am I dead?"

Many years have passed and my daughter is now a young adult. When I told her about the event about ten years after it happened, it was the first time I had mentioned it to anybody since that day. She had absolutely no recollection of any of it, not the near-miss or the question she had posed to me—but I can tell you I remember every moment as vividly as if it happened yesterday.

Over the years, I've tried to come up with theories as to what happened that morning. There's the "Many Worlds Theory" that posits that reality is a "many-branched tree" where every possible outcome of an event happens. In one universe, my daughter is struck by the car. But mercifully in this world, the one I am aware of, she came through unscathed, though she had some inkling of this alternate vision of reality—explaining why she had asked me that haunting question.

Still I wonder, on that day, at that moment, had the Divine interceded here on earth, saving one life and preventing the ruination of my life and the life of my wife? Was this a sign of God making his or her presence known?

I believe so, but I'll let you be the judge.

# A Guide to Reading
## *Wake Up Call*

You may have played the game in which everyone chooses the five people they would invite to a dinner party. Or maybe you'll like my version better: "If you could have a beer or coffee with just one person, who would that person be?" Think of this book as a means to finding new answers to that question. By the time you get to the end of the book, you will have been introduced to over a hundred people of various spiritual stripes, many of whom you'll want to get to know better. Consider *Wake Up Call* an introduction. You might want to have an imaginary drink with them, or perhaps pick up one of their books. I hope you'll choose a few of the fascinating people you're about to meet and take the time to learn more about them and their work. If they're still alive, you might even reach out to them, as I did to a few people featured in this book. You never know; they might just reply.

As you begin to read *Wake Up Call*, you'll find the stories are spread across seven broad categories, one for each day of the week. If you read a story a day, that adds up to sixteen weeks-worth of stories or roughly the length of a college semester. My editor thought it would be a cool idea to present this book as a course in everyday spirituality—not just for college students, but for lifelong learners. But don't be compelled to read one story a day. Feel free to read multiple stories each day. Skip a few days. Or binge read the entire book. Read at whatever pace is comfortable for you.

The categories of stories in *Wake Up Call* are broken down like this:

**Day 1: Inspiration**

**Day 2: Awareness**

**Day 3: Character**

**Day 4: Calling**

**Day 5: Practice**

**Day 6: Inner Work**

**Day 7: Contemplation**

Next, I'll give you a brief explanation as to what you can expect to find in each of these categories. But I should warn you that sometimes the lines between these categories can get a little hazy and in a funny way, each category connects to the next. For instance, you might be inspired (day 1) to become more aware (day 2). Your self-awareness can lead to a renewed calling in life (day 4), which may lead you to develop new spiritual practices (day 5). For the spiritually engaged person, it's all connected.

I think of this as 360-degree approach to spirituality. I hope that by reading this book you develop a richer and fuller spiritual life by realizing that spirituality is a part of every phase of life. To become more spiritual, you don't have to quit your job, shave your head, or trade in your jeans for a saffron robe. If you want to do those things, go for it!

But I've found it is possible to engage and embrace the spiritual side of your self—often called "the inner life"—all day, every day, from the moment you wake up in the morning to the time you go to bed at night—and all the moments in between. Occasionally, it may even pop up in your dreams.

Here's a quick rundown of the daily categories in this book:

**Day 1. Inspiration.** We all can use an inspiring read now and then. These stories are designed to lift your spirit, get you ready for the day ahead, or help you reflect once the day is done. Many of these stories offer you direct advice, while a few give you a glimpse of what others do to get inspired.

**Day 2. Awareness.** If inspiration is about looking outward, these stories are more about looking inward and navigating your own interior landscape. Sometimes seeing a fresh perspective is all it takes to change the way you view the world around you.

**Day 3. Character.** What do you bring to the people in your life? Are you humble, kind, and compassionate? Are you true to yourself? Do you regularly express gratitude? These stories will help guide you to becoming the best possible version of yourself.

**Day 4: Calling.** Are you on the right path in life? From setting a course, to reevaluating your path, to making the most of your years on this planet—these stories reflect the ways spirituality intersects with the major choices we all make in life.

**Day 5: Practice.** Spirituality doesn't happen in a vacuum; we often need a gentle prodding to help us both recognize and celebrate our spiritual nature. These stories can guide you in recognizing your own spiritual essence and help you develop, or strengthen, your personal spiritual practice.

**Day 6: Inner Work.** As spiritual people, some of the most important work we can do centers around engaging in specific spiritual activities. These stories explore various types of prayer, meditation techniques, mindfulness and breathing exercises that can help ground you and connect you with the Divine life force within us all.

**Day 7: Christian Contemplation.** The final day of the week is about God, religion and faith. I'll also touch on Jesus, with atypical stories that explore the Jesus they often don't tell you about in church. With sources that include the gnostic gospels, Christian mystics, and transcendentalists like Ralph Waldo Emerson, you'll get a taste of the contemplative dimension of the Christian faith.

Are you ready? Let's get started.

# WEEK ONE

## How to Squeeze More Juice from the Orange That Is Life

When was the last time someone asked you how you were doing, and you responded, "I'm busy." We seem to do it all the time. The essayist and cartoonist Tim Kreider has an interesting take on the pride we seem to feel about our "busy" lives. He points out that while this busyness may make us feel important, there's also a huge downside to our nonstop activity—it takes away from our ability to be lazy.

Now, one person's lazy is another person's downtime, and Kreider is no slouch. He's an accomplished author who writes and draws at least five hours a day before indulging in more leisurely pursuits. He refers to this downtime as a necessity. Here's why: When we're being lazy it allows us to step back, survey the world, and figure things out before moving on to our next order of busyness.

There's just one problem for many of us: As much as we'd like to, we don't have time to be lazy. We're busy with kids, a never-ending series of "to do" lists and time-eating, forty-plus-hour-a-week jobs. So how do we squeeze more juice out of our busy lives? How do we live a more fully engaged and spiritual life, when our hectic schedule is always threatening to overwhelm us?

## IF YOU CAN'T ESCAPE THE BUSYNESS, TRY STOPPING OR SLOWING THE CLOCK.

If it feels like your life is going by in a blur, it may be time to reset your internal clock. The Catholic Benedictine monk David Steindl-Rast has a phrase he uses each morning upon awakening: This is a wonderful day. I've never seen this one before. This very simple act has a way of pointing out that no day is the same; each one is new and deserves our rapt attention.

Steindl-Rast also has advice on how we should look at the day ahead. We should be grateful for each moment, even the ones we might normally see as busy-work. It's a three-step process called Stop-Look-Go and it works like this. When you find yourself mindlessly not tuned in to your actions or surroundings:

1. Stop what you're doing; freeze in place for a moment.
2. Look around you; be fully present with your sight, your ears, your touch.
3. Go ahead with your activity but do it alert and aware of each move you make.

*"We only live in one space: the present. It is important to live where we are at this very moment as fully as we can." — Ivon Prefontaine*

What's it like to live fully in the moment? In his book *Becoming Who You Are*, bestselling author and Jesuit priest James Martin tells the story of the writer Andres Dubus and his reflections on encountering the holy in his daily life. It started innocently enough when Dubus was making lunch for his children one morning before school, something most of us would see as a chore. He sensed that there was more to his actions than he realized:

Each moment is a sacrament, this holding of plastic bags, of knives, of bread, of cutting board, this pushing of the chair, this spreading of mustard on bread, this trimming of liverwurst, of ham. All sacraments.

Finding the sacred in sandwich-making is a hint as to how we might look at many of our "I'm busy" activities. Might giving your kid a ride to a friend's house be a chance for conversation and bonding? Might washing the dishes be an opportunity to engage in silent prayer or meditation? Might even the dullest workplace chore be a chance to notice and connect with those around you?

Much like Dubus, in his groundbreaking book *A Religion of One's Own*, psychotherapist (and former monk) Thomas Moore talks of consciously engaging in sacraments in our everyday lives. He tells us that Henry David Thoreau believed that "just getting up early can be a sacrament, a spiritual act." Moore advises us to plan for these moments each day, tacking them on to our regular schedule:

> Instead of just letting your days unfold spontaneously or being at the mercy of an inflexible, busy schedule ... set up a few regular activities, like meditation before breakfast, listening to music before lunch, being quiet after ten p.m., eating simply in the morning and taking a quiet walk afterward, if only for five or ten minutes.

If you find yourself in the midst of a long workweek and have a ton of obligations outside the office to boot, there's just one option. Start getting more out of each moment, being mindful of each step and each action you take. We are best served by remembering the wise words of the Persian philosopher Omar Khayyam: "Be happy for this moment. This moment is your life."

## WEEK ONE / DAY 2: AWARENESS

# The Greatest Gift You Can Give Another (Today and Every Day)

I'm sure that at some point you've witnessed this scene. You're out to dinner and glance over at the table next to you—only to see the entire family with their heads buried in their phones. Mom, Dad, teenage daughter, even preteen son. If you're like me, you find something unsettling with this picture.

In my own home, we have an unspoken rule that bans smartphones and iPads from the dinner table. I once had someone tell me that she goes a step further— she and her husband ban Internet devices from the bedroom. No TV either. This may sound over-the-top, but maybe it's not. Because when you take away the external distractions, that allows you to be fully present to the person you're with. That's important because as author Richard Moss points out:

**THE GREATEST GIFT YOU CAN GIVE ANOTHER IS THE PURITY OF YOUR ATTENTION.**

Giving someone your full attention includes listening to what they have to say. As my wife occasionally reminds me, **there's a difference between listening and waiting to speak.** When you're truly listening, you're tuning in not just to the words of the speaker, but also to the feelings behind the words. You can sense the true meaning of what the person across from you is trying to get across.

The fact is, the person you're communicating with can usually sense when you're paying full attention, as opposed to allowing their words to pass through one ear and out the other. When the person talking to you senses you are truly listening, they know their words and thoughts are valued. It enhances their feelings of self-worth, making them feel better about themselves—and about you.

Do you have trouble listening to others? Moss advises us that one key to being good at undistracted listening is to engage in a regular meditation practice. This helps build "the muscle of attention." When we strengthen our ability to observe our thoughts and calm our mind through meditation, we're better able to focus on the person conversing with us, without "spacing out" or having our minds wander off.

Moss tells us we can then go a step further with a practice he calls "Sacred Attention." In this exercise, while conversing with another, keep your focus on your breath and visualize positive energy or "God's infinite love." Then, let this love flow through your entire being to the other person. For both parties, the result can be "sensations like warmth or heat, tingling or pressure, as well as a sense of love."

## Two Small Gifts You Can Give to Any Stranger: REP and The Wave.

Paying better attention to friends and loved ones is one thing. But how can you better connect with those you meet in passing, perhaps at the library, or local supermarket, or while driving through town? Here are two ideas.

One way to affably engage with the people you encounter daily is through a practice centered around the acronym REP. It stands for Recognize, Encourage, Praise and it works like this.

- **Recognize** by saying hello, making eye contact, and smiling
- **Encourage** by saying a kind word
- **Praise** those adding anything of value to the world, like complimenting the job they're doing or even their sense of fashion.

There's another small gesture you can make that increases civility and our connectedness to those around us. It's called the wave. The idea comes from the author and life philosopher Seth Godin and it's a simple act that can help each of us do our small part to make the world a better place. Here's Godin's short essay on "The Wave" in its entirety:

> When someone lets you into the flow of traffic,
> or holds a door,
>
> or takes a second to acknowledge you,
>
> it's possible to smile and offer a wave in response.
>
> This, of course, costs you nothing.
>
> It creates a feeling of connection, which is valuable.
>
> It makes it more likely that people will treat someone else well in the future.
>
> And it might just brighten your day.
>
> The simplest antidote to a tough day is generosity.
>
> Waves are free, and smiles are an irresistible bonus.

**WEEK ONE / DAY 3: CHARACTER**

# Five Essential Laws for Living a Righteous Life

As we grow spiritually, we can sometimes get ahead of ourselves. We may think of ourselves as spiritual, because we're reading the latest spirituality best-sellers, taking yoga classes, or engaging in a meditation practice. But we can sometimes forget the basics—the simple daily acts that can enrich our lives and the lives of those around us.

I was reminded of this recently by one of Sir John Templeton's writings. While best known as one of the great financial masterminds of our time, Templeton was also a life-long spiritual seeker and teacher. He took the lessons he learned throughout his life and turned them into several classic books, including *The Worldwide Laws of Life* and *Wisdom from World Religions*.

In *Discovering the Laws of Life*, Templeton laid out "200 basic laws" that might be considered rules to live by. They're comprised of "universal principles present in every society and every religion" and each has the ring of truth. In fact, five of the first six laws Templeton mentions should be etched on our daily "to do" lists—and become an integral part of our personal spiritual journey.

## FIVE ESSENTIAL LAWS FOR LIVING A RIGHTEOUS LIFE

1. **Treat others as you would like them to treat you.** It's known as the Golden Rule and may be the most important law of life. We can't expect others to treat us with kindness and respect unless we offer the same to them. And while they may not always reciprocate, by leading with a smile and a friendly demeanor you greatly enhance the odds they will.

2. **Really listen to those who talk to you.** Instead of simply waiting for your turn to talk, be an active listener, staying focused on the person speaking to you. In Templeton's words: "When you truly show an interest in another person and really listen, without constantly referring to yourself, you have begun a relationship that will only grow stronger over time."

3. **To be loved, love others.** According to Templeton, like the sun, love is a source of limitless energy that "lies deep at the

center of our being." When we allow this energy to flow from us to others "our lives become brighter" and so do the lives of others. To get love, give love. This applies to loved ones, friends, acquaintances and even strangers. And don't forget your pets.

4. **Give thanks and you'll have more to be thankful for.** Each morning or night, say a prayer of gratitude for all the good that is in your life. The late religious scholar Huston Smith had a simple but effective daily prayer that covers all the bases: "God you are so good to me." As Templeton says, when you have "an attitude of gratitude" and praise the good, you draw even more goodness into your life.

5. **Give to life and you'll find life gives back to you.** Just like a mirror, what you reflect out to the world is reflected back to you. So, Templeton advises us to "reflect love, joy, peace, patience, kindness, goodness." It lets others know they can trust you and can make each encounter you have with another person a positive experience.

I've listed five of the first six laws Templeton wrote about in *Discovering the Laws of Life*. The one I left out is a pretty good as well: You cannot be lonely if you help the lonely. If you find yourself spending more time alone than you want to, reach out to anyone you know who may be in the same situation. The benefits work both ways.

**WEEK ONE / DAY 4: CALLING**

# Five Clues to Knowing Your Path in Life

How do you walk through life? Are you sure-footed with a specific destination in mind? Or do you meander, unsure of your direction or exactly where you're headed?

Every now and then, you'll hear about a friend or acquaintance who has "found their calling." And when you hear those words spoken, it might cause you to wonder: Does everyone really have their own calling, even me? Spiritual philosopher David Spangler says yes! In his words: "We *all* possess a gift or talent that we are attracted to and enjoy doing ... this gift ultimately connects us to others. This is our calling."

Yet, while Spangler may make it sound easy, determining the precise "gift or talent" that connects you with others can be difficult. Here are just a few of the questions that might come up when looking for your life's purpose:

- How do I know which gift or talent is my calling?
- How do I incorporate this gift or talent into my life?
- What if following my calling makes my life more difficult?

There are no flashing road signs to alert us that we're on the right path—or tell us when it's time to make a mid-life course correction. We need to figure this out for ourselves and determine how we can build a life with meaning and purpose, one that makes the most of our own potential.

The five clues below don't provide all the answers, but they may help you get closer to discovering your calling. They may also provide you with the motivation you need to put your calling into practice.

## CLUE #1. WHEN LOOKING FOR YOUR PATH, THE FIRST PLACE TO SEARCH IS WITHIN.

From Ram Dass to Jon Kabat-Zinn, many spiritual leaders believe the answers we all seek can be found within. So, what's the secret to tapping into this internal source of knowledge? You can start by quieting your mind, through meditation or prayer, and once settled, contemplate what you were meant to do in this life. Spiritual author Carolyn Myss tells us that, with patience, "the path will reveal itself."

There's another important component to finding the answers you seek: have faith that you will find them. You need to believe the answers are available to you or they will continue to remain a mystery. In *The Spirit of Happiness, Discovering God's Purpose for Your Life*, the scholar T. Byram Karasu describes faith like this:

"To believe—to have faith—in God means trusting there is a reason for the existence of everything in his world and beyond, and there is a meaning in its mystery. It means believing that there is a Holy Purpose for you."

## CLUE #2. YOU CAN SEEK HELP FROM A MENTOR OR SOMEONE YOU ADMIRE.

If you don't have a person to emulate or seek advice from in your own life, find a public figure you admire—then read all you can about him or her, including any available autobiographies. Doing this may help you intuit how these people might have seized opportunities similar to those occurring in your own life.

The inspirational blogger James Altucher, who has written a lot about mentorship, came to a similar conclusion. His takeaway: You don't actually need a living, breathing mentor at your side to receive the expert guidance you need. According to Altucher:

Everyone wants a mentor. I picture some old guy saying, 'Ha ha, here's how we did it in my day. Here's what you should do.' and then he lays out the secret mystical formula for life fulfillment. It doesn't work that way. Everything in life is your mentor. Think of everything you see or do as mentoring you.

## CLUE #3. YOUR PATH OR PURPOSE CAN EMERGE IN ONE OF MANY DIFFERENT WAYS.

In her book *The Wisdom to Know the Difference*, Eileen Flanagan tells us of an Episcopalian group of laypeople on a mission: to uncover the best way to find "God's purpose for our lives." To do this, they read through a ton of scripture and spiritual autobiographies. Their conclusion? Our purpose comes to us not in one way, but in one of many ways. Flanagan writes:

"Our purpose can emerge through a gnawing feeling that we need to do a specific thing. On occasion, it can burst forth as a sudden awareness of a path that God would have us take. Our call may be emphatic and unmistakable, or it may be obscure and subtle. In whatever way our call is experienced, God has chosen to speak to us and bids us to listen."

## CLUE #4. DON'T LET OBSTACLES STOP YOU, JUST KEEP MOVING FORWARD.

Pastor Joe Quatrone, Jr. writes that at some point in life we may be on the right path—and then the going gets tough. Our path may not move in a straight line and we may even find it littered with stones or boulders we have to climb over or around to get back on track. In Quatrone's words:

"The journey of life is not paved in blacktop; it is not brightly lit like the 'Yellow Brick Road.' It is a rocky path through the wilderness. It is not a linear road where we take one step after another in a straightforward progression. That is not what the road is like. Rather, it is a series of twists and turns, and there is nothing simple or straightforward about it."

Indeed, even the "Yellow Brick Road" was filled with danger and uncertainty. Yet once we get past the rough patches, we almost always come out stronger on the other side, learning character-building lessons along the way. The important thing is to keep your eye on your destination. Should you ever feel you have lost your way, pause for contemplation and renewed direction. And remember: Patience is key.

## CLUE #5. WHEN YOU ARE ON YOUR TRUE PATH, YOU'LL KNOW IT. (LIFE BECOMES EASIER.)

———

*"It is the toughest task you will ever face. But once you define your purpose, the meaning of your life will become clearer and all other tasks, no matter how difficult they may seem, will become easier."* — Bryan Karasu

———

The quote above points out that the sooner you're able to uncover the gift or talent that connects you with others, the better. Once your purpose is uncovered, you get to practice getting better at it each day. You can work at being a better coach or mentor, a better veterinarian or volunteer, a better baker or painter, a better [*insert your calling here*].

When you're on your true path, you'll find that you're not only helping to enrich the lives of others, but that this is the key to your own happiness as well. You're doing what you're supposed to be doing, making your own small contribution to the betterment of the world. It's a satisfying feeling.

# A Ten-Step Guide to Leading a More Spiritual Life

*"We are spiritual beings having a human experience."*
— *Pierre Teilhard de Chardin*

Were you once part of a religious tradition that failed to meet your spiritual needs? Did you leave the tradition you grew up with because you found you couldn't relate to the stale rituals and centuries-old dogma? Or have you never been a part of any tradition, but consider yourself a spiritual person?

If you answer yes to any of these questions, you might classify yourself as "spiritual but not religious" (SBNR)—and you may also feel there's a void in your life. You have a spiritual yearning at your core that often goes unfulfilled, a thirst that isn't quite quenched. You may have even tried to satisfy that yearning by trying new houses of worship, only to come up empty.

The key to satisfying this deep-seeded spiritual yearning is to start your own spiritual practice. This practice doesn't replace organized religion, it becomes your religion. It involves engaging in a series of regular activities that both enrich your spiritual awareness and feed your soul—and can be the difference between a satisfying life or one where it feels like something integral is missing.

In the book *A Religion of One's Own,* psychotherapist and best-selling author Thomas Moore lays out a blueprint by which you can develop your own spiritual practice, a set of rituals you can partake in on a regular basis. It's Moore's belief that "we need a new way to be religious, a really new way. A way that honors the traditions of the past but moves on."

13

What follows is a summary of the main tenets found in *A Religion of One's Own*, a ten-point list provided by Moore (with my thoughts following each numbered point). Moore lays out the keys to developing your own daily spiritual practice, by carving out time to accomplish specific, simple tasks or mini rituals throughout the day. He also offers a glimpse of what a "spiritual but not religious" life can be.

## A 10-STEP GUIDE TO LEADING A MORE SPIRITUAL LIFE

1. **Meditate**. Learn a formal way of meditating, or be contemplative in nature, alone, at work, or at home. Meditation is easier than you think. In its most basic form, it centers around one key idea: breathe. During our harried lives, we often begin to breathe shallowly, taking short breaths. Whenever you feel stressed, or sense that life is moving too fast, remember to b-r-e-a-t-h-e. Try it now. Take a deep breath. Repeat.

2. **Live ethically**. Do no harm and make your life a positive contribution to humanity. Work ethically for ethical companies or organizations. Change work if necessary. At least, stay on track toward a highly moral life work. I don't have to tell you there's a lot of bad stuff going on in the world today. It can be hard to figure out how you can personally have an impact. To get started, think small. Focus on the modest acts and activities you can do, in your home, neighborhood and workplace, to make the world a little bit more caring, a little bit better.

3. **Live responsively**. Read the signs for who you are to be and what you are to do. There's a centuries-old Christian devotional exercise called "examen" that involves "discerning God's direction." Each evening, at bedtime, reflect on the day's events and ask yourself two questions: When was I most alive today?

When was I most drained today? Find out what in your life brings you closer to God (a happy place) and which actions take you further from God (an unhappy place).

4. **Have a dream practice**. Dreams give you strong hints about what's going on and how you can adjust. Without them you have no guidance but your own consciousness, which is too limited. Keep a dream journal next to your bed where you can jot down your dreams. They can sometimes give you a glimpse into a deeper part of yourself, illuminating your hopes, desires or deep-seated concerns. To help remember your dreams, before your head hits the pillow, hold a pen and pad in your hands and declare "I will remember and write down my dreams the moment I wake up." Place the pen and pad in an easy to reach place and see if the alternate reality of dreamland is trying to tell you anything.

5. **Be a mystic**. Expand your sense of self through art and wonder. Achieve special states of awareness. Have a greater sense of self through losing yourself. This doesn't have to be complicated. You can be a mystic this evening by sitting outside and gazing up at a sky full of stars. Or by rising early in the morning, when your home is dark and quiet, and engaging in contemplation. Or by spending an afternoon taking a long, slow trek through an art museum, even if that museum is online.

6. **Be intimate with nature**. Especially take daily note of the sky: sun and moon, clouds, weather, planets, stars. Learn from animals. Be astonished by geology and plant life. Getting closer to nature means you need to get outside. Depending on where you live, this may involve a walk through a park, around a lake, along the ocean. As you walk, be perceptive, take in the trees, notice the rhythmic movement of any water, tune in to the sounds and activities of the wildlife. Open your senses wide.

7. **Be a monk (or monkess).** Adapt monasticism of any variety to your daily life and to the world in which you live. Spend time carefully. Read deeply. Study. Honor the book, good food and community. Be especially aware of time and how you use it. Could some of the time you spend mindlessly scanning social media be better spent satisfying the needs of the soul? Read a book or listen to a podcast by someone who inspires you, cook an intricate meal you've always wanted to prepare, or engage in a long conversation with an old friend—not just talking, but really listening.

8. **Aim for bliss.** Not superficial happiness or possessions or wealth. Not entertainment. But bliss: knowing you are in the right place and doing what you are meant to do. Don't settle for shallow material gains. Aspire to deep happiness. And remember, happiness is often found not in our own self-centered actions, but by reaching out to, connecting with, and helping others. When we give to others, we often receive even more in return.

9. **Develop a philosophy and theology of life.** Think about your life. Work out some principles for yourself. Don't follow the crowd. Take the road less taken, the narrow gate, the path you see behind you. Find your own personal path, one that's not dictated by society or family. Your path will be associated with a special gift or talent you have, something that you enjoy and that connects you with others. As I heard someone recently say, we all have at least one superpower. What is yours?

10. **Learn from the world's religions and spiritual traditions.** You don't have to join or believe. Find insights and methods and beautiful expressions and images. Don't separate secular from sacred. Make your own collection of truths and art works. Read the works of the great spiritual leaders from a va-

riety of traditions. If you're interested in Hinduism, check out the *Bhagavad Gita*. If you want a fresh take on the teachings of Jesus, pick up *The Gnostic Gospels* by Elaine Pagels. If you want to know more about Jewish mysticism, read *The Essential Kabbalah* by Daniel C. Matt. Build your own spiritual library, one you can be inspired by again and again.

# Meditation Made Easy (For Those Who Say They Can't Meditate)

Have you ever tried to meditate and found you just couldn't do it? Maybe you like the idea of meditation, are well aware of its benefits, but you just can't get your racing, over-thinking mind to calm down long enough to engage in the practice. This story may help.

Several years ago, I wrote a column titled *How to Meditate Like a Monk in 10 Easy Steps*. The practice was based on a slim paperback book called *Deep Meditation* by Yogani that was (and still is) far and away the best book on meditation I've ever read.

One of the things I like about *Deep Meditation* is Yogani's empathetic approach to meditation. He realizes that we can tend to start thinking about other things when we meditate, self-sabotaging our own meditation practice. So, the author gently, and continuously, reminds the reader that when your mind starts to wander, no problem, just come back to the mantra.

Here are some of Yogani's words which I've paraphrased from the book. I've added a few additional thoughts in parentheses.

## AN EASY NINE-STEP MEDITATION PRACTICE

For most people, twenty minutes is the best duration for a meditation session. (But it's okay to start with five to ten minutes and work your way up from there.) Try it twice a day, once before the morning meal and the day's activity, and then again before the evening meal and the evening's activity. (I make sure, at minimum, to get a morning session in each day.)

1. When sitting for meditation, the first priority is comfort. Don't sit in a way that distracts you from the act of meditation. (Stay away from positions where you might fall asleep.)

2. For your meditation practice, use the thought *I am*. This will be your mantra. (More on mantras below.)

3. While sitting comfortable with your eyes closed, relax. You'll notice thoughts, stream of thoughts. That's fine. Just let them go without minding them. After about a minute, gently introduce the mantra.

4. As soon as you realize you're no longer thinking of the mantra, come back to it.

5. If you get lost in a stream of thoughts, no matter how mundane or profound, just go back to the mantra. Don't make a struggle of it. It's okay not to be on the mantra all the time.

6. Thoughts are a normal part of the meditation process. Just ease back to the mantra again. Deep meditation is going toward, not pushing away from.

7. No struggle. No fuss. No iron willpower or mental heroics are necessary for your meditation practice. All such efforts take away from the simplicity of your practice and will reduce its effectiveness.

8. When you realize you've been off somewhere, just ease back into the mantra again. Go inward with your attention to progressively deeper levels of inner silence.

9. The cycle of thinking about the mantra, losing it, and coming out into a stream of thoughts is a process of purification. It is very powerful and will ultimately yield a constant experience of inner silence in your practice and, more importantly, in your daily activity.

### TRIED THE 10-STEPS AND STILL HAVING TROUBLE MEDITATING?

After using the practice above for several months, for me there was just one hiccup. I found myself falling off the mantra constantly and thinking about anything and everything else, from the workday ahead to the repairman I had to call to an upcoming weekend getaway. My meditation sessions turned into very choppy affairs, my "monkey mind" continuously losing focus and interjecting random thoughts, as many as twenty, thirty, a hundred times over a twenty-minute meditation session.

Then, I discovered the problem. My mantra wasn't working. In *Deep Meditation*, Yogani recommends focusing on the word *Ayam*, or *I am*, while meditating. Most Buddhists favor using "Aum" or "Om" which in your head winds up sounding like *Ommmmmmmmmm*. And that was my issue. The sound just wasn't strong enough for this Western mind to keep random thoughts from flowing in. So, I tried a new mantra, one that had personal meaning to me:

### GOD IS LOVE. LOVE IS GOD.

I repeat this mantra over and over (sometimes replacing it with "Love is Good. Love is God.") There's something about this longer, more verbal mantra that locks me in. As, I repeat the words they create a circular pattern. I sometimes see the words visually flowing as if in a figure eight. And it works. I am now able to go through twenty-minute meditation sessions with nary a disruption, the new mantra acting like a shield that fends off random thoughts.

Now, there's no need to take my mantra as your mantra—unless these words also have special meaning for you. Your words may be "Jack and Jill went up a hill" repeated over and over. Find the phrase that works best for you, something that's easy to repeat and could be as simple as "I love my family, my family loves me."

Why meditate? I don't know how or why it works, but for me it's like a reboot to the system. I compare it to restarting your smartphone or computer when you're having technical issues, then somehow the issues disappear. After meditation, it's as if my mind is working from a clean slate. I'm suddenly in a better place to deal with whatever obstacles or opportunities life may send my way.

**WEEK ONE / DAY 7: CONTEMPLATION**

# When God Talks, Do You Listen?

*"Let us be silent, and we may hear the whispers of the Gods." — Ralph Waldo Emerson*

What if someone told you they regularly talked to God: had a give and take, where they asked God a question and got an answer in return. Would you think they were nuts? Or would you think they had tapped into a secret wisdom that you didn't know about?

In a *Daily Beast* story titled "We Talk with God: What Evangelical Christians Hear," anthropologist T.M. Luhrmann reported that after ten years of research on the issue, she was convinced evangelicals were having a regular dialogue with God. Or at least they believed they were. In her words:

"They believe that prayer is a conversation in which they talk to God and God talks back. They will say that God 'told' them to do something—to talk to the stranger next to them on the bus, or move to Los Angeles."

Luhrmann reports that many of the evangelicals she spoke with can pinpoint the exact time and place when God began to speak with them, often while they were engaged in prayer. Once this conversation begins, it continues throughout their lives. In most instances, Luhrmann says it works like this:

"They would talk to God with their inner voice, about something that was vexing them, and they would wait for his response—some inner word or image that would give them guidance. Sometimes it came immediately; sometimes it took time. They call this practice listening."

Of course, when one hears these stories, they may bring to mind the tales of those who hear God tell them to do evil deeds, say kill the neighbor's dog or worse. But Luhrmann says that for starters, one does not act on a faint notion, only on the certainty that what one has heard is the true voice of God. She explains:

> The church teaches congregants to pay attention only to certain of these striking thoughts—to good thoughts, thoughts that are the kinds of things God should say. That is, those thoughts should be relevant, wise, and loving. ("God does not tell you to hurt yourself," people said.) You should feel calm when you have them. When you hear God correctly, you should feel peace, and if you didn't feel peaceful, it wasn't God.

Ralph Waldo Emerson, who is widely recognized as one of the great American philosophers, had a similar way to communicate with God. A former Unitarian minister, Emerson left the church after finding its rigid doctrine and rules too stifling—but he took his spirituality with him.

Emerson posited that there was a source of guidance available to us all called the "divine soul." He had his own way of communicating with this source, which he referred to as "lowly listening." It's not too different from what many evangelicals practice today. Emerson wrote:

> There is a soul at the center of nature and over the will of every man ... we prosper when we accept its advice ... we need only obey. There is guidance for each of us, and by lowly listening we shall hear the right word.

The first step in "lowly listening" is to quiet the mind and be still. You might do this through centering prayer, meditation, or even a brisk workout. After you're in a relaxed state, you then put your concerns and questions out to God and, while not trying too hard, "listen" for the answers within. Emerson discussed the process in an essay he penned titled "Spiritual Laws":

> Place yourself in the middle of the stream of power and wisdom which flows into you as life, place yourself in the full center of that flood, then you are without effort impelled to truth, to right, and a perfect contentment.

As explained by Emerson scholar Richard Geldard, it's at this point that we reach a place where we can receive the word of God: "Solitude, stillness, reflection, judgement and understanding all come together to guide us."

Perhaps influenced by Emerson, in the early 1900s Ralph Trine, a leader of the New Thought Movement, sang from the same hymn sheet. In the spiritual classic *In Tune with the Infinite*, a runaway bestseller in its time, Trine wrote that there is a "divine inflow" that we can all tap into for guidance. In his words: "It is through your own soul that the voice of God speaks to you. This is the interior guide."

The idea that there is a quiet inner voice we can access, one that belongs to God, is still prominent today and not just in evangelical circles. In fact, it does not require you to belong to any specific religious group or to have any special powers. The Canadian poet and sage Ivon Prefontaine explains it this way:

> Regardless of faith and even when we do not have it, there still exists a source deep within each of us that when we touch it and let it speak to us is able to guide us in wonderful and amazing ways.

Additional guidance on listening to God comes from author and mystic Llewellyn Vaughan-Lee. In his book *Prayer of the Heart in Christian and Sufi Mysticism*, he writes: "Learning to pray is learning to listen. Within the heart we learn to wait with patience for God's words, which may come even when we have not asked."

The most important part is learning to separate the false voice of the ego from the true voice of God. Vaughan-Lee advises:

> Such listening requires both attentiveness and discrimination, as it is not always easy to discriminate between the voice of the ego and the voice of our Beloved. But there is a distinct difference: the words of the ego and mind belong to duality; the words of the heart carry the imprint of oneness. In the heart there is no argument, no you and me, just an unfolding oneness.

It is in this oneness that we find the voice we are looking for and the guidance we need.

# WEEK TWO

## Seven Ways to Be Better Than You Were Yesterday

*"You don't need to be better than anyone else. You just need to be better than you used to be." — Wayne Dyer*

At the end of our days, we all want to be able to look back and say, "I led a good life." But what exactly is the measure of a good life? And how do we know we've achieved it?

Wayne Dyer points us in the right direction. To have lived a good life has nothing to do with comparing our possessions or our accomplishments with anyone else. It's all about comparing where we started (as adults) and where we wound up.

Yes, we may stumble along the way, but we want to be able to honestly say we made slow but steady progress from point A to point Z. That means continually striving to be a better person than we were last decade, last year, last month, last week—even a better person than we were yesterday.

**WE ALL WANT TO BE THE BEST POSSIBLE VERSION OF OUR SELF. BUT HOW?**

In *The Road to Character, New York Times* columnist and best-selling author David Brooks presents several examples of people who lived lives of moral strength and honor, many overcoming difficult challenges to become the best person they could possibly be. Brooks also offers a series of life tips, standards to live by. I've taken what I think are the most important components of this list and added a few of my own. While they may not change your life immediately, they can help you find a path with meaning, while strengthening your character and fortitude.

### SEVEN WAYS TO BECOME THE BEST VERSION OF YOURSELF, STARTING TODAY.

1. **Nourish your soul daily.** At least once each day, break away from your work or home routine and take a little time to feed your soul. This may involve a walk out in nature, reading a spiritual text, taking a yoga class or spending fifteen minutes in quiet contemplation.

2. **Be grateful.** Find something to be thankful for each day, even if it's just to give thanks for the food in your refrigerator or the roof over your head or the fact that you lived to see another day. I like to say a prayer of gratitude each morning, giving thanks first for my family and friends.

3. **Be humble.** In Brooks's words, "Humility reminds you that you are not the center of the universe, but you serve a larger order." This also means keeping your ego and pride in check. "Because of pride we try to prove we are better than those around us. It makes us more certain and close-minded than we should be." Be willing to hear others. Be open-minded.

4. **Don't be led astray.** This may seem obvious, but avoid the big four sins of lust, fear, vanity and gluttony. This means: Stay away from temptation. Be brave when the situation calls for it. Don't look down on others. Try not to overindulge in food or drink.

5. **Trust in a force greater than yourself.** The world can be a tough place and we need all the help we can get. Whether you believe in a specific God, a greater life force or a set of moral

principles, we all need someone or something to lean on. According to Brooks, "You have to draw on something outside yourself to deal with the forces inside yourself."

6. **Know how to quiet the inner self.** Brooks writes that, "Only by quieting the self can you be open to the external sources of strengths you will need. Only by muting the sound of your own ego can you see the world clearly." That means engaging in a regular practice of meditation, contemplation or centering prayer.

7. **Determine what life is asking of you.** We spend much of life focused on what we want—but we also need to discover what the world wants from us. That means finding a need in the world, one you have the skills or passion to address, and serving it. This is a hard one, but a question you should ponder daily—the answer may take weeks or even years to arrive, but it eventually will.

And as you grow in wisdom and spiritual maturity, consider the words of the late great poet Maya Angelou: "Do the best you can until you know better. Then, when you know better, do better."

# Are You Giving Life Your Full Attention? Or Cheating It?

I was almost in a car accident the other day. In a hurry, I was making a right turn into traffic, not realizing that from the other side of the road another car was trying to turn into the same lane. The blare of the other driver's car horn stopped me just short of impact—and when I caught my breath and realized what had just happened, I blamed myself.

Maybe technically I had the right of way. But I had not taken in the complete picture. Instead of widening my gaze to take in the full view, seeing a car across the road entering the same lane I was driving toward, I was narrowly focused on what was directly in front of me. I ignored a danger that lurked just outside my self-imposed limited range of vision.

I'll ask you the same questions I asked myself after that near-miss wake-up call: Are you giving life your undivided attention? Or are you living with blinders on, not fully taking in all that's around you? Are you distracted by a mind that's too jammed with random thoughts or a schedule that's all busy-ness, without enough time for yourself?

A few years ago, I listened to a podcast where businesswoman Ariana Huffington talked about her crazy, workaholic life as the head of the *Huffington Post*. At the time it was one of the fastest growing media companies in the world and, by most societal measures, Huffington was wildly successful. But it was all at a steep personal cost.

After one particularly grueling stretch of work she literally passed out in her office, gashing her head on a desk in the process. She recalls that when she was with her adult children, she was totally preoccupied, thinking about her next meeting or her "to do" list at work. It was when a daughter called her out for not really listening to her, that Huffington came to the following realization:

**ANYTHING THAT MATTERS REQUIRES YOUR FULL ATTENTION.**

Sometimes we stop paying attention because our lives are dulled by our daily routine. You might be working at a mundane job, traveling the same route to your workplace, and performing similar tasks each day. Or you might be at home, handling the same daily chores and running the same errands day in and day out.

It's at these times that we can tend to walk through daily life in a self-induced fog, not paying enough attention to the people and things around us. I can testify to doing this myself from time to time, tuning out the interesting things on the margins, the people I did not come in direct contact with, the beautiful elements of nature just outside my peripheral vision, the artwork and keepsakes that line my home. That's a mistake.

When we go through life as if we have seen, done, and heard it all before—or are so busy that we ignore the people and environment around us, we stop being fully human. We lose the ability to tune in to the small details of life that have the power to surprise and delight us. We miss the nuances that add texture and meaning to our lives.

## WHAT IF WE WOKE UP EACH DAY AND SAW LIFE FOR THE FIRST TIME?

It's an idea that the author Alan Lightman put forward in his book *Einstein's Dreams*. In one memorable chapter, a daydreaming Albert Einstein imagines a world where people awake each day with no memory, unaware of who they are or what role they play in life. Each morning, they need to consult notebooks to uncover the details of their lives.

They go to a job that is new and full of promise with co-workers they meet with interest. They return home to spouses they have never seen before and children they have never met. With great curiosity, they reacquaint themselves with each other and tell stories about the day's events. When the children go to bed, husband and wife look into each other's eyes and talk as if for the first time.

In this world, everyone's life is full and rich because as Lightman puts it, "It is only habit and memory that dull the passion for life."

Without habit and memory, we would live each day as if it were a new and exciting adventure. Is it possible that we too could start each day with a similar perspective on life?

### WHAT IF WE ADDED MORE AWE TO OUR LIVES?

A recent story on awe appeared in *The Guardian* online. Awe is a word we don't use very often. It's defined as "a feeling of reverential respect mixed with fear or wonder," as in "they gazed in awe at the small mountain of diamonds" or "the sight filled me with awe."

We're told that the Irish philosopher Edmund Burke had a revolutionary take on awe. You see, it was previously thought that awe was something felt only during religious ceremonies, when God was perceived to be present. But in 1757, Burke stated his belief that awe could be found in "everyday experiences like music, patterns of light or a crack of thunder."

So how do we create a feeling of awe in our everyday lives? The article's primary suggestion is to go on "an awe walk." *The Guardian* tells us of a 2020 study showing that "participants taking weekly 15-minute awe walks for eight weeks reported less stress and increased emotions like compassion and gratitude." So how do we take an awe walk? According to the article, it's pretty simple:

> Take a short walk in your immediate neighborhood and observe details you wouldn't normally notice: plants pushing through concrete or fences, the textures of a wooden bench, the structural patterns of high-rise buildings.

In other words, pay attention.

### THE GOOD NEWS: SOLVING OUR ATTENTION-DEFICIT PROBLEM IS EASY.

In a nutshell,

- Make a conscientious effort to live at a slower and more thoughtful pace, open to the people and places and experiences we encounter.
- Talk through life alive and alert, our eyes wide open, looking a little bit longer, listening a little more intently, digging a little deeper.
- Start interacting with life as it interacts with us.

When we teach ourselves to look past the things we know and expect, we may be surprised by what we see. We may find that our lives are richer and full of more interesting and rewarding experiences than we ever imagined. We may notice that the happiness and fulfillment we've been chasing have been with us all along.

**WEEK TWO/ DAY 3: CHARACTER**

# Why You Should Be the Truest Version of Yourself

*"Let the world know you as you are, not as you think you should be, because sooner or later, if you are posing, you will forget the pose, and then where are you?"*
— *Fanny Brice*

From the outside looking in, James Martin was living the good life. He was twenty-nine years old and had a good job working for a Fortune 500 company. He had a fancy apartment, hip friends, wore stylish suits to work, and had begun to climb the corporate ladder. But there was a problem: he had the gnawing feeling that something wasn't right.

When James began taking a closer look at his life, he couldn't overcome a feeling he had long tried to suppress. He was miserable. In his words, he was "overworked, stressed and lonely." While some saw him as a successful young business professional, he viewed his life as having no meaning or purpose.

Yet wasn't James Martin living the American dream? He had graduated from a top-tier college and landed a good-paying corporate job. If he followed the path of his peers, he would get married, buy a big house in the suburbs and raise a family. He would stay in his career for forty or so years and retire with a robust retirement account. The only problem:

"This way of living simply wasn't for me ... my heart knew that as much as I wanted to want this, I wasn't made for the life I was supposed to want."

Martin found a solution to his crisis when he stumbled upon Thomas Merton's autobiography *The Seven Storey Mountain*. There he found a kindred spirit, "a man roughly my own age, who had struggled with the same things I did: pride, disappointment, confusion, doubt, sadness, loneliness." There was one passage that was especially resonant with Martin:

"Why do we have to spend our lives striving to be something we would never want to be, if we only knew what we wanted? Why do we waste our time doing things which, if we only stopped to think about them, are just the opposite of what we were made for?"

**MARTIN ASKED HIMSELF A QUESTION WE ALL MIGHT ASK: ARE WE LIVING OUR TRUEST LIVES?**

---

*"Before coming to know the true self, one must confront the false self that one has usually spent a lifetime constructing and nourishing."* — James Martin

---

In the book *Becoming Who You Are*, Martin writes "The person I had presented to others—the person interested in climbing the corporate ladder, in always being clever and hip, in knowing how to order the best wines, in attending the hottest parties, in always being, in a word, cool—that person was unreal. That person was nothing more than a mask I wore."

Martin made a bold move. He left the corporate world to become a Jesuit priest, effectively shedding his false self to fully realize his true identity.

Why did Martin pursue the role of "corporate suit" in the first place? Like many of us, Martin had created a persona he thought would be pleasing to his family and friends. His "false self" was sure a life in corporate America was the right path. As Franciscan friar Richard Rohr put it, "Our false self is who we think we are. It is our mental self-image … which most people spend their whole lives living up to … or down to."

### How about you? Are you presenting your "true self" to the world?

Much like Martin, many of us adopt the mannerisms and persona of the "false self" each day we walk out the door and head out into the world. I know all too well because for years I wore "the mask" of the false self, climbing the corporate ladder until one day I stopped to take in the view up ahead—and not liking what I saw, began the slow descent back down, a process that continues today.

What might be most puzzling in the whole process is this: What is our true self and how do we find it? While Martin does not answer these questions directly, he believes that our true self is the role that God wants for us, which means it may be in direct opposition to the role society expects from us. In Martin's words:

God desires for us to be the persons we were created to be, simply and purely ourselves ... the more we live as our true selves, the more we become the person whom God intended.

It's important to note that Martin asserts that our path may be quite different than his and doesn't have to entail leaving our everyday lives to join the priesthood or enroll in a Buddhist monastery. According to Martin, the paths we are called to are all different, all unique in their own way:

The path to sanctity for a young mother is different from that of an elderly priest. Moreover, the path to sanctity for an extroverted young man is probably different from that of the introspective middle-aged woman who likes nothing better than to sit at home with a good book and a pot of chamomile tea. One's personal brand of happiness becomes clearer once the true self is revealed.

Once this true self is revealed and realized, it becomes harder to live a life that is guided by the false self, the one created by the pull of society and our peers. As Richard Rohr says, "Once you learn to live as your true self, you can never be satisfied with this charade again: it then feels so silly and superficial."

### HAVE YOU LOOKED INSIDE AND ARE STILL HAVING TROUBLE FINDING YOUR TRUE SELF?

Try answering the five questions below, which I tweaked from a list created by Dr. Ilene Strauss Cohen. They should put you in the right headspace—and may cause you to realize that who society thinks you are, and who you really are, are two very different things.

1. What is the accomplishment in life you're most proud of?
2. What do you enjoy doing when no one is watching?
3. If there were no such thing as fear and failure, what would your life look like?

4. If money were no object, what would you do?

5. Who is your role model?

**WEEK TWO/ DAY 4: CALLING**

# Oprah and Coelho on Finding Your Personal Calling

On *Oprah's Super Soul* podcast, there's a conversation in the archives that features two of the leading spirituality figures of our time. The first is Oprah Winfrey herself, the famous inspirational talk-show host, and the second is Paulo Coelho, author of *The Alchemist*, one of the biggest selling spirituality books of our time.

Over the course of a fascinating hour-long discussion, Oprah asks Coelho about some of the spiritual principles found in *The Alchemist* and how to interpret them. The book's primary message: everyone should live in the singular pursuit of their dreams.

Oprah and Coelho's thoughts frequently merge as one, albeit with subtle shadings in the language they use. I took copious notes during my listen, writing down the key points they discussed. I then rearranged these points into the narrative you see below, with some editing on my part to shape the story.

## FINDING YOUR PERSONAL CALLING

- Every person has a personal calling in life.
- Your calling is your destiny or purpose. It is the reason you are here.
- Your only job in life is to discover, honor, and fulfill this calling.
- Your calling is a potential given to you by God. Your job is to realize this potential.

- If you're like most people, your calling is related to what makes you enthusiastic and happy.
- Though you may know your calling, this does not mean you will fulfill it.
- To fulfill your calling, takes courage. You need to move forward without fearing the unknown.
- You must listen to your heart. Give in to your fears and you will no longer hear the voice of the heart.
- Ask yourself: Is my heart open to embrace every moment, every person, every element of my life?
- When necessary, be prepared to fight for your dream. In your pursuit, don't take "no" for an answer.
- Use every bit of your willpower, desire, and enthusiasm, then surrender to the flow of life.
- Look at everything like you are seeing it for the first time.
- You may be tested, but don't lose faith. While there may be obstacles, you can always get back on track.
- God will guide you, even if you take wrong steps; especially if you take wrong steps.
- Listen. Pay attention to the world for cues and signs.
- The Universe is on your side and will rise to meet you and help fulfill your destiny.

**WEEK TWO/ DAY 5: PRACTICE**

# The First Fifteen Minutes: Ten Steps to a Better Day

How do you start your day? After you hit the alarm, do you immediately reach for your phone and start scrolling through email or social media posts? Or do you ease into your day, making sure your head is clear and you're spiritually centered before facing the world?

Author and podcaster Tim Ferriss is a big proponent of a regular morning practice. He has found that if he can do five specific activities each morning, he can practically guarantee he'll have a great day. Here are four of his five activities below. I've left off his use of an inversion table and my commentary follows each point on his list.

1. **Make your bed**. It may sound silly, but it sets the tone for the day. Ferriss believes this small accomplishment can lead to bigger ones.

2. **Meditate**. While he recommends the Headspace meditation app, my favorite is the Waking Up app from Sam Harris. His basic meditation course includes twenty ten-minute sessions and you can try the app on a free trial basis.

3. **Enjoy a cup of good, brewed tea**. I prefer a good cup of coffee and preset my coffeemaker the night before. There's nothing like sitting in a comfortable chair, when the house is still dark and quiet, and enjoying that first sip.

4. **Write in a journal, including making a "to do" list**. Interestingly, on his list, Ferriss includes all the people he needs to give thanks to that day.

Ferriss points out that due to his busy schedule, he often finds he can't do all five activities. But he has found that if he can check off at least three items from his list, the whole day seems to go better. While I use two of the four activities listed above, I include two additional activities in my daily routine:

5. **Stretch**. I've found that as I age, my body feels stiffer upon waking up. That's why the first thing I do is lie down on a yoga mat and stretch my back, arms and legs.

6. **Read spiritual literature**. This activity always seems to put my head in a good place for the day ahead. I've most recently been reading *The Universal Christ* by Richard Rohr, though I often return to what for me are the classics like *The Alchemist* by Paulo Coelho.

A recent story at AARP.com also provided five steps to get your day off to a good start, suggesting they be done in the first five minutes of your day. To avoid repetition, I've listed three here:

7. **Wake up to music.** Your alarm clock or smartphone's ringtone can jolt you out of a sound sleep. Try setting your phone or alarm to something more soothing that eases you into the day.

8. **Find a saying that resonates.** You may have a favorite quote that reflects your personal hopes and ambitions. As a reminder, put in on a sticky note near your bed and silently say it two or three times upon waking. The AARP story says it can be as simple as "breathe in love, breathe out hate."

9. **Have an attitude of gratitude.** Always be giving thanks. According to the story, a recent study suggested listing three things you are grateful for every morning can have the same effect on you neurologically as taking an antidepressant.

Finally, a recent story in *The New York Times* details the morning activities of ex-NFL football player and current TV analyst Tony Gonzalez. His morning ritual covers some of the same ground as above, including stretching and a morning meditation where he feeds "gratitude and love into his heart," thereby opening it. (He also engages in spiritual reading and by chance happens to be reading the same Rohr book I am.) He also stresses one additional point:

10. **Sleep as much as you need.** This is something you'll need to get a head start on by getting to bed at a good hour the night before. Gonzalez believes proper sleep is "the number one

thing you can do to create a better life." I find seven-and-a-half hours a night is good for me (when I can get it); Gonzalez prefers nine hours.

Consider developing your own list of morning activities, based on what feels right to you. If you consider yourself a spiritual person, you can also replace meditation with a prayer. A morning practice is easy to start and to follow through on, and by devoting fifteen to twenty minutes to your practice each morning, you may feel the positive effects all day.

# The Prayer Banned Six Centuries Ago—and Its Amazing Return

What do you do when it feels like your prayers are going into a deep, dark void and you aren't connecting with the Divine?

Well, in the fourteenth century an English Christian mystic had an answer, an alternative to traditional prayer that he believed offered a direct connection to God. The mystic, who has never been identified, put his or her thoughts down in a book titled *The Cloud of Unknowing*. It includes guidance like this:

> This is what you are to do: Lift up your heart to the Lord, with a gentle stirring of love desiring him for his own sake and not his gifts. Center all your attention and desire on him and let this be the sole concern of your mind and heart.

The anonymous author had described the foundation for contemplative prayer, which for centuries was largely forgotten—and for good reason. According to Trappist monk Father Thomas Keating, one of the prayer's great modern-day proponents, when the Inquisition began to expand in the late 1400s, the prayer was judged to be heretical. He tells us that "a negative attitude prevailed with growing intensity from the sixteenth century onward" and it was effectively banned from the Catholic church.

But in the past few decades, the prayer has made an amazing comeback. When the church began to lose members to Eastern philosophies and the lure of meditation in the 1960s and '70s, a small band of renegades on the fringes of the church began reintroducing the idea of contemplative prayer. They were inspired by Thomas Merton, who wrote "the simplest way to come into contact with the living God is to go to one's center and from there pass into God." The practice became known as centering prayer.

## WHAT IS CENTERING PRAYER AND HOW DOES IT WORK?

Essentially, it is a prayer without words, or more accurately a prayer with a single word. Its aim is to help you establish a deeper relationship with God (or for some practitioners, Jesus) to the point that God becomes a living reality in your life, available to you at all times.

Thomas Keating explains the powerful effect of centering prayer this way:

> It is the opening of the mind and heart—our whole being—
> to God, the ultimate mystery, beyond thoughts, words, and
> emotions. Through grace, we open our awareness to God
> whom we know by faith is within us, closer than breathing,
> closer than thinking ... closer than consciousness itself.

There's an excellent book on the subject titled *The Path of Centering Prayer* by David Frenette. The author describes the practice as *"a state beyond walking, sleeping or dreaming."* With help from his writings, I've developed a six-point "how to" guide on the subject.

## CENTERING PRAYER IN SIX STEPS

1. Choose a one- or two-syllable word such as God, peace, love, or faith. (I sometimes cheat and use a sentence, like this mantra borrowed from Huston Smith: "God you are so good to me," repeated over and over.)
2. Sit comfortably still with your eyes closed. Silently introduce the word as the symbol of your consent to allow God's presence.
3. Repeat the word a few times, moving deeper and deeper within yourself.
4. If your mind wanders, gently return to the word.
5. Rest and simply be with God, "as if you put your head back down on the pillow after waking." Sense the presence of God within you.
6. As your prayer ends, let go of the sacred word and rest your mind for a minute or two before going about your business.

As with most things you want to be proficient at, the key to success in centering prayer is practice, practice, practice. Another modern-day expert on the subject, Trappist monk Basil Pennington, who along with Father William Meninger collaborated with Keating in developing the modern form of the prayer, recommends two twenty-minute sessions a day: "The first in the morning, introduces into our day a good rhythm … the second, after eight to ten hours of fruitful activity, is a period of renewal to carry us through."

## THE NEXT STEP: PRAYING WITHOUT WORDS.

Frenette writes that the next step is to engage in centering prayer without any words, to just rest and simply "be" in God. He says that the sacred word or symbol you use is really like a life preserver you might need when entering deep waters for the first time. He recommends that as you become better versed in centering prayer you "let go of the life preserver and just float."

It's easy to see the parallels between centering prayer and secular meditation. But while the calming effect is much the same as meditation, there's an added element in centering prayer. It's the sense that in the vast nothingness within, there's a presence, one that's part of the soul but greater than the soul. And that presence is what many refer to as God.

**WEEK TWO/ DAY 7: CONTEMPLATION**

# Ten Jesus Quotes Hidden by the Church—and What They Reveal

What if I told you some of the most meaningful and compelling things Jesus said during his lifetime can't be found in the Bible? That's because they're part of the Gnostic Gospels, a loose collection of almost sixty ancient texts that some early Christian referred to as "the secret sayings of the savior."

Many of the Gnostic gospels were written in the first through third centuries, about the same time as the four gospels found in the New Testament. Once in wide circulation, these gospels were passed around early fledgling churches throughout the Mideast and show the rich diversity of Christian beliefs in the years following the death of Jesus.

## THE GNOSTIC TEXTS WERE BANNED BY THE CHURCH IN THE 4TH CENTURY.

The early Roman church wanted to centralize authority and literally get all of western Christianity on the same page. So, they did things like make December 25th the official birthday of Jesus, even though he was more likely born in March or April. They also declared the Gnostic texts to be heretical and ordered that all books about the life of Jesus, not named Matthew, Mark, Luke or John, be destroyed.

Despite the best efforts of this book-burning regime, many of these texts survived. In 1945, a treasure trove of them were discovered in Egypt at Nag Hamadi. But you probably won't find them included in your Sunday church service, as they are still largely ignored or even considered taboo by mainstream Christianity.

What are these Gnostic books all about? I've read several of them and, like much of the Bible, they can be rather dry and difficult reading. The subjects include everything from creation mythology to the feminine side of God to wild tales of a coming apocalypse—but most interesting, and perhaps most controversial, are the passages that directly quote Jesus.

I've selected ten short passages from the Gnostic texts and grouped them by theme into three categories. I believe they reveal extraordinarily important messages that Jesus only hinted at in the canonical gospels. In total, they inform us we can skip the priest or middleman, and that each of us can have a direct and personal relationship with God.

After each quote, you'll find the Gnostic book from which it originated. Some passages are trickier than others, challenging us to think outside the box to decipher their meaning.

**THEME 1. THE FIRST STEP TO KNOWING GOD IS TO KNOW YOURSELF.**

1. "He who has known himself has ... already achieved knowledge about the depth of all." — The Book of Thomas the Contender
2. "That which you have will save you if you bring it forth from yourselves." — Gospel of Thomas
3. "Those who have come to know themselves will enjoy their possessions." — Gospel of Philip

**THEME 2. ALL THE ANSWERS YOU SEEK CAN BE FOUND WITHIN.**

4. "What you seek after (is) within you." — The Dialogue of the Savior
5. "Beware that no one lead you astray, saying 'Lo here!' or 'Lo there!' For the Son of Man is within you. Follow after him! Those who seek him will find him." — The Gospel of Mary
6. Matthew: "Lord, when I speak ... who listens? The Lord said: "It is the one who speaks who also listens, and it is the one who can see who also reveals." — The Dialogue of the Savior

**THEME 3. YOU CAN FIND THE KINGDOM OF GOD HERE ON THIS EARTH.**

7. "The Kingdom is inside of you and it is outside of you." — Gospel of Thomas
8. "The disciples said, 'What is the place to which we are going?' The Lord said, 'Stand in the place you can reach.'" — The Dialogue of the Savior
9. "His disciples said, 'When will the Kingdom come?' It will not come by waiting for it. It will not be a matter of saying here it

is or there it is. Rather, the kingdom of the father is spread out upon the earth and men do not see it." — Gospel of Thomas

This final Gnostic passage reinforces the message that God can be found right in our midst. We just need to look and listen, our eyes open to see and our ears open to hear.

10. "Recognize what is in your sight, and that which is hidden from you will become plain to you. For there is nothing hidden that will not become manifest." — Gospel of Thomas

# WEEK THREE

## What Can Bill Murray Teach You About Life? Plenty.

A few years ago, there was an article in *Rolling Stone* titled "Being Bill Murray." It told the story of how the comic actor has a habit of engaging in sometimes mischievous, often beguiling public acts.

For instance, there's the time he stopped to read poetry to a group of construction workers in New York City. Or the tale of how, while in a cab in San Francisco, he engaged the driver in conversation and found out he was an aspiring saxophonist who rarely got the chance to play. Murray took over the wheel, driving himself to his destination so the cabbie could play his sax in the backseat.

Why does Bill Murray do it? In a recent article published in *The Guardian*, the actor explains himself this way:

> I'm not acting like this for the purpose of being exciting—I do it because it's fun. If there's life happening and you run from it, you're not doing the world a favor. You have to engage. It's almost sad that people are not expecting others to engage, that it's a surprise.

Murray believes that "no one has an easy life" so he goes out of his way to surprise and delight those around him. His aim is to help "lessen their load." These small acts have an effect on those he encounters, making their worlds "a little weirder, the mundane routines of everyday life a little more exciting." Murray's motivation is personal:

"If I see someone who's out cold on their feet, I'm going to try to wake that person up. It's what I'd want someone to do for me. Wake me the hell up and come back to the planet."

## BILL MURRAY MAKES WAKE-UP CALLS EVERYWHERE HE GOES.

He has been known to stroll around Charleston, South Carolina, where he owns part of a minor-league baseball team, and make impromptu, spontaneous appearances at public and private events. He "photobombed" a couple taking wedding pictures in a local park; he stopped by a birthday party in a bar to give an off-the-cuff speech and toast.

But perhaps what is most interesting is the fact Murray performs these acts not just for the pleasure of others, but also for himself. In his words:

"My hope, always, is that it's going to wake me up. I'm only connected for seconds, minutes a day, sometimes. And suddenly, you go, Holy cow, I've been asleep for two days. I've been doing things, but I'm just out."

Now you might say, this is Bill Murray and he can get away with this kind of wackadoodle behavior. But the fact is, we all have the ability to break away from our preconceived ideas of how we should act and behave in public. We all can engage in activities that add a little more light and joy to the world.

The businessman and life philosopher John Templeton tells the story of a friend who was sitting in a park one day when she noticed an elderly man stroll by wearing a bright red cardigan, a red cap, and checkered pants. The man smiled and said hello, then proceeded to walk to a playground. There, he got on a swing and began vigorously and joyfully swinging back and forth.

The dapper gent later stopped by to explain that he swung on that same swing exactly fifty times a day while on his daily walk. The woman noticed that the man "glowed with the fullness of life" and that his eyes "sparkled with the joy of living." His age was clearly of no concern to him, nor did he worry what others might think about his behavior.

## TEMPLETON POINTS OUT THAT WE OFTEN CURTAIL OUR CHILDLIKE WONDER AND JOY UNNECESSARILY.

We do this because we're concerned about "our self-imposed limitations of age, the appropriateness of our behavior, the images we hold of ourselves." This robs us of our ability to fully engage in life. He mentions the example of Jesus who asked us to "become as little children" so that we might enter into the fullness of life.

John Templeton was known by some as a staid businessman, but he also had a contrarian streak, zigging while others zagged. He showed that he is a kindred spirit with Bill Murray when he made the following challenge, one we might all take to heart:

"When did you last do something "outrageous" that pushed you beyond your present boundaries and radiated to the world that you are fully alive? When did the childlike spirit within you run free in joy and excitement? Age is no excuse; other people's opinion of you is no excuse; and your own limiting opinion of yourself is no excuse for not embracing the gift of life and living it to its fullest expression."

WEEK THREE/ DAY 2: AWARENESS

# How to "Shush!" the Critical Voice in Your Head

Have you ever become aware of a voice talking in the back of your head? You know, the one that critiques and analyzes your every move—and it … just … won't … shut … up? You're not alone, this voice is a constant companion for many of us.

German-born spiritual teacher Eckhart Tolle identifies this narrator in our heads as "the egoic self." The ego is a voice you might falsely identify as yourself, "a mind-made me" in the words of Tolle, as opposed to the other voice that lives within you—the deep and steady awareness at your core that is the real you.

What's the problem with the ego? It overanalyzes. It overreacts. It complains a lot. It likes to be in conflict with something or someone. It always wants to be right so it can feel superior. And when you acknowledge the ego by going along with what it has to say, you only make it stronger.

In *Stillness Speaks*, Eckhart Tolle tells us that due to the unsteady nature of the ego, it's hard to feel real peace or contentment when we place the egoic voice in charge. Your moments of happiness are fleeting, because the ego is always moving on to the next thing, never satisfied, always looking for new conquests and conflicts.

### MICHAEL A. SINGER SAYS THE EGO KEEPS US FROM LIVING OUR BEST POSSIBLE LIVES.

In *The Untethered Soul*, Singer takes a look at "the self" and the barriers the ego puts up that prevent us from fully living our lives. I've reordered the content of Singer's book into nine key points. While much of the language below belongs to Singer, I've interspersed his thoughts with some of my own.

## POINT 1. THERE'S A VOICE INSIDE YOUR HEAD THAT NEVER STOPS TALKING.

It never shuts up. It talks nonstop, like an annoying roommate. It even talks to you in the shower. It analyzes. It criticizes. Its constant chatter puts a buffer between you and life, instead of allowing you to live life to its fullest.

You're not the only one who hears this chattering voice. It's an issue that plagues almost everyone. Former publisher of *The Washington Post* Katherine Graham once wrote that she was always wondering: "Did I say the wrong thing? Did I wear the right clothes? Am I attractive?" The voice second guesses your every move.

But for all the attention you pay to it, most of what the voice says is meaningless. It doesn't improve your life or make you a better person. All the chattering is a waste of time and energy and a heavy anchor that can prevent you from living your best life.

That's a burden nobody needs to bear. You shouldn't have to constantly mull over what you just said or did or what this or that person thinks about you. You shouldn't have to experience constant insecurity, anxiety and self-consciousness. You should be able to live your life without this prevalent voice questioning your every move. But how?

## POINT 2. REALIZE THAT YOU ARE NOT THE VOICE INSIDE YOUR HEAD.

———

*"When you notice the voice, you realize that who you are is not the voice—the thinker—but the one who is aware of*

*it. Know yourself as the awareness behind
the voice." — Eckhart Tolle*

———

This idea requires a little bit of introspection, so you might want to read it slowly. There are two distinct aspects of each person, including you, and you need to separate them.

- The first you is the shallow you, the ego, the person you put out into the world. This is the domain of the egoic voice and the source of the incessant, often critical chatter in your head. It is located in the mind.

- The second you is the deeper you, the awareness, the witness, the center of your intentions. Some might call this the soul or true Self. It is located at the core of your being and is located close to the heart.

The second you sits back and watches the first you. Think about that. There's a you that's deep inside that notices the voice in your head talking. It is separate and not the voice itself.

There is nothing more important to your personal growth than realizing that you are not the voice. The real you is the one who hears the voice. The listener. The one who observes. When you come to this realization, you diminish the power the egoic voice has over you.

**POINT 3. STOP FOR A MOMENT AND LOCATE
THE REAL YOU, THE AWARENESS AT YOUR CORE.**

———

*"The mind itself is not awareness. It is only a machine. We
are the awareness." — Yogani*

———

It's so easy to get caught up in the world of thoughts, emotions, and physical sensations that you don't even know you're in there. Your consciousness just follows whatever catches its attention like a cat chasing a flickering light. That's the normal state for most people.

The key is to be quiet. It's not your mind that has to be quiet. It's you, the one inside watching the neurotic mind, that has to be quiet. You are the awareness.

There are ways to get to this quiet place and find the awareness. For many, this happens through meditation, breathing exercises, yoga, or a vigorous workout, when you're able to quiet the shallow you and silence the voice. When the voice is silenced, what remains is the real you, the watcher, the true Self.

## POINT 4. TO TAP INTO THE REAL YOU, YOU NEED TO BE CENTERED AND AWARE.

---

*"You are the sky. Everything else is just the weather."*
*— Pema Chödrön*

---

You want to live with a separation between you and your thoughts. Your thoughts may happen, you're aware of them, but you're not affected by them. They're out there, like clouds floating by a window, and you're sitting back observing them.

When you live your life with awareness, you're no longer completely immersed in the events around you. Instead, you inwardly know that you are the one who is experiencing both the events and the corresponding thoughts and emotions.

Instead of getting lost in a thought, you remain aware that you are the one who is thinking the thought. The world ceases to be a problem. It's just something you're watching. You can pull back from the angst, the worry, the second-guessing, and see everything.

## POINT 5. DON'T FIGHT YOUR THOUGHTS, JUST LET THEM GO.

We tend to let ourselves get bothered by the little, meaningless things that happen each day. Just decide that no matter what the mind says, you aren't getting involved. When you feel the pull, like somebody pulling on your heart, just let go. Fall behind the thought. Gently disengage. Do not fight your mind. Just don't listen to it.

Your consciousness is always drawn to the most distracting object: the loudest noise, the hurting heart. This is a reminder to let go. If you don't let go, you'll get sucked in.

Drop back and hang out with the true Self instead of hanging out with the mind's disturbances. You don't have to get rid of a negative emotion; just cease to be involved with it. Sit back and watch.

## POINT 6. WHEN A NAGGING OR QUESTIONING THOUGHT ARISES, LET IT GO.

The moment you feel your consciousness getting drawn to a questioning or negative thought, relax your shoulders and relax the area around your heart. Letting go means falling behind the energy instead of going into it. Just let go.

When you start to sense there's a problem with the thinking mind, relax and release. When you see this stuff going on in your mind, relax your shoulders and relax your heart. Fall behind the noise. Watch it float by and then disappear.

Once you've learned to let go, every minute of every day, that's where you'll live. You'll learn to stay there. You'll sit in the seat of centered awareness. You'll be at peace.

## POINT 7. YOU MIGHT STUMBLE ALONG THE WAY. THAT'S OKAY.

If you fall, just get up and forget it. Use the lesson to strengthen your resolve. Let go right then and there. Move on.

If you feel fear, let it go. If you feel shame, let it go. No matter what it is, let it go.

The bigger the disturbance, the higher the reward of letting go and the worse you'll feel if you don't.

## POINT 8. THE ULTIMATE GOAL IS TO LIVE WITH THIS AWARENESS ALL THE TIME.

-------

*"You find peace not by rearranging the circumstances of your life, but by realizing who you are at the deepest level." — Eckhart Tolle*

-------

Remember, you are not the thinking mind; you are the one who is aware of the thinking mind. When you pull back behind the mind, then you—the awareness—are not involved in the process of thinking. Thinking is something you watch the mind do. You're just in there, aware that you are aware.

The more you sit in the Self, the more you'll feel a change within. When you're no longer absorbed in your own melodrama, instead sitting comfortably deep inside the seat of awareness, you'll start to experience a positive feeling.

Awareness does not fight. Awareness releases. Awareness is at peace and simply observes while everything in the universe parades before it.

## POINT 9. WALK THROUGH LIFE WITH YOUR HEART OPEN.

Do not let anything that happens in life be important enough that you're willing to close your heart over it. If you love life, nothing is worth closing your heart over. No matter what events take place in your life, it is always better to let go than to close.

Don't live in fear. Fear is caused by blockages in your energy. When your energy is blocked, it can't come up and feed your heart. Your heart becomes weak. Problems ensue.

If you sit within the Self, you will experience the strength of your inner being even when your heart feels weak. You may feel inner disturbances—but they no longer disturb the seat of your consciousness, the place where the real you lives.

Follow this path and you will live a life that is less burdensome, more rewarding, more in tune with the person you were meant to be. You will be a person living your fullest potential.

## WEEK THREE/ DAY 3: CHARACTER

# Sage Advice from the Fourteenth Dalai Lama: Don't Be a Jerk.

I'm thinking there should be a prequel to "Five Basic Rules to Living a Righteous Life," a story that appeared earlier in this book. Let's call it Rule Zero, the rule before the rules, the one baseline behavior all of us should follow to be a part of the human community.

The intent of this rule is expressed in the words of the and current Dalai Lama. He's a wise man who has written many books on the general theme of being a compassionate and good person. They include many quotable lines, perhaps none better than this: "Our prime purpose in this life is to help others. And if you can't help them, at least don't hurt them."

I've taken the liberty of translating the Dalai Lama's message into more colloquial language, distilling it down to just a few words. It's a statement that's more suited for our coarse times, when civility seems to be a relic of a different era. The translation:

## Do good. Don't be a jerk.

Don't bully. Don't belittle. Don't be petty. Don't be mean. Don't yell or shout. Don't be rude. Control your anger. Be considerate. Be friendly. Be helpful. Be kind. Encourage. Inspire. Treat others as you would want to be treated. Do good. Don't be a jerk. Be a good human being.

It doesn't matter whether you're playing the role of supervisor at work, mom or dad at home, or you're in situations where you're dealing with people in a service capacity, be they waiters, bank tellers, or customer service reps. Take a moment to consider this challenge from the business marketer and life philosopher Seth Godin:

> In the moment, when you have power, no matter how momentarily, how will you choose to act? More than just about anything else, what you do when you have the chance is what people say about you and remember about you. (People) pay careful attention to the restraint (or lack of it) that you show when the opportunity arises.

In other words, we need to THINK before we act, considering the repercussions of our actions and how we're communicating with those around us. This is especially true if you're in a position of power—because what you do when you're in power ultimately inspires and encourages those around you to act in kind, for better or worse.

I'm not sure when I first jotted down the list below, and Google was not a big help in determining its origin. The important thing is the simple point it makes. We need to THINK before we speak, text, or email. Whether you're talking to friends or family, chatting with co-workers, or engaging in any exchange with another, you should ask yourself the following questions before you communicate:

T – Is this true?
H – Is this helpful?
I – Is this inspiring?
N – Is this necessary?
K – Is this kind?

When we take the time to ask ourselves these questions, we become more human and allow the best parts of ourselves to come through. Most importantly, we wind up adding to the world around us, not detracting from it, by uplifting the spirits of those we encounter. When you THINK before you act, your small portion of the world becomes a better place.

WEEK THREE/ DAY 4: CALLING

# Are You Playing a Role or Living Your Best Life?

Have you ever heard of impostor syndrome, also known as the fraud syndrome? I hadn't until it was brought to my attention by the blogger and cartoonist Carl Richards. For starters, here's a paraphrased description from Wikipedia: Impostor syndrome is a psychological pattern in which a person doubts their accomplishments and has a persistent internalized fear of being exposed as "a fraud." Despite external evidence of their competence, those experiencing this phenomenon remain convinced that they are frauds and do not deserve all they have achieved.

People with "impostorism" attribute their success to sheer luck, or as a result of tricking others into thinking they're more intelligent than they really are. They feel like an actor playing a role on stage or screen. While the syndrome is prevalent among high-achieving women, research shows that it affects men almost equally.

Richards points out the curious thing about impostor syndrome— it really doesn't hit you until you've achieved a level of success. In his words:

> It doesn't just show up in beginners. High achievement doesn't solve the problem — it can actually make it worse! And the reason is that as you get further and further off the ground, achievement often acts as air beneath you. You may be more skilled, and more confident. But at the same time, you've got further to fall.

This may explain why Jodie Foster "thought it was a fluke," when she won an Oscar. In Foster's words, "I thought everybody would find out, and they'd take it back. They'd come to my house, knocking on the door, 'Excuse me, we meant to give that to someone else. That was going to Meryl Streep.'"

It may also be why Maya Angelou once said, "I have written eleven books, but each time I think, 'Uh oh, they're going to find out now. I've run a game on everybody, and they're going to find me out.'"

### IF IT CAN HAPPEN TO JODIE FOSTER AND MAYA ANGELOU, IT CAN HAPPEN TO YOU.

While Richards doesn't offer precise advice on beating the syndrome, he references the expression "fake it until you make it." In other words, the feelings of inadequacy you're feeling, aren't apparent to everyone else. They're just thoughts inside your head that don't represent the real you and may require you to reset how you view the world around you.

## THERE ARE OTHERS WHO SEE THEMSELVES AS ACTING THEIR WAY THROUGH LIFE.

In *The Second Mountain*, author David Brooks describes another group of individuals who believe they're in roles that they weren't meant to play. They might be best described as the discontented. If you're part of this group, you believe the life you're living doesn't represent who you really are or who you were meant to be.

Brooks references writer Ada Calhoun, who tells us that many people in their thirties and forties feel adrift, like they're misleading their lives. One forty-four-year-old woman told Ada that while she sometimes has moments of contentment, she often hears a voice deep inside her head that shouts "What are you doing? This is pointless and boring! Why aren't you out there doing something you love!"

The writer Veronica Rae Saron spins a similar tale: "Those among us with flashy Instagram accounts, perfectly manicured LinkedIn profiles, and confident exteriors are probably those who are feeling the most confused when it comes to the future. The stuck-ness sensation is everywhere, and there's a correlation between those who feel it and those who put off a vibe of feeling extremely secure."

So how do you relieve the feeling of "stuck-ness," the feeling you're attached to a life that's not really your own? You need to take action. Soul expert Thomas Moore spells out what your primary goal should be in his book *A Life at Work, Discovering What You Were Born to Do*: "You want your life to match your sense of self—your values, your hope, your style, and your deep needs."

He points out that matching your life with your true self is not an easy path. It is the road less traveled. To navigate this path, you must frequently consult your inner compass to determine if you are headed in the right direction. Moore goes on to caution:

> You might go through more phases than people think are standard. Many men and women wake up one morning ... to discover that they have changed in some way. Suddenly they crave more meaningful work and activities. ...

Brooks also talks about the importance of living an authentic life, one that is guided by the still voice within. Again, the key is to take action, moving your life forward each day. In his words:

> As you make your own personal journey, you learn to better express your own unique self. You learn to get in touch with yourself, find yourself, and live in a way that is authentic to who you really are. The ultimate source of authority is found inside, by listening to the authentic voice within.

We all strive to live authentic lives, so ask yourself: What do I believe in? Where do I belong? What changes do I need to make to live the best possible life, the one I was truly meant to live?

# Finding Your Own Spiritual Mentor (Living or Dead)

While the spiritual path is often best navigated as a solo journey, it can also be helpful to have a mentor. Think of a mentor as a guiding force who, when needed, dispenses valuable advice and counsel. He or she becomes the equivalent of a map or compass you take into the woods, helping ensure that you, the spiritual journeyer, stays on course.

## To find your personal mentor, look to your heroes.

The marketer and philosopher Seth Godin has an interesting take on mentors, pointing out that a mentor can be anyone—living or dead. Godin says we merely need someone whose example we live up to and honor, "even if we never meet them, even if they've passed away." Since most of us don't have mentors within our reach, "for the rest of us, heroes will have to do." The good news is there's a vast supply available. In Godin's words:

"I find heroes everywhere I look. I find people who speak to me over my shoulder, virtual muses, who encourage me to solve a problem or deal with a situation the way they would. This is thrilling news, because there are so many heroes, so freely available, whenever we need them."

Once you find your own personal hero to emulate, Godin even coined an expression that can help guide you in your life decisions:

## WWHD. What Would my Hero Do?

Commiserating with a dead hero may seem like an unusual way to receive guidance, but consider that Napoleon Hill, author of the motivational classic *Think and Grow Rich*, gave similar instruction. Buried deep in Hill's long-time bestseller, there's a chapter devoted to "The Sixth Sense: The Door to the Temple of Wisdom" that addresses this topic. His initial comments on mentorship mirror those of Godin:

"My experience has taught me that the next best thing to being truly great is to emulate the great, by feeling and action, as closely as possible."

At this point, Hill ventures into more esoteric territory, which may surprise those who view him as a straight-laced, uber-capitalist.

He reveals that "every night over a long period of years," he "held an imaginary council meeting" with a group he called "the Invisible Counselors." Who were his counselors? Some of the greatest minds of all-time including Ralph Waldo Emerson, Abraham Lincoln and Thomas Edison.

Hill says that his communications with the panel of counselors worked like this:

> Just before going to sleep at night, I would shut my eyes and see, in my imagination, this group of men seated with me around my council table ... here I had the opportunity to sit among those whom I considered to be great ... I called on my cabinet members for the knowledge I wished each to contribute.

What made Hill's counseling sessions easier was the fact he had extensive knowledge of each of his "cabinet members," which also included Henry Ford and Napoleon, having studied their lives in detail. He knew their backgrounds, their manner of thinking, and their individual characteristics. This makes it easier to see how he may have conjured up conversations with them using his imagination.

But Hill's story goes a step further. After a few years of regular evening sessions, Hill notes that he "was astounded by the discovery that these imaginary figures became, apparently, real." In his book, he details several encounters that moved beyond give-and-take conversations, where his counselors begin giving him unsolicited advice.

Hill awoke one night to find Abraham Lincoln standing at his bedside. Lincoln informed him that "the world will soon need your services. It is about to undergo a period of chaos that will cause men and women to lose faith and become panic stricken. Go ahead with your work ... this is your mission in life." Hill followed this advice (and who wouldn't listen to a direct appeal from Abe Lincoln) which led him to write the aforementioned *Think and Grow Rich*.

As time went on, Hill discontinued these regular nightly meetings, but throughout his life he went back to the counselors whenever he needed mentoring or advice. They were always there for him:

"On scores of occasions when I have faced emergencies—some of them so grave that my life was in jeopardy—I have been miraculously guided past these difficulties through the influence of my counselors."

### READY TO FIND YOUR OWN SPIRITUAL COUNSELOR?

As mentioned, Hill was a voracious reader and in effect knew well the counselors he enlisted. So it only makes sense for you to choose a mentor whose teachings, and life, you're well versed in—or to kick off the process by studying books by and about your preferred mentor.

Additionally, Hill believes the earliest one can encounter the counselors is the age of forty—and that in most cases, they're usually not accessible "until one is well past fifty" and only after one has gone through "years of meditation, self-examination and serious thought."

It's also important to note here that Hill's list is comprised entirely of men, perhaps partially due to the fact Hill came of age in the early 1900s. Your list might include women as well, following the lead of renowned interspirituality author Mirabai Starr. She draws inspiration from the likes of Teresa of Avila, a Catholic saint who lived in the 1500s, and Julian of Norwich, an English female mystic who lived two centuries before that. (Starr has written about and translated the works of several Christian mystics.) Mentors can be female or male, old or young, and come from any time or place.

Who are your spiritual mentors? And if you say you have none, consider the historical spiritual figures or spiritual writers you most admire. Then, do a deep dive into their history and writings. It could be the start of a rewarding long-term relationship.

WEEK THREE/ DAY 6: INNER WORK

# The Single Step We Can Take to Be More Mindful

Are you busy? In today's modern world, it seems we all are. We cram our lives with so much busyness that we, in effect, become spiritually lazy. We don't allot the time, or have the willpower, to engage in a regular spiritual practice—including the recommended two daily meditation sessions that can lead to greater mindfulness, the ability to focus our attention on the present moment.

There may be an easier way to be mindful, and it comes from Google. Not through an online search, but via a former Google engineer who has taught his ideas on mindfulness to thousands of the company's employees. His name is Chade-Meng Tan, though he goes by Meng, and in his book *Search Inside Yourself*, he explains the biggest obstacles many of us face to being more mindful. It starts with an inability to meditate.

### WE OFTEN HAVE TROUBLE MEDITATING BECAUSE WE'RE TRYING TOO HARD.

Meng explains that meditation is like trying to fall asleep, in that it shares one important feature: they both rely on letting go. The better you are at letting go, the easier it is to fall asleep or meditate. The key is to get into a relaxed state, which is often easier said than done.

Meng offers tips on meditation technique and wise advice: start small. He writes of a single step we can start taking today to help us live a more relaxed life. It involves our breathing and it goes like this:

> Take one breath a day. Commit yourself to one mindful breath a day. Just one. Breathe in and breathe out mindfully,

and your commitment for the day is fulfilled. Everything else is a bonus.

Sounds too easy, doesn't it? Well, Meng notes that when we stop to become conscious of our breath and take a deep and focused breath in and out, we can immediately feel a sense of calm. Try it a second, third, and fourth time throughout the day, and you have a way to instantly calm yourself, which is especially important when you're feeling overwhelmed or stressed.

When it comes to more formal meditation, Meng has a fix for those of us who don't have the time or desire to add a twenty-minute sit-down session into our lives. It's called a walking or moving meditation. And we can work it into our daily comings and goings, whether we do it while walking from our car to the office or supermarket, or anytime we take a stroll from point A to point B.

Meng reminds us that when walking we should "bring full moment-to-moment attention to every movement and sensation in the body, and every time attention wanders away, just gently bring it back" to walking. Here is his approach, slightly modified and broken down into four easy steps.

1. Start by standing still. Become aware of the pressure on your feet as they touch the ground. Become aware of your whole body touching the ground.

2. Take a step forward. Lift one foot mindfully, move it forward mindfully, plant it down in front of you mindfully, shift your weight to this foot mindfully. Repeat this process with the other foot.

3. If you like, you can synchronize your movement with your breathing. When moving one leg, breath in, when moving the other leg, breathe out.

4. When you stop, become mindful of your body in a standing position. You can repeat silently to yourself, "standing, standing, standing."

If you're feeling more ambitious, walking meditation can also become a running ("step, step, step") meditation or swimming ("stroke, stroke, stroke") meditation—opportunities to put your mind at rest and relax into the motion of the body. These actions become the equivalent of a refreshing nap, recharging our brains with the added benefit of strengthening our hearts. For many of us, they help make meditation doable.

## WEEK THREE/ DAY 7: CONTEMPLATION

# The Fifty Miracles of Jesus: Fact or Fiction?

In the early 1810s, a newly retired Thomas Jefferson took on a project that no one had undertaken before him. After ordering two copies of the New Testament, he took out a razor and painstakingly cut out the portions of the text he preferred. He then rearranged these passages and glued them into the pages of a blank book. The result is what Jefferson called *The Philosophy of Jesus of Nazareth*, though today it is better known as *The Jefferson Bible*.

What was Jefferson's motive for deconstructing the Bible? Jefferson wanted to differentiate between what he saw as the true and false teachings of Jesus. He discarded "things impossible, of superstitions, fanaticisms and fabrications." He instead looked for passages that "place the character of Jesus in its true and high light." In short, Jefferson removed the miracles.

## THERE ARE MORE THAN FIFTY MIRACLES MENTIONED IN THE NEW TESTAMENT.

Jefferson was deeply skeptical of the supernatural acts of Jesus that were mentioned in the Bible. By one count, there are at least fifty of them. Consider that by the time Jefferson created his Bible, scientific knowledge was beginning to expand. Anything that could not be proven through experimentation could be called into doubt. And while Jefferson fully believed in the moral principles of Jesus, he found the unexplainable events in the Bible to be hogwash.

In *The Miracles of Jesus*, H. Van der Loos breaks down the miracles of Jesus found in the New Testament into two distinct groups:

- Miracles that affect people. Jesus healing the blind or exorcising evil spirits and raising people from "the dead," including Lazarus and later himself.
- Miracles that control nature: Jesus walking on water, turning water into wine, or feeding thousands of people with only five loaves of bread and two fish.

## DID THESE MIRACLES REALLY HAPPEN?

Most mainstream Christians (who view Jesus as a fully divine human), as well as Muslims (who view Jesus as a prophet of God), will tell you the miracles did happen. Some outside the mainstream believe these miracles began happening when Jesus was a youth. In both the Gnostic *Infancy Gospel of Thomas* and in stories passed along in the Muslim Sufi faith, there are tales of a precocious young Jesus pulling off incredible feats.

Sufi authors make frequent reference to Jesus as "a Master of the Way" with abilities that transcended those of normal human beings. In the tale that follows, which appears in slightly different forms in several Sufi texts, a young Jesus shows off his ability to do the unexplainable:

> One day Jesus, the son of Mary, was fashioning small birds out of clay. Some other youngsters, who could not do so, ran to the elders and told them, "This work cannot be allowed on the Sabbath," for it was a Saturday. The elders went to the pool where Jesus was sitting and asked him where his birds were. He pointed to the birds he had made and they flew away. "Making birds which fly is impossible, therefore it cannot be a breaking of the Sabbath," said one elder. So, the Sabbath was not broken.

### WAS JESUS A MAGICIAN? OR WORKING IN WAYS WE DO NOT UNDERSTAND?

Writing in *Jesus, A New Vision,* Whitley Strieber points out that the original gospel writers were "at pains to identify the miracles as originating from Jesus's divinity and not from magical practice." The reason? During the time Jesus lived, the practice of magic was looked down upon and could result in imprisonment. In fact, an ancient Roman text on the life of Nero reveals that "penalties were imposed on Christians, a sort of men who practice a new superstition involving magic." Another ancient text identifies Jesus as "a Galilean magician."

Strieber questions whether "the miracles were not supernatural but caused by natural forces that remain to this day little understood." He speculates that Jesus was able to "bend the rules of nature" and work with them in ways we cannot understand today—and perhaps in ways even Jesus did not totally understand.

One such example would be in Mark 8:22–26, where Jesus heals a blind man by rubbing spit in his eyes—twice. Strieber calls out the fact that in ancient medical texts, including *The Egyptian Book of the*

*Dead*, "there are many examples of medical spitting, and one way it was used was to cure weak vision." So, was the man that Jesus healed actually blind?

There are Christians today who believe the various miracles of Jesus were meant to be taken figuratively, not literally. For instance, when Jesus helps the blind to see, they believe this is not meant to be taken at face value—the person had actual sight, but Jesus helped him see the light of God within. (As in the lyric from "Amazing Grace," "I once was blind, but now I see.")

### THE CONNECTION BETWEEN MAGIC AND JESUS EXISTS TODAY.

Attend services in a Roman Catholic church and at a certain point during the sacrament of communion, a process called transubstantiation happens. Through a ritual that dates to the time of the Apostle Paul, a priest turns bread and wine into "the body and blood of Christ." It is akin to enacting a magical spell, similar to something you might see in a Harry Potter movie.

But perhaps the biggest miracle of all is the fact that Christianity, from its humble beginnings, is still around today. To paraphrase Whitley Stieber:

> Around forty years after the death of Jesus, a truly striking phenomenon took place. People decided to commit the stories that were circulating about him to the written word. They were then amplified into a religion that has changed human life and human history. That may be the greatest miracle of all.

It's a sentiment that even a nonbeliever in miracles like Thomas Jefferson might agree with.

# WEEK FOUR

## The Magic of Thinking Big

The title above is borrowed from a book by the same name, *The Magic of Thinking Big* by David J. Schwartz. Though it sold three million copies, you've probably never heard of it and for good reason. It was published way back in 1959.

*The Magic of Thinking Big* was part of a wave of self-help books that came out in the middle of the twentieth century with a similar message. Like *Think and Grow Rich* by Napoleon Hill and *The Power of Positive Thinking* by Norman Vincent Peale, Schwartz's book claimed to have found the key to success and happiness in life. The idea went something like this:

**BELIEVE YOU CAN SUCCEED AND YOU WILL.**

Schwartz's philosophy closely mirrors a sentiment expressed by Napoleon Hill: "What the mind can believe, the mind can achieve." According to Schwartz, Peale, and Hill, the biggest stumbling block to getting ahead in life is our own doubting mind. If we could just think positively and live confidently, we could be successful, as evidenced by these passages:

**Schwartz**: "Think Big and you'll live big. You'll live big in happiness. You'll live big in accomplishment. Big in income. Big in friends. Big in respect."

**Peale**: "Believe in yourself! Have faith in your abilities! Without a humble but reasonable confidence in your own powers you cannot be successful or happy."

**Hill:** "There are no limitations to the mind except those we acknowledge. Both poverty and riches are the offspring of thought."

### The Four Steps to Thinking Big

In *The Magic of Thinking Big*, Schwartz credits belief as "the driving force behind all great books, plays, scientific discoveries." He says it's the one ingredient that can be found in all successful people, that if you "believe, really believe, you can succeed, ... you will." He then lays out a four-point plan to help us achieve success.

1. **Think success; don't think failure.** Let the thought "I will succeed" dominate your thinking process. Thinking success conditions your mind to create plans that produce success. Thinking failure does the exact opposite.

2. **Remind yourself regularly: You are better than you think you are.** Successful people are not supermen or superwomen. They're just ordinary people who have developed belief in themselves and what they do.

3. **Believe big.** The size of your success is determined by the size of your belief. The bigger your dreams, the bigger your accomplishments.

4. **Stop making excuses.** Schwartz refers to it as "excusitis, the failure disease." In his words, people with mediocre accomplishments are quick to explain "why they haven't, why they don't, why they can't, and why they aren't." Each time someone makes an excuse, it becomes embedded in their subconscious.

## WAIT A SECOND YOU SAY, THAT SOUNDS TOO EASY. IS THAT ALL THERE IS TO IT?

Here's my take: I do believe there's something to the idea of thinking positively and/or thinking big. After all, I can't think of a single story in our popular culture about a businessperson, athlete, musician, or actor who thought they were going to fail miserably, but somehow succeeded. Yet, I also believe success is predicated not just on our beliefs—but on our actions.

Had Schwartz been alive today, he might have known about the writer Malcolm Gladwell and his "10,000-hour rule." Gladwell asserts that the key to success in any field is simply a matter of practicing a specific task over and over. While there is debate whether ten thousand hours is the actual number of hours needed, the idea is that you have to work at something to be good at it. In turn, once you're good at it you're more likely to succeed.

Writing in the book *Mastery*, George Leonard tells the story of the legendary golfer Jack Nicklaus. The man known as "The Golden Bear" spent years on the golf course before making his mark, but in an interview for *Esquire* magazine in his later years, he credited one factor for his great success: visualization.

Nicklaus claimed he never hit a golf shot without first visualizing the ball reaching its desired destination, "sitting up there high and white and pretty on the green." Nicklaus said the perfect shot was 50% visualization, 40% setup, and only 10% swing.

Think about how that might apply to any endeavor in life, whether it was applying for a job, looking to complete a project at home or work, finding romance, or achieving any milestone. We do the preparatory work (40%), we visualize the result (50%) and then make the effort (10%) to achieve success.

The net: Yes, think big. But be sure to put in the work to make big things happen.

## WEEK FOUR/ DAY 2: AWARENESS

# Is Your Inner Critic Holding You Back?

What keeps you from doing the things you want to do in life? Are you penned in by the expectations of others? Or is it your own doubting self that keeps you from fully expressing who you are and what you were meant to do in this life?

Seth Godin tells us that the culprit is often within us and labels it "our inner critic," a voice inside us that "comes from the shadows." We're not talking about the voice of reason or intuition warning you against doing something dumb or misguided, but the voice that comes from the place where "we store our shame, our insufficiency, our fraudulent nature."

Godin advises us on how to deal with the intractable fearmongering of this inner voice, via an anecdote from the Tibetan Buddhist teacher Pema Chödrön:

> When the inner critic arrives, invite him to sit for tea. Instead of running, welcome him. Dance with him, talk with him, take him along for a long, boring car ride. Suddenly, you'll find he's not so dangerous. He's sort of banal, actually.

You need to see the inner fear for what it is, an impostor posing as your real self. Godin informs us the truth is, "the critic isn't nearly as powerful as you are, not if you are willing to look him in the eye." When we confront and face down this fear, a funny thing happens. It crawls back into the shadows and leaves us to our own more astute powers of reasoning.

## THERE'S ANOTHER WAY TO LOOK AT AND DEAL WITH FEAR.

It comes from John Templeton. He too realizes that it is important to distinguish between the fears that help us and those that hurt us. Some fears, when it comes to our personal safety or the well-being of our family, community, or the planet, are justified. But what Templeton is talking about is the fear that keeps us from being our best selves:

> If you have a given fear, ask yourself: What's the worst possible thing that can reasonably happen? If the worst happens, is it manageable or reversible? Because in most cases, the worst that can happen is usually not that bad.

As Templeton points out, many times we fear things that cannot hurt us. "We fear the unknown and can often experience fear and anxiety about the future. We believe there is the potential for terrible things to happen to us and we don't know when."

When that happens, we are unable to live a full life, as the fear takes root in anticipation of the worst possible scenario. Nothing good comes of this:

- Fearing possible humiliation, we decline to make a contribution.
- Fearing rejection, we avoid asking the things we need to ask.
- Fearing nonconformity, we relinquish our individuality.

Irrational fear holds us back from the fullest expression of ourselves. It locks us in an invisible prison. It causes us to compromise and settle for less and can even prevent us from loving ourselves and others.

But the truth is that when we approach life without fear, things tend to work out for the best. When we put fear in its proper place, we eliminate the filter that prevents us from seeing a world that's filled with possibility and opportunity.

As Templeton says, "Like the child who discovers that ghosts are not real or worthy of fear, we can come to see that most of our fears are also phantoms." They are invisible barriers to becoming who we want to be or become. When we address these fears, we move forward with courage and discover we are capable of more than we think.

# The Seven-Step Guide to Being a Kinder Person

Late in his life, the famed Russian author Leo Tolstoy began compiling a book titled *A Calendar of Wisdom*. Subtitled *Wise Thoughts for Every Day*, it contained a series of quotes and insights that might be looked at as rules to live by.

They include pearls like, "When joy disappears, look for your mistake," and "Instead of saving humanity, every person should save himself." But as pointed out by Maria Popova in her *The Marginalian* e-newsletter, many of these insights have to do with kindness. For instance, Tolstoy writes: "The kinder and the more thoughtful a person is, the more kindness he can find in other people. Kindness enriches our life ... and is for your soul as health is for your body."

Tolstoy believed that we live our best, most fruitful life when we can sacrifice our own narrow self-interests for the benefit of others. He considered this to be the essence of true love. In his words:

> Only when a person forgets himself for the sake of another, and lives for another creature, only this kind of love can be

called true love, and only in this love do we see the blessing and reward of life. Nothing can make your life, or the lives of other people, more beautiful than perpetual kindness.

### "What I regret most in my life are failures of kindness."

The above sentiment comes from *Lincoln in the Bardo* author George Saunders, who goes on to point out that "it is a regret we all have from time to time." How true. Who hasn't come out of an uneasy encounter with a store clerk, a co-worker, or loved one and thought, *hmmm, I could have handled that a little better!*

So how do we shift our mindset into what Tolstoy calls "perpetual kindness," a place where being kind to others becomes our second nature? Richard Rohr, Franciscan friar and the head of the Center for Action and Contemplation, has some suggestions. In a recent edition of his weekly newsletter, the topic was the practice of "loving kindness," a major component of which is compassion. Rohr writes that in Buddhism:

"Compassion includes a willingness to identify so fully with someone that you would be willing to carry a little of their suffering. It is a quality that increases with practice and use. If you don't choose daily and deliberately to practice loving kindness, it is unlikely that a year from now you will be any more loving."

Rohr tells us that the qualities of compassion and kindness are limitless because they are already abundantly within you. There's no place to go and find compassion and kindness, no book to read. They are part of our inherent nature and just need to be brought to the forefront.

He recommends that we use a practice for growing loving kindness that was created by the Tibetan Buddhist teacher Pema Chödrön. She suggests we "set aside a quiet period to go through these simple steps with intention and openness." Here's a paraphrased version of Chödrön's steps based on the Buddhist *metta* practice.

### Seven Steps to Being a Kinder Person

1. Recognize the place of loving kindness inside yourself. It is there. Honor it, awaken it, and actively draw upon it.

2. Drawing upon the source of loving kindness within, think of someone for whom you feel sincere goodwill and tenderness, someone you love very much. From the core of your being, send loving kindness toward this person and bless them.

3. Awaken loving kindness for someone who is a casual friend or associate—someone not in your inner circle, but a bit further removed, someone you admire or appreciate. Send love to that individual.

4. Now send loving kindness to someone about whom you feel neutral or indifferent—for example, a waiter who served you dinner. Send your blessing to this person.

5. Think of someone who has hurt you, who has talked badly about you, whom you find it difficult to like or you don't enjoy being around. Bless them. Send this would-be enemy your love.

6. Bring the previously mentioned individuals into the stream of flowing love that includes yourself. Hold them there for a few moments.

7. Finally, extend this love to embrace all beings in the universe. It is one piece of love, one love toward all, regardless of religion, race, culture, or likability.

Of course, merely reading these steps will do little to help your sense of compassion and kindness. You must practice them. Consider going back to the top of the list and conjuring up the appropriate person for each step. When complete, you may find you feel a little better about the people around you. Rohr offers one additional reminder:

> Remember, spiritual gifts increase with use. Love, compassion, kindness and joy will grow as you let them flow. You are simply an instrument, a conduit for the inflow and outflow of the gifts of the Spirit.

**WEEK FOUR/ DAY 4: CALLING**

# The Mayoruna: On Finding Your Path in Life

Have you ever heard of a book titled *The Encounter, Amazon Beaming*? It tells the story of *National Geographic* photographer Loren McIntyre, and how he made contact with the elusive Mayoruna (also known as Matsés) tribe in the deepest jungles of Brazil in 1969. McIntyre was one of the first "outsiders" to ever have contact with the tribe.

For several years, Simon McBurney brought *The Encounter* story to the stage as a one-man show, including a run on Broadway. Before doing so, McBurney retraced the steps of McIntyre's journey and visited the indigenous tribespeople who to this day have little contact with the outside world. McBurney has a special interest in "consciousness" and how people think. So, he asked some of the tribespeople:

#### "WHERE IS YOUR CONSCIOUSNESS LOCATED?"

Now if you ask most people, they will tell you that consciousness is located somewhere behind the eyes in the area of the brain. But when McBurney asked the question of the Mayoruna, they pointed to the forest. He thought they didn't understand the question, so he asked them again. They pointed to the forest again. He then deduced that for the tribespeople, the inner world is not separate from the outer world around them. The forest and inner self are one.

This story may help explain how the photographer Loren McIntyre communicated with the tribespeople, not with words, but through his consciousness. McIntyre spent several weeks with the Mayoruna living as a de facto member of the tribe. He did not speak their language and came to realize he could hear what the tribespeople were telling him without the need to speak. They primarily communicated through thought. He, too, soon became an expert in telepathy.

But telepathy is just one attribute that made the tribe interesting. Known as the "cat people," McIntyre reported that the Mayoruna believe they're descended from jaguars—and pierce their faces with thin wooden spikes that mimic whiskers. The tribesmen found McIntyre fascinating, this light-skinned man wearing clothing. They wore none. But rather than ask him his name or where he came from, they specifically wanted to know one thing about him:

## "What is your ca'ah?"

McIntyre did not know what the term "ca'ah" means so eventually asked an interpreter for an explanation. He was told that a person's ca'ah is their "direction in life." It is "contained in your spirit" and is "controlled by your conscious decisions." Each of the tribespeople had their own specific ca'ah or role within their tribe, and they wanted to know what his role is in his tribe. He explains that his ca'ah is "to find things and photograph them" which the tribe found a satisfying answer.

## HOW WOULD YOU ANSWER THE QUESTION "WHAT IS YOUR CA'AH?"

If you're unsure how to answer, the key may be to look at your own "tribe." See where you fit in and what you offer now. What do you provide of value? How can you be of greater value? You may find that you're already offering a service or activity of importance, but that you can expand on and become even better at it. To this end, the Beat-era poet Gary Snyder (who, at this writing, is still kicking at age ninety-two) advises us to: "Find your place on the planet, dig in, and take responsibility from there."

Finding your own "place on the planet" means setting down roots and giving to the people and community around you—in whatever way you can and with as much devotion and love as you can. Wondering how much can you give? Snyder tells us that within your own tribe: "The size of the place that one becomes a member of the tribe is limited only by the size of one's heart."

I've recently been thinking about a person with a big and giving heart. He was a good friend of mine, Terry Tomalin, and it is now several years since he passed away. He lived the fullest life possible, one that was abruptly cut short by a sudden and unexpected heart attack at the age of fifty-five. (A reminder that we are all on this earth for a limited amount of time.)

Terry's passion was the outdoors, specifically in his adopted home state of Florida, but he did more than fish, dive, paddle, and hike. As the long-time Outdoors Editor for the *St. Petersburg Times*, he shared his adventures, using his column as an opportunity to teach as well as tell. He was a strong advocate for the environment and educated his readers on how they could prepare for virtually any out-in-the-wild situation.

Yet, to peg Terry as purely an outdoorsman is to only tell part of his story. He married the love of his life, Kanika, and was a devoted and caring husband and father, which he understood was his most important role in life. He committed himself to causes and organizations that bettered his community. And he motivated those around him to become better people. In my late-twenties, I was living a sedentary life when he persuaded me to start running. More than three decades later, I still run a few days a week.

Terry gave his all to those around him, so to say Terry's ca'ah was to teach us to love and respect the outdoors only covers one facet of his life—just as our own vocation is just one slice of our own lives. I believe Terry's calling was a bit broader: to give 100% of himself—to his family, friends and community. That was his ca'ah and a goal he accomplished. And that's a goal you and I can accomplish, as well.

Have you identified your ca'ah? If not, what might it be? It could be something as simple as being a great listener to those who need counsel or a friendly ear. Is there a way you can nourish and expand on your ca'ah and make it a more integral part of your life?

WEEK FOUR/ DAY 5: PRACTICE

# How to Improve Your Spiritual Well-Being—Morning, Noon and Night

January is often the time to make big resolutions, and for many of us this includes a pledge to become healthier and more physically fit. But what if for the next year, whether you're reading this in January or July, you resolved to improve your spiritual health as well?

You may have already read about starting a morning ritual, a practice that can have a positive effect on your mental and spiritual well-being. When we start our days with a regular morning routine, it nourishes us both body and soul. It can calm and center us, better preparing us for the day ahead. So, no matter what challenges life puts in front of us, we can deal with them from a place of greater compassion, humor, kindness, and love.

## THERE'S ANOTHER TOOL YOU CAN USE TO MAINTAIN YOUR SPIRITUAL HEALTH—A SHORT EVENING RITUAL.

If you're like a lot of people, each morning you meditate (or like me, engage in silent contemplation) for a ten- to fifteen-minute period—and while a second "meditation" session is recommended toward the end of the day, we often can't find the time. That's why I'd like to share a simple, five-minute practice you can engage in each night at bedtime to cap off the day and put your head in a good place before dreamtime.

This concept comes from Facebook COO Sheryl Sandberg who, while grieving the sudden death of her husband several years ago, began a simple practice. Before she went to bed at night, she wrote down three things she did well that day. The list started with small acts like making a good cup of tea. She found that by focusing on things she had done well, even if small, she was able to record something positive each day and rebuild her confidence.

Sandberg then moved on to the next step. In *USA Today*, she stated that after engaging in the "three things done well" practice for about a year, she transitioned to a new practice: Instead of recording three things she did well, Sandberg said her resolution was to write down three joyful moments because, to quote Bono, "joy is the ultimate act of defiance."

What a great idea—appreciating the good that happens by writing down three joyful moments each day before they're forgotten. This aligns with another practice I heard about via the pastor Steve Wiens of Minnesota, a centuries-old ritual called *examen*. It involves "noticing God's presence and discerning God's direction" each evening by reflecting on the day's events and asking ourselves two simple questions. To quote Wiens:

"At the end of each day, take ten minutes to stop and review the day's events, becoming aware of God's presence all through it." Then ask yourself two simple questions:

1. When was I most alive today?
2. When was I most drained today?"

You can write down your answers in a journal or simply contemplate them. (Wiens recommends "praying through them.") Either way, the point is to find out what in your life is bringing you closer to God (a happy place) and which actions take you further from God (a negative place). By noticing these patterns, you can then make the necessary adjustments to help ensure your good days outnumber the bad.

By ending the day with the practices suggested by Sandberg or Wiens, we bring our day full circle. With our morning ritual, we ready ourselves for the day ahead. With our nighttime ritual, we reflect on the day's events and learn to appreciate all that is good and right in our lives. Put together, they help us lead our best possible lives.

**WEEK FOUR/ DAY 6: INNER WORK**

# The Simple Breathing Exercise That Works Like Meditation

I once read a story that asked a singer/performer, I think it was Bonnie Raitt, "What was the best piece of advice you ever received?" Her response consisted of a single word:

---

*"Breathe."*

---

The songstress had been given this tip from her father, who had pointed out that when we're stressed or feeling a little bit tense, we tend to shorten our breath. And at those moments, there's nothing better we can do to steady ourselves than to take a big, deep gulp of air.

I was reminded of this advice when reading *The Last Barrier*, the autobiography of the late English author and spiritual teacher Reshad Feild. In the book, Feild is told by his spiritual mentor that learning to breathe properly is "the study of a lifetime" and the rhythm and quality of your breathing "can help change the course of your life."

It was instruction that Feild took to heart, and as part of his life work, he continually stressed the importance of breathing. Feild was also the founder of the Sufi-inspired Chalice School and if you go to the school's website, in large ninety-point type, you will be greeted by the following message:

## "ALL IS CONTAINED IN THE DIVINE BREATH, LIKE THE DAY IN THE MORNING'S DAWN."

There is a section of the Chalice School site that is devoted to the importance of breathing, titled "Breath is Life." Here, Feild echoes the lessons he was taught as a young man, telling us:

"The secret of life is in the breath. We come into this world on the breath and we go out on the breath; but if we are not awake to breath, we will surely die asleep to the reality of life itself. Breath is life."

Feild recommends that we engage in a practice he calls the "7-1-7 Breathing Exercise," also known as the "Mother's Breath," a simple exercise that originates from ancient Egypt. I have edited Feild's words on the subject and put them into the eight-step practice below.

### PRACTICING THE 7-1-7 BREATH

1. Sit in a hard-backed chair. Keep your back straight, without forcing it. Feel the flow of energy move through you. (*I imagine it moving up and down my spine.*)

2. Place your feet flat on the floor, with heels together and toes apart forming a triangle. Legs should be uncrossed. Your arms should be relaxed and your hands should rest on your knees.

3. Before you start the conscious breathing practice, visualize the most beautiful object in nature you can imagine. It could be a plant, a tree, a waterfall, the sea, or whatever has special meaning to you.

4. Your eyes can be open or closed. Either way, focus on a point approximately eight feet in front of you. If your eyes are closed, imagine the picture of what you've chosen. If you're focusing on an object, put it as close to eight feet away from you as you can.

5. Next comes the sacred rhythm, the 7-1-7 rhythm of the Mother's Breath. The method is simple, though initially it may seem difficult since we are used to breathing without any form of attention or consciousness.

6. Breathe into the solar plexus (the pit of your stomach) for the count of seven, pause for one count, then for another seven counts radiate out breath from the "heart center," the point in the center of your chest. *Important note:* When counting to seven, you do not have to count in precise measured seconds. It's not the speed that matters, it's the actual number of counts. Choose the speed, fast or slow, that suits you.

7. Having breathed in for the count of seven, pause for one count and at the same time, bring your attention to the center of the chest. Then breathe out for the count of seven. As you breathe out, radiate love and goodwill from your center.

8. To complete the practice, return to your senses. Come back to your body and be awake to the room and your surroundings.

The whole exercise should only take you about ten minutes and Feild recommends trying it a few times a day. I find it's a great companion to and substitute for meditation, with many of the same calming and revitalizing effects. As Feild says, it will leave you with a "tremendous sense of wonder and gratitude."

## WEEK FOUR/ DAY 7: CONTEMPLATION

# The Woman Who Can Feel God in Her Bones

Is God a continual presence in your life? Or does the sense of the Divine within you, the feeling that you have a deep connection to something greater than yourself, come and go?

I believe for most spiritual people it is the latter. Some days the heavenly spark in our hearts burns brightly, while at other times it seems to flicker and is barely perceptible. It is during these times that we need to fan the flame and there may be no better person to ignite it than the author and teacher Mirabai Starr.

There's an expression my wife Laney uses when the bitter cold days of winter arrive here in the Northeast. "It's so cold I can feel it in my bones." I think of Mirabai Starr as a person who can feel *God* in her bones, a presence that permeates her being and can be sensed with each breath she takes.

Before reading Starr's recent book *Wild Mercy: Living the Fierce and Tender Wisdom of the Women Mystics*, I decided to revisit a previous book of hers from a decade ago, an energy drink for my soul titled *God is Love: A Guide to the Heart of Judaism, Christianity and Islam.*

Starr comes from a diverse religious background and practices what is known as interspirituality. She participates in not one, but several spiritual traditions, which in her case include, but are not limited to, the religions called out in the subtitle of *God is Love*. She does this because she believes in "the oneness at the heart of all religious traditions" and finds meaning in all their teachings. In her words: "When I drop down into these ancient texts, I feel the breath of the God of Love on my face. It makes me crazy. In the very best way."

As you may be able to tell, Mirabai Starr is not your average spiritual seeker. She pursues God with a passion and sensuality that would make the more puritanical among us blush. She is a woman on a mission to find God, the "source of Love itself," and become one with this love. She writes: "The soul spends all her life longing for union with the Divine. And when at least she reaches the object of her desire, she disappears into Him."

Starr is bold and daring and her love for God comes leaping off the page. Her enthusiasm is so great, it's hard not to get caught up in it. Through the sheer force of her writing, you begin to view God in a new light, as the all-encompassing source of love:

> This God of mine is not mere emptiness. It is imbued with the energy of love. It is an overflowing of love into the entire container of the cosmos. I call it the Sacred, and there is nowhere it is not. I am in awe of this God of Love, who breaks through ordinary moments with a dazzling radiance and melts the boundaries of my individuated consciousness and reminds me that I am not separate from the source of Love Itself.

Starr advocates for the active pursuit of the Divine in everyday life. Like one of the Christian mystics whose writings she has translated, Teresa of Avila, she says that "what the beloved wants from us is action." And she takes this advice to heart, describing what it's like to live a life encompassed by the love of God:

> Your heart is so drenched in love for the Beloved that it overflows into everything you do. You are incapable of making distinctions between the sacred and the profane; each act has become an act of prayer.

As she makes clear, the good news is that this divine love is not hard to find. It is with us always and can be accessed by any of us at all times:

> We can feed the fire of divine love by cultivating simple practices that expand our hearts and raise our consciousness, such as meditation and chanting, reciting ancient prayers or conversing with the Beloved ... each sunrise, each meal, every challenge and triumph in work and human relationships, are opportunities to praise God.

For a life so saturated by so many religious faiths, Starr's main message rings loud and clear: "Each faith tradition is singing the same song in a deliciously different voice. God is love."

# WEEK FIVE

## An Eight-Step Guide to Living Your Life with Gumption

These days, it can be easy to lose your *joie de vivre* (joy of living) or at least feel like it's missing in action. And who can blame you? It seems like there's been a seemingly endless stretch of bad news that has lasted for months, from political turmoil to mass shootings to a string of natural disasters related to climate change.

So, with all that's going on, how can you stay actively engaged with life? Should you sit back and wait for things to improve? Or should you step up right now and try to make life around you a little bit better?

I suggest you try to make life a little bit better by taking a different approach to living, one that comes from the novelist J.C. Hutchins. In a short story he wrote several years ago, Hutchins decries the fact that we lead lives that are far too laid-back: "Most of us settle in and settle for what we have. Rather than pursue, we accept. Our lives become unwitting celebrations of passivity...we pine for better lives but live vicariously through our televisions."

Hutchins believes that what we need is a little gumption, a wonderful term that means "a spirited initiative and resourcefulness." (Brings to mind Forrest Gump, doesn't it?) In effect, this approach means we need to actively engage with life to get the things we want, including happiness. Hutchins asks us to take action:

Let's declare war on passivity. Hush the inner voice that insists you're over the hill, past your prime, unworthy of achieving those dreams. Get fired up. Find your backbone and your wings.

But how do you get "fired up" when you're feeling less than confident about the future? What do you do when you're thinking that your best days may be behind you? You might try this easy eight-step guide that for me epitomizes what gumption is all about. (Source unknown.)

### An Eight-Step Guide to Living Your Life with Gumption

1. Miss somebody? Call.
2. Wanna meet up? Invite.
3. Wanna be understood? Explain.
4. Have questions? Ask.
5. Don't like something? Say it.
6. Like something? State it.
7. Want something? Ask for it.
8. Love someone? Tell them.

Simple, isn't it? To me, this list illustrates that you have to be an active participant in your life. Each question is followed by an action verb, a step you need to take. These angst-filled times are no excuse to lock yourself—and your heart and soul—behind a closed door. Even meet ups these days can be done virtually using Zoom.

I was recently reading about a real-life example of a person with gumption. Unfortunately, it was the obituary of a man who died from complications due to COVID-19, but his words live on here. His name is Joseph Michael Novi and he passed away at the age of fifty-seven. His obituary in the *New York Times* mentioned his "Joseph's Pearls of Wisdom," which include these words: "Let those you love know you love them, share your knowledge and always ask for one more hug."

Three distinct actions are recommended in that sentence:

1. Talk to those you love and tell them you love them.
2. Share the wisdom you've gained over the years with those who need it.
3. When appropriate, hug those who are closest to you.

May Joseph rest in peace—and may the rest of us get busy living.

# Is The Cure for our Aches, Pains, and Fatigue Right in Front of Us?

How are you feeling today? Healthy and alert with, to borrow a phrase from fitness guru Jack LaLanne, pep in your step? Or are you suffering from aches and pains, feeling tired, or even mildly depressed? There's a fellow from a small town on the eastern shore of Maryland who may have a cure for what ails you. His name is David Mercier.

Mercier's resume includes a masters' degree in acupuncture, two years of study under renowned psychologist Stanislav Grof, and a teaching gig as an integrated medicine professor at John Hopkins University. He also has a deeply spiritual side, having spent two years living as a monk in a Buddhist monastery, and he currently conducts classes in meditation and mindfulness.

In *A Beautiful Medicine, A Radical Look at the Essence of Health and Healing*, Mercier posits that the cure for much of what ails us lies within us. He believes the great majority of the aches and pains we experience need to be looked at in a fresh way—as symbols of deeper issues within our bodies and within our souls.

While Mercier concedes that some symptoms can be signs of serious illness, he also asserts that symptoms are the equivalent of "a flashing light on the dashboard, the wailing of a smoke alarm, a baby's cry in the night." A symptom, like a headache or feeling of melancholy, is not the problem. It merely points to a problem. That's why he says:

"When we have a backache, a migraine or a case of the blues, we need to be curious about the symptom's intent and ask ourselves four questions:" They are:

1. What's the message?
2. What am I being asked to do?
3. Is there something missing that I need to add?
4. Is there something present that I need to subtract?"

Mercier points out that the most common way we approach these symptoms or messages from the body is to blunt them, without trying to understand their purpose. We do this through "medications, herbs, denial, overwork or alcohol." We never get to the core issue, the problems or stress that lie behind the symptoms.

He also has an interesting take on what our symptoms want from us and why they appear. Mercier writes:

> Since our bodies can't form words and sentences, they gesture with insomnia, headaches, a pain in the belly, an ache in the shoulder, a shroud of weariness ... our symptoms are often asking us to purge our bodies of grief, resentment, fear, and sometimes, plain boredom.

**DAVID MERCIER HAS MET THE ENEMY. IT'S THE WAY WE LIVE TODAY.**

In his own practice, Mercier often finds that once he deals with the outward symptoms, he can discuss with his patients the true root of their problems. In other words, what's really going on. Sometimes these problems are caused by poor lifestyle and work choices. He writes:

> Headaches and insomnia can come from the contours of our lives, which are in turn shaped by our values and priorities. The headaches and insomnia can come from eating poorly and not exercising, which come from not having enough time, which comes from being too busy at work, which comes from the desire to have a certain income.

Some of our problems may be self-induced. The author blames this on "the myth that happiness is the freedom to indulge without limits our overindulgent lives." Mercier points out that "watching a sitcom with beer and chips in hand doesn't inspire us to lead our best lives, or to seek the heights of human possibility." We are often our own worst enemies. He concludes:

> The most common proximal sources of inertia are the allure of the sugar fairy, the siren call of daily drink, and the gravitational pull of the American couch. For many others, the inertia in taking care of their health comes from being under the whip of constant work overload and a frenzied schedule. They choose a lifestyle which allows them insufficient time to do good things for their bodies.

For our health and well-being, we may need to live a simpler life. While we can always run to a doctor for a quick fix of what ails us, ultimately this does not address the underlying issues. We need to find the motivation, courage, and discipline to make the changes

95

WAKE UP CALL • TOM RAPSAS

necessary to improve our lives. Mercier tells us that when we commit to becoming fit and healthy, it's part of a bigger plan:

> You're taking out spiritual insurance and increasing the chances that the generosity of your soul will be more durable and available longer to those who need it most. We're here for a purpose, and that purpose is grander than our own individual designs for our lives … living with a meaningful purpose, perhaps even one you would die for, paves the potholes of daily living.

And isn't fulfilling your purpose what life is all about?

WEEK FIVE/ DAY 3: CHARACTER

# The Day Mahatma Gandhi Threw His Sandal off a Train

I've always been interested in college commencement speeches and when I see them in print, I'll check them out, curious as to what wisdom our elders have to pass on to our youth. One speech that caught my eye was from U.S. Senator Cory Booker of New Jersey, given to a graduating class at the University of Pennsylvania. Booker is an excellent storyteller, and he kicked off his speech with an anecdote about Mahatma Gandhi that I'll paraphrase below.

Mahatma Gandhi had a busy schedule and was often rushing from place to place. One day he was literally running late for a train. He ran down the tracks as the train was leaving the station and leapt into the third-class section that he normally travelled in. People were there to grab him and help him aboard, but as they did one of his sandals fell off. Everybody watched with disappointment as the train pulled away. Gandhi had lost a sandal.

Before anyone could react, Gandhi reached down quickly, grabbed his other sandal and threw it out the train door onto the tracks. People were curious as to why he had done this and asked, "Mahatma, why would you throw your other sandal out there?" He was both confused and bemused by the question and answered, "I threw the other sandal because whoever finds that first sandal, wouldn't it be nice if they found the other one as well?"

This is an example of what Booker calls "creative compassion," an ability to find ways to help others that might not be quite so obvious. It's part of his belief that if we use our imagination, we all have ways to make a difference in the everyday lives of those we encounter.

To illustrate this idea, here are five key points from Booker's speech that encapsulate his main message:

1. **How you live your days is how you live your life.** As you're chasing after your goals and dreams, it's the small things you do every single day that define you.
2. **The biggest thing you can do on any given day is a small act of kindness.** Do you miss opportunities to offer the people around you decency, love, and compassion?
3. **Your real power is not necessarily to change the world, but to make a world of change.** Offer the people you encounter a smile, a kind word. Find a way to throw a sandal onto the track—that is the power you have today and every day.
4. **Life is not about celebrity; it's about significance.** In turn, life is not about popularity, it's about purpose.
5. **"Do a little bit of good where you are,"** in the words of Desmond Tutu. It's those little bits of good, put together, that overwhelm the world.

Booker closed his speech by talking about one of his mentors, a public-housing advocate named Frank Johnson, who spent decades helping those in need in Booker's home city of Newark, New Jersey. Johnson had failing eyesight and by the end of his life he was totally blind. When Booker would encounter Frank, they would exchange a verbal greeting: "I see you. I love you." He worked this expression into his parting words to the UPenn class:

"You're going to go out for the big challenges, the big fights. I see you. I love you. You're going to have tough days, you're going to fall, you're going to fail but I see you and I love you. May your vision and your love not just change the world but make a world of change for everyone that you can."

**WEEK FIVE/ DAY 4: CALLING**

# Where Are You in the Seven Stages of Life?

When we look at our lives, we often tend to view them as broken into three distinct phases: school, work, and retirement. But these days, when our jobs have become more fluid, when the delineation line between work and retirement is often hazy, these terms seem to come up short.

That's why when I saw the following list in Thomas Moore's book *Ageless Soul,* I thought: finally, here's a guide that more accurately describes the phases of life as they relate to our modern age. From Moore's perspective, life is comprised of seven stages as follows:

1. Educating yourself and developing talents and skills
2. Looking for a job that employs these abilities
3. Developing a career
4. Dealing with endings and turning points in the career
5. Achieving success in your own way

6. Shifting into the older years with an emphasis on service
7. Creating a legacy for future generations

Notice how stages four and five allow for the fact that it is rare for anyone to stay at one job for their entire careers. We may occasionally bounce back to stage three, because in this day and age we often reshape our careers mid stream. In fact, it is not uncommon for some in our society to jump back to stage one in their thirties, forties and even fifties to purse an entirely new career direction.

**WHAT ESPECIALLY INTERESTS ME IN THIS LIST IS THE STAGE SEVEN ACT OF LEGACY.**

While it may occur in the final stage of our life, I believe the idea of leaving a legacy is fluid and can occur along the way. (Think of a teacher whose lessons are so valuable they stay with you for life.) A legacy is all about our generosity and involves leaving behind something of value for others to benefit from or enjoy. Moore points out that his act has the power of giving our own lives greater value because it enables each of us to become "a bigger and deeper person."

The author cites the example of Elizabeth Marshall Thomas, who in 1993 published the bestselling book *The Hidden Life of Dogs*. Thomas used part of the money she made to purchase Cunningham Pond in Peterborough, New Hampshire, and stipulated that there be two beaches there, one for humans and one for dogs. To this day, you can visit the site and watch dogs playing on a beach that's all their own.

Moore reminds us that "legacy is not about the size of our impact on those who will come after us, but only the fact of having been significant to someone." So, while a legacy can involve a grand gesture, like passing on a home to a new generation or contributing a sum of money to a cancer research center, it can also involve much smaller and more intimate acts.

Leaving a legacy can mean passing along a treasured piece of family jewelry and the story behind it, or even more importantly, passing along a part of yourself. It's easy to self-publish these days, and your legacy may include a short book that's comprised of the important events that shaped your character and your innermost thoughts on what you've learned in this life.

It's never too early to start thinking about your legacy. What will you leave behind?

**WEEK FIVE/ DAY 5: PRACTICE**

# Is Your Head Full of Noise? Or "Inner Music"?

*"We seem so frightened today of being alone that we never let it happen. We choke the space with continuous music, chatter, and companionship to which we do not even listen. It is simply there to fill the vacuum. When the noise stops there is no inner music to take its place."*
— *Anne Morrow Lindbergh*

I can recall an acquaintance once remarking that each of us is troubled by something and that's often the dominant thought in our head. It could be an argument with our spouse, a perceived public slight, our finances, or a conflict at work. And once we resolve whatever issue is at the forefront, our next most pressing conflict comes rushing in. We go through life moving from one worry to the next, our heads full of noise.

**NOISE HAS A WAY OF DISTRACTING US FROM WHAT REALLY MATTERS.**

To the Trappist monk and noted author Thomas Merton, noise represented one of the biggest problems of our modern society—because when our heads are filled with noise, whether it's self-generated or it comes from our immediate environment, we go through life off balance and disconnected from our spiritual nature. In the book *No Man Is an Island*, Merton writes:

> Everything in modern city life is calculated to keep man from entering into himself and thinking about spiritual things. Even with the best of intentions, a spiritual man finds himself exhausted and deadened, debased by the constant noise of machines, the dead air and glaring lights of offices and shops, the everlasting suggestions of advertising and propaganda.

Christian musician John Michael Talbot, who is also founder of the Brothers and Sisters of Charity based at Little Portion Hermitage in Arkansas, explains the problem in a similar manner: "The world's noise has a way of deflecting people from the deeper realities of life. It keeps us preoccupied with the superficial at the expense of the meaningful." Or, as Anne Morrow Lindberg so eloquently states, noise stops us from hearing the "inner music."

**HOW DO WE HEAR THE INNER MUSIC? BY MAKING TIME FOR STILLNESS AND SOLITUDE.**

Talbot encourages us to take breaks from the stresses of the everyday. He writes that places like monasteries, retreat centers, and hermitages (which literally means the dwelling place of hermits), were created "so that people who wanted to hear the still, small voice of God could turn down the deafening and disquieting cacophony of sounds coming from a busy, bustling world."

But since most of us have families and jobs and a retreat is out of the question, how do we find the space to hear our thoughts? Where can we access the silence and solitude that, in the words of Merton, allow us to "recuperate spiritual powers that may have been gravely damaged by the noise and rush of a pressurized existence"?

## WE NEED TO SET TIME ASIDE TO RECHARGE OUR SPIRITUAL BATTERIES.

You can do it in your own home. For me, this especially holds true on Sundays as I get ready for the new week. It's a time to detach from work, and as Merton says "see all things in the light of faith." This means expressing gratitude for the good in our lives, asking for guidance with the things that trouble us, and trusting that our needs and concerns will be addressed. Merton also writes: "[People] need enough silence and solitude in their lives to enable the deep inner voice of their true self to be heard at least occasionally."

Is your schedule jam-packed with work, chores, and other responsibilities? You might consider carving out some alone time early in the morning or later at night. Set your alarm clock fifteen to thirty minutes earlier a few days a week. Or, after saying goodnight to your significant other, retreat to the den or the quietest part of your home for a few moments. Find the time for solitude. Talbot puts this in a spiritual context:

> There's nothing magical about solitude that makes God suddenly appear. God is everywhere all the time. It's just that most of the time we are so busy with everything else that we don't notice. But by practicing the discipline of solitude, we are creating a space in our lives where God can be with us.

Will you make time to hear the "inner music"?

## WEEK FIVE/ DAY 6: INNER WORK

# Can the Prayer the Dalai Lama Says Daily Help You?

It's hard to think of a more compassionate person than the Dalai Lama. As the spiritual leader of Tibetan Buddhism, living in exile from a country where religious and political freedom have long been repressed, he carries a heavy load on his shoulders. Yet, to see him in public, is to witness a man who appears care-free.

The Dalai Lama has been described as "witty and effervescent," "the personification of compassion" and "the most peace-loving person on earth." He sincerely seems more concerned about the well-being of others than about himself, as illustrated at the website "His Holiness, the 14th Dalai Lama of Tibet":

> [He] is concerned with encouraging people to be happy—helping them understand that if their minds are upset, mere physical comfort will not bring them peace, but if their minds are at peace even physical pain will not disturb their calm. He advocates the cultivation of warm-heartedness and human values such as compassion, forgiveness, tolerance, contentment, and self-discipline.

What makes this guy tick? How is he able to remain so happy and offer such great compassion and do-gooding-ness, day-in and day-out? I have written about the Dalai Lama's ever-present smile (he has called smiling more important than meditating), but one wonders how he is able to tap into this constant stream of good will without pause. One clue may be in the prayer he recites daily.

I have read conflicting reports whether the Dalai Lama says this prayer in the morning or at bedtime. Perhaps he recites it both upon awakening and at night. Yet, to read its words is to realize that some people are called to, and live up to, a higher spiritual standard.

## THE BODHISATTVA PRAYER FOR HUMANITY

May I be a guard for those who need protection

A guide for those on the path

A boat, a raft, a bridge for those who wish to cross the flood

May I be a lamp in the darkness

A resting place for the weary

A healing medicine for all who are sick

A vase of plenty, a tree of miracles

And for the boundless multitudes of living beings

May I bring sustenance and awakening

Enduring like the earth and sky

Until all beings are freed from sorrow

And all are awakened.

It's easy to read this prayer and feel the positive energy contained within it. I am reminded of a story I once wrote titled "If You're Not Drowning, You're A Lifeguard." The fact is, no matter how difficult your own life may sometimes feel, there are others in greater need, people around you who are suffering and can use your guidance, support, or help.

Consider: Who do you know in your own life who can use your assistance, even if it's just a kind word? Our role in life should not be to tend solely to our own needs, but also to tend to the needs of our families, friends, and community. The payoff is huge because, in the words of author Florence Scovel Shinn, what you do for others, you are also doing for yourself.

**WEEK FIVE/ DAY 7: CONTEMPLATION**

# The Mystics on Finding God within Yourself

At some point in time, have you wondered if God really exists? You may have asked God to show you a sign, any sign, that he or she is real. You want to know your prayers aren't going out into an empty void, that your faith isn't a sign of some deeply ingrained ignorance, that there truly is someone or something looking over our messy lives and world.

**THE MYSTICS SAY THEY KNOW GOD EXISTS BECAUSE THEY HAVE EXPERIENCED GOD FIRSTHAND.**

There are those, past and present, who have made a personal connection to a greater force. They claim to have not only sensed the presence of God, but also to have felt the Divine within themselves, permeating their entire being. They are labeled mystics, and they have been around since the dawn of religion.

Mysticism is the knowledge of God that comes from a direct experience of God. This knowledge is not learned from years of religious study or by following a specific faith-based protocol. It is an experience that is felt deeply and convincingly within, sometimes unexpectedly, a vision or sense of something that is far outside the normal experiences of life.

In the book *Mysticism, A Study and an Anthology*, author F.C. Happold points out that mystical experiences are common to all religions. What stands out is not so much the differences in these experiences but their similarities. They often come out of nowhere and can be fleeting, but they leave an indelible mark on the recipient.

Happold writes of several modern-day mystics he has studied and how through their supernatural experiences, they have found "an illumination and certainty which can rarely, if ever, be reached by the rational consciousness." Two common themes emerge:

- **Mystics discover the unity of all things or what Happold calls "a consciousness of the oneness of everything."** When describing his experience, one contemporary mystic described it like this:

  > A great peace came over me, I was conscious of a lovely, unexplainable pattern in the whole texture of things, a pattern of which everyone and everything was a part; and weaving the pattern was a Power; and that Power was what we faintly call Love.

- **Mystics realize that the God we are looking for, and call out to in our times of need, is actually within us.** Here's another modern-day testimonial via Happold:

  > The room was filled by a Presence, which in a strange way was both about me and within me, like light or warmth. I was overwhelmingly possessed by someone who was not myself, and yet I felt I was more myself than I had ever been before...overall there was a deep sense of peace and security and certainty.

Happold largely focuses on the Christian mystics and highlights more than a dozen, that span several centuries and countries. As previously noted, what stands out are the similarities of these experiences, each stressing a deep and personal connection with something greater than the self. Here are a few of my favorite first-hand accounts.

The French abbot St. Bernard of Clairvaux:

> My curiosity took me to my lowest depth to look for Him, nevertheless, He was found still deeper … he had passed into my inmost parts. Only by the movement of my heart did I recognize his presence.

The philosopher Meister Eckhart (here referring to the soul as the feminine "she"):

> She plunges into the bottomless well of the divine nature and becomes so one with God that she herself would say that she is God … where God is, there is the soul and where the soul is, there is God.

The cloistered nun Julian of Norwich:

> God is nearer to us than our own Soul; for He is (the) Ground in whom our Soul stands … our Soul is kindly rooted in God in endless love.

The parish priest John of Ruysbroeck:

> Grace flows from within, and not from without; for God is more inward to us than we are to ourselves. God works in us from within outwards … not from without.

All these different mystics, separated by time and place, in the days before religious texts were widely circulated, come to conclusions that sound surprisingly alike. It is a stirring reminder that if you are seeking the presence of God in your own daily life, it makes sense to pause each day and locate and engage with the Divine within.

Here's one more passage, from the English priest William Law and a book he wrote in the 1700s titled *The Spirit of Prayer*. Law believed in what he calls an "indwelling presence" and wrote that heaven is "as near to our souls as this world is to our bodies." What follows are his lightly edited words, updated to contemporary language:

> You see, hear and feel nothing of God, because you seek God outside yourself. You look for God in books, in the church and outward exercises, but you will not find God until you have found God in your heart. God is already within you, living, stirring, calling, knocking at the door. Look for God in your heart and you will never search in vain, for he lives there.

# WEEK SIX

## Was the Secret to Life Discovered in 1897?

Every few years, a spirituality bestseller comes out that captures the imagination of the public. Over the years, there's been *The Secret* by Rhonda Byrne and *A New Earth* by Eckhart Tolle. Before that, you might remember *The Celestine Prophecy* by James Redfield or *Jonathan Livingston Seagull* by Richard Bach.

Once upon a time, there was a spirituality book even bigger than those classics. It was first published in 1897 and because it is now 125 years old, there's a good chance you've never heard of it. It's titled *In Tune with the Infinite* by Ralph Waldo Trine and it's considered by some to be the greatest spirituality book of all time.

A pioneer in the era's New Thought movement, Trine wrote over a dozen books. However, it was this one that caught fire with the public and went on to sell more than two million copies. Just how popular was *In Tune with the Infinite*? I own a used copy that dates to 1909, and on the worn dustcover here's what the publisher had to say:

> It has become a world classic. One traveler writes that he came across a man reading it while sitting on the banks of the Yukon; another that he finds it in the shops and even the little railway stations in Burma and Ceylon (now Sri Lanka). An American reviewer said: "For one to say that he has never heard of *In Tune with the Infinite* is similar to saying that he has never heard of the Constitution of the United States."

For a book that achieved such worldwide popularity, its main message was relatively simple. It was repeated again and again, because the author believed this knowledge was the secret to a happy and fulfilling life. It had to do with a realization—that God is everywhere and always present. Trine wrote that:

> God is the "Infinite Spirit" of life and is present in and through all things. This spirit surrounds us on all sides. You and I have the power, within us, to open or close ourselves to this divine inflow exactly as we choose.

The key to realizing "the power within us," what Trine alternately refers to as the Infinite Spirit, Infinite Power, and Infinite Life, was to recognize that it is always there and accessible at all times. By getting "in tune with the infinite" we can then access "a divine source of love and guidance," and our lives can be changed for the better.

What follows are eight of my favorite passages, which I've organized by subject. I've also done a little editing, including updating some of the language and using gender-neutral pronouns where possible. By reading these passages, you'll get the gist of Trine's message. Much of what he wrote all those years ago still has the ring of truth today.

### #1. Find Your Center.

Find your center and live in it. Surrender it to no person. The more you do this, the more you will find yourself growing stronger. How can you find your center? By realizing your oneness with the Infinite Power, and by living continually with this realization.

### #2. Listen to the Voice of the Soul.

When we recognize our true selves, and our oneness with the Infinite Life, then the voice of intuition, the voice of the soul, the voice of God speaks clearly. When you listen to, and obey it, it speaks even more clearly, until there comes a time when it is absolutely unerring in its guidance.

#### #3. BE AN OPTIMIST.

The optimist is right. The pessimist is right. The one differs from the other like the light from the dark. Yet both are right. Each is right from their own individual point of view, and this point of view is the determining factor in our lives. It determines whether you have a life of power or of impotence, of peace or pain, of success or failure.

#### #4. LIVE IN LOVE.

Live only in the thought of love for all and you will draw love to you from all. Live in the thought of malice or hatred, and malice and hatred will come back to you.

#### #5. KNOW YOURSELF.

There is no better way to help yourself than to know yourself. Become aware of the power lying dormant within your own soul, for it is through your own soul that the voice of God speaks to you. This is the interior guide. This is the light that lights every person. This is intuition. This is the voice of the higher self, the voice of the soul, the voice of God.

#### #6. SEE THE GOOD IN ALL.

The moment we recognize ourselves as one with the Infinite, we become so filled with love that we see only the good in all. And when we realize that we are all one with this Infinite Spirit, then we realize that in a sense we are all one with each other. Wherever we go, whenever we come in contact with other people, we are able to recognize the God within. We thus look only for the good, and we find it.

#### #7. FOLLOW THE LAW OF PROSPERITY.

This is the law: When apparent adversity comes, don't let it get you down, but make the best of it. Always look forward for better things, for more prosperous conditions. To hold yourself in this attitude of mind is to set into operation subtle, silent, and irresistible forces that sooner or later will actualize in material form that which is today merely an idea. Ideas have power, and ideas, when rightly planted and rightly tended, are the seeds that actualize material conditions.

#### #8. BRING JOY EVERYWHERE YOU GO.

Carry with you this inspiration and continually offer a good word and blessings wherever you go so that your friends and all people will say your coming brings peace and joy. As you pass the tired and weary and even sin-sick people along the street, they will feel a certain divine touch that may awaken a new life in them. Such are the subtle powers of the human soul when it aligns itself with the Divine.

**WEEK SIX/ DAY 2: AWARENESS**

# Finding the Magical Missing Ingredient to a Happy Life

Are you happy? Chances are, if I caught you on a good day, you'd probably say yes. But on other days, you might feel as if something is missing, as if there's a small void in your life that you couldn't quite put your finger on. A magical missing ingredient.

This sense of subdued discontentment is one of the many areas author Benjamin Riggs explores in the book *Finding God in the Body*. Its subject matter extends well beyond its title and invites us to take a close look at who we are, what makes us tick and how we can come closer to happiness and contentment by finding God (and ultimately, ourselves) within.

I previously wrote how medical professional David Mercier has attributed many of our ailments and symptoms, from our aches and pains to fatigue and the blues, to the stress and worries of our modern daily lives.

Riggs continues this argument. He writes of the busyness that controls our lives as we continually move from task to task in both our work and personal lives. The author points out how, for many of us, life feels like "a never-ending project. We are forever trying to improve our self, our job, our relationships, and no matter how much we try, happiness escapes us."

## SO WHY DO WE FEEL COMPELLED TO STAY SO BUSY?

It seems we consistently put ourselves in situations that are stressful and take us further away from the happiness we desire. Riggs blames our actions on the "false self" or ego, the exterior part of ourselves that we present to the world. (As opposed to our true self which resides within.) He writes that we need to "be on guard against the false self's agenda," because:

> Our true life cares nothing about projects, plans, fears or ambitions of the false self. It is our job to cut through the stress, anxiety, aggression and depression and come back to our Self, over and over again.

The good news is there's a simple cure for our stress and anxiety. We need to focus our search for happiness away from the outside world and place it on the self.

To do this, Riggs has a few ideas, starting with a return to "wakefulness." It involves preparing ourselves for whatever life throws at us with "a daily practice of self-analysis, prayer and meditation." This includes checking in with our interior selves regularly to be sure we are calm, centered and actively awake to the people and world around us. The author advises us to:

> Sit with the simplicity of your breath for a few minutes. Throughout the day, return to the immediacy of the present moment by reconnecting with the breath. We must do this in the face of busyness.

If we feel like there's a missing ingredient in our lives, we need to discover it for ourselves—through introspection. We need to look within, past the false self which is the ego, to the center of our beings. It is where the real you lives and, not coincidentally, it is where you may sense the presence of the Divine. It is the only place we can find the thing that stands between us and a happier, more contented life.

Riggs reinforces this point, saying, "Happiness evades us because it is found in the one place we have been unwilling to look. We have looked everywhere, except for within ourselves." And until we figure out how to really look within, we will also have trouble spreading love and goodness to those around us. Riggs writes:

> Spirituality does not begin with love and compassion for others. We can't give away what we do not have. Before we can love those around us, we have to cultivate a loving kindness toward our Self.

It is up to us to set our own paths. In Riggs's words: "Others can walk beside us, hold our hand, and be there. What they cannot do is live our lives." It is up to us to act, to take charge of our own lives. I am reminded of a bold, all-capitalized line in a recent post by the music and life critic Bob Lefsetz:

YOU'VE GOT TO RESCUE YOURSELF!

There simply is no other way.

# Three Steps to Being a More Compassionate Person

What's going on these days? When did we lose our sense of simple human decency and respect for other people, regardless of our differences in opinion or politics or ethnicity?

I could point to a certain former resident of the White House for introducing an ugly and divisive tone into our public discourse. But perhaps it was coming to fruition just before then, most notably in online message boards where, under the cover of anonymity, rude and hateful language has been legitimized.

**IT'S GOT TO CHANGE—AND THE CHANGE STARTS WITH YOU.**

"What?" you say, I'm not involved in the rancor coming out of Washington, DC, or caustic online discussions. Neither am I. But that doesn't mean we can't take a fresh approach to our own individual interactions. We can choose to respect the opinions of others, even if they're in opposition to our own. Our words matter.

We can follow what is known as "Thumper's Rule." Ever hear of it? In the Disney film *Bambi*, a young rabbit named Thumper remarks that the fawn Bambi is "kinda wobbly" and "doesn't walk too good." Well, Thumper's mother doesn't go for that kind of language and gives him a piece of advice we all can use, a sort of verbal golden rule:

## "IF YOU CAN'T SAY SOMETHING NICE, DON'T SAY NOTHING AT ALL."

In *The Lessons of St. Francis, How to Bring Simplicity and Spirituality into Your Daily Life*, John Michael Talbot tells us other ways we can change the way we interact with family, friends, co-workers, and acquaintances we encounter each day. It's a small step that at minimum can make our little corner of the world a better place. I've distilled Talbot's thoughts, which were influenced by the life of St. Francis, into three primary steps:

## LOOK. LISTEN. FORGIVE.

1. **Look**.

   Nothing shows that you're interested in another person like giving them your full attention. That means phone down, preferably off and nestled in your pocket or purse, and eyes focused on the person across from you. The writer G.K. Chesteron explains St. Francis's approach to eye-contact this way:

   > There was never a person who looked into the eyes of Francis without being certain that Francis was really interested in them; in their own individual life from the cradle to the grave; that they themselves were valued and taken seriously.

   Can't we do the same when we talk to others? Eye contact helps show the person across from us that they are valued, and we care about them.

2. **Listen.**

When listening to another person, we've got to resist the all-too-human urge to critique what they're saying. As Talbot states:

> Compassion isn't about whether you approve or disapprove of what someone is saying; it's about understanding another person. It isn't about promoting your agenda; it's about comprehending someone else's.

That means putting the other person first, listening instead of simply waiting to talk.

3. **Forgive.**

Forgiveness simply means stepping down from a throne of judgement and releasing those who have offended you from any hostility or anger. Everyone deserves a second chance. Your most important relationships may deserve a third and fourth chance. Talbot quotes Frederick Buechner, who writes that forgiveness is a way of saying:

> You have done something unspeakable, and by all rights I should call it quits between us. Though I make no guarantees I will be able to forget what you've done, I refuse to let it stand between us. I still want you for my friend.

And as Ralph Waldo Emerson once said: "For every minute you remain angry, you give up sixty seconds of peace of mind."

I'm reminded of a poem St. Francis wrote to a close friend about the nature of God. I have paraphrased it below. There may be no human being alive today that encapsulates all these traits, but I think they are qualities we all can strive for each day of our lives.

You are love.

You are wisdom.
You are humility.

You are endurance.
You are rest. You are peace.
You are joy and gladness.
You are justice and moderation.
You are gentleness.
You are our guardian and defender.
You are our courage.

You are our haven and our hope.


**WEEK SIX/ DAY 4: CALLING**

# Taking the Next Step in Life (A Ten-Step Guide)

Have you ever felt stuck? As if your life is stuck in neutral, making no forward progress? Believe me, I've been there, and it's at these times that you need to call a time-out and take stock. You need to determine what steps you can take that will allow you to approach life with a renewed sense of purpose and vigor.

**THERE'S NO BETTER TIME TO START PLANNING FOR TOMORROW THAN TODAY.**

In Eiman Al Zaabi's 2015 book *Finding Grace*, the author was almost prescient when she wrote the following passage that speaks directly to our troubled times, from our messy politics to pandemics past and future. She also tells us how we might use this period to uncover our personal path in life:

> When we witness the chaotic, violent, and unpredictable events taking place, it's natural to be deeply troubled. We may wish to be of service but not know what to do or where to begin. How can we make a difference? Each of us has a vital role to play in restoring peace and harmony to the world. To fulfill the intention of your creation, you must discover your unique role.

Eiman goes on to point out that "times of change and unpredictability can lead you to your life purpose." The time to start planning your next move is now because "every one of us is meant to add to the world in a way no one else can. If you do not act, that contribution is lost." You can choose to do nothing—or you can choose to contribute to the betterment of the world around you.

## OKAY, YOU MIGHT BE THINKING, BUT WHERE DO I START?

The next step is determined by you, by doing a deep dive into your heart and soul. The goal is to find the place where your passions (what you like) and abilities (what you're good at) meet. This means doing what feels right for you, not necessarily what others want you to do, or what society expects from you. Eiman advises us to "take the steps to bring your vision into reality."

I've listed ten key steps below that I discovered in *Finding Grace* that can help you create your own path. The words are lightly edited and the points are in a different order than they appear in the book, and I've added a few thoughts of my own in italics.

## A Ten-Step Guide to the Next Phase of Your Life

1. Every human life counts. Every contemplation, every word of truth you say, and every action in service of others counts. Your contribution matters. *We are all here for a purpose and your number one responsibility is to find it.*

2. Your purpose will always be something bigger than yourself. Your job is to surrender to its pull. *You won't find this purpose on your smartphone. Contemplate. Meditate.*

3. Let your actions be guided by both knowledge and knowing. Knowledge is based on history, study, and past experiences. Knowing, on the other hand is intuitive. *To make the right move for you, use both your head and your heart.*

4. The soul longs for expression. It is here that we embody our talents, our abilities, and our most hidden desires for ourselves and the world. What does your soul long to express? *You might even look as far back as your childhood dreams. What did you most want to become or accomplish? Why not pursue this dream now?*

5. Every time you have an insight or make a decision, be aware of your soul's needs. Ask yourself: Does this support my well-being? Am I acting in love and kindness? *Will the steps I'm about to take satisfy my innermost yearnings?*

6. Heed your soul's call to express its gifts. Share your uniqueness, your brilliance, and your light. *Think about the point where "your talent meets service." Put to use what you are good at and most passionate about.*

7. Don't be discouraged by the amount of work to be done. Take one small step at a time. Your sincere actions go further than you realize. *Say "I can do it" as opposed to "I can't."*

8. Every action ripples outward. You can change the world from within your circle of influence, wherever you are and however you are called to help. *Be the light.*

9. Instead of asking "How can I save the world?" ask "What are the unique things I have to offer? How can I be a force of good, right here, right now?" *For a world that needs healing, sometimes the greatest gift is your own compassion. Where can you bring comfort to those in need?*

10. Your life is a precious gift that should not be squandered. Every one of us has the power to make a difference. *To quote Mary Oliver, "What is it you plan to do with your one wild and precious life?"*

# The Simple Prompt That Can Help You Stay Mindful All Day

We all want to live a mindful life, being fully present in each moment. But too often, we are distracted. Rather than being totally tuned in to our surroundings, or the people in front of us, we are often there in body, but not in mind or spirit.

For some, this is due to an addiction to our smartphones. The small screen in the palm of our hand steals our attention from the more vital big screen of life. Other times, our monkey mind is on the loose, skipping from one random thought to another. We're thinking about work, our to-do list, an incident from our past, all distracting us from the present moment.

In the past, I've sought out books on mindfulness for tips and pointers. The most well-known is probably Jon Kabat-Zinn's *Wherever You*

*Go There You Are*. Its primary message is hinted at in the title; true contentment is found at any place and any time. But if you're like me, you can read this book and similar titles, feel like you know what mindfulness is all about—and then find that once you get caught up in a hectic day, all that wisdom dissipates like the morning dew. What we really need is:

## A SIMPLE DAILY PROMPT THAT CAN HELP US BE MORE MINDFUL.

Wouldn't it be great if, when you find yourself not fully present, there were a few words you could use to get immediately back on track? I may have found them courtesy of Dan Millman, author of the long-ago spiritual classic *Way of the Peaceful Warrior*. Millman later wrote a follow-up called *No Ordinary Moments: A Peaceful Warrior's Guide to Daily Life*.

Millman discloses that as a young man, he was once struck by a realization so profound it changed the course of his life. His story goes like this: Millman was outdoors in a park, and after practicing a disciplined t'ai chi routine, he went to put on a pair of sweatpants over his running shorts. As a group of teenagers watched, he began to coolly pull up his sweats, only to lose his balance, stumble backward and fall on his butt.

The author realized: "I had given my full attention to the movements of t'ai chi, but not to the ordinary moments of putting on my pants. I had treated one moment as special and the other as ordinary." To repeat the key phrase, he "treated one moment as special and the other as ordinary." From this brief experience, Millman came to the follow conclusion:

**THERE ARE NO ORDINARY MOMENTS.**

Millman goes on to tell his teacher from *Way of the Peaceful Warrior*, an odd fellow named Socrates, about his experience falling down in front of others. The teacher informs him:

> Athletes practice their athletics; musicians practice their music; artists practice their art. The peaceful warrior practices everything. That is a secret of the Way, and it makes all the difference.

Millman takes this lesson to heart and teaches us that "walking, sitting, breathing, eating, taking out the trash, all deserve the same attention." Life is a series of moments, and each moment deserves the same amount of personal awareness and respect. To that end, as we go through life, we are either awake or asleep, "fully alive or relatively dead." In his words:

> The quality of each moment depends not on what we get from it, but from what we bring to it. And by treating every action with respect and every moment as sacred, you will find a new relationship with life, filled with passion and purpose.

For those who say they'd like to live a more mindful life but the demands of work, kids, etc., are too strenuous, Millman reminds us that all moments, even the stressful ones, are what make up our lives. Each moment is precious and counts for something. In his words:

"Your relationship with your (partner), the responsibilities of children, the pressures of your job—*are* your spiritual practice. When you recognize this, every moment takes on a greater purpose."

So how do we stay more mindful? Remind yourself of these words daily, hourly, every five minutes if needed. Write them on sticky notes and place them on your bathroom mirror, the fridge, the dashboard, or in your notebook:

———

There are no ordinary moments.

———

# An Eight-Step Guide to Meditation — and Deep Inner Peace

While this book has already presented one way to meditate, the fact is there are many, all with slightly nuanced ways to achieve the meditative state. The approach that follows comes from the writer Sam Harris. In 2005, he wrote the bestselling book *The End of Faith* that, in a nutshell, portrayed religion as little more than a collection of myths and superstitions that could be blamed for much of the world's ills.

It was with some trepidation that I picked up his book *Waking Up, A Guide to Spirituality Without Religion*—but I knew that Harris was an excellent writer and the title grabbed me. And in this fascinating study of meditation and consciousness, my only difference with Harris is this: Where he finds self-transcendence, I sense the presence of God.

It turns out that Harris spent much of his young adult life traveling the world and studying with some of the best meditation teachers of our time. (His main focus was Buddhist meditation due to its relative lack of religious content.) Harris shares with us his own eight-step guide to meditation, which is similar to centering prayer, but with a few nuances. Here's my summary of Harris's method:

## AN EIGHT-STEP GUIDE TO MEDITATION

1. Sit comfortably with your spine erect, either in a chair or cross-legged on a cushion.

2. Close your eyes, take a few deep breaths, and feel the points of contact between your body and the chair or cushion. Notice the sensations of sitting—pressure, warmth.
3. Gradually become aware of the process of breathing. Pay attention to where you feel the breath most, either in your nostrils or rising and falling in the abdomen.
4. Allow your attention to rest on your breath, as you let it come and go naturally.
5. Every time your mind wanders, gently return it to the breath.
6. As you focus on your breath, you may perceive sounds, bodily sensations, emotions. Simply observe these phenomena as they appear and return to the breath.
7. The moment you find yourself lost in thought, observe it as an object of consciousness, release it, and return to the breath.
8. Continue in this way until you merely witness objects of consciousness—sights, sounds, emotions, thoughts—and allow them to rise and pass away.

Harris sees meditation as creating a deeper sense of well-being and inner peace. He strongly advocates that we need to overcome the conventional sense of ourselves, which is merely an illusion. We can do this by taking a pause from our jittery, overthinking selves and paying closer attention to the present moment.

He relates our lives to watching a film in a movie theater. When we're totally immersed in the film, we forget our surroundings and the fact we're merely looking at light on a wall. In Harris's words: "Most of us spend every waking moment lost in the movies of our lives." Meditation allows us to step out of the movie, return to our seat, and observe our lives from a distance. It helps us overcome the illusion of the self, by placing us squarely in the present moment.

**THE REALITY OF YOUR LIFE IS ALWAYS NOW.**

Harris points out that we often forget or overlook this truth. We become preoccupied with thought, dwelling on the past, pondering the future, questioning, analyzing everything, until we are "spellbound by the conversation we are having with ourselves." He self-effacingly confesses:

> It seems to me that I spend much of my waking life in a neurotic trance. My experiences in meditation suggest that an alternative exists. It is possible to stand free of the juggernaut of self, if only for moments at a time.

What's important to note here is that a regular meditation practice can also extend benefits into our everyday lives, not just at the moment of meditation itself. This ability to calm and unclutter our mind becomes an attribute we can always fall back on, simply by remembering to breathe. Harris refers to this as "mindfulness" and a "state of clear, nonjudgmental, and undistracted attention."

When we reach this state, Harris tells us that what remains is consciousness itself, with "its attendant sights, sounds, sensations, and thoughts appearing and changing in every moment." We exit the "self" and become more tuned in to the people and world around us. We become more fully present in our lives.

**WEEK SIX/ DAY 7: CONTEMPLATION**

## The Secret Teachings of Jesus

What if we got the true message of Jesus wrong? What if his real message was hiding in plain sight, in familiar parables whose meaning we take at face value, but that contain deeper and more meaningful truths?

That is one of the primary themes in *Jesus, A New Vision* by the bestselling author Whitley Strieber, a book that forces us to look at the life and teachings of Jesus in a fresh light. Strieber asserts that "for too many of us, the promise of the Jesus teaching has slipped away, encrusted in religious doctrine or dismissed because we find that doctrine impossible to accept."

## You may need to look beyond the Bible to find the real Jesus.

Strieber believes that the most important sayings and key teachings of Jesus are found in two gospels not included in the Bible, the *Gospel of Thomas* and the *Gospel of Mary*. They are a part of the fifty-two "Gnostic" texts discovered at Nag Hamadi in 1945 and represent some of the earliest Christian teachings. In fact, the *Gospel of Thomas* may predate all four of the New Testament gospels.

One of the key takeaways from these two Gnostic texts is the notion that "Jesus was not giving us the answers we seek but beseeching us to look within ourselves." Jesus wants us to use our own "self-knowledge" for answers and insights. This idea was propagated by many early Christians sects, including the Valentinians, who claimed their fellow Christians were making a mistake by reading the scriptures only literally. This was especially true with the parables that Jesus used to teach his disciples. Strieber explains that: "Once one understands how to use the parables, which is by seeing them internally, their role as the hidden path 'to the realm that is within you' is made plain."

## For starters, let's look at the meaning of the "kingdom of heaven."

In her book *The Gnostic Gospels*, religious scholar Elaine Pagels informs us that three of the four Biblical gospels say the Kingdom will come in the near future. But there's an outlier. It's the *Gospel of Luke* and in its pages Jesus explicitly states "the kingdom of God is within you." In other words, "the kingdom" should not be viewed as a literal geographic location, a belief that is amplified in the *Gospel of Thomas*.

As Pagels points out, "In the *Gospel of Thomas*, Jesus ridiculed thinking of the "kingdom of God" in literal terms, as if it were a specific place." The kingdom cannot be found in the sky or in the afterlife but is "a state of self-discovery." One can find it while here on Earth through internal transformation. While containing some of the same language found in Luke 17:21, Thomas expands on the notion of the kingdom:

> The kingdom is inside of you and it is outside of you. When you come to know yourselves, then you will be known, and you will realize that you are the son of the living Father.

Strieber writes that "The disciple who comes to know himself (or herself) can then discover what even Jesus cannot teach." It is what the early Christian leader Simon Magus (mentioned in Acts 8:9-24) called "a dwelling place (of) infinite power… the root of the universe." It is no different today. To paraphrase Strieber, Jesus offers a realm of heaven that we can discover within us right now, not in the afterlife. No matter how difficult our lives may be, we can bring the peace of the kingdom into our hearts in the present moment.

It's an idea that is echoed by the Franciscan friar and prolific author Richard Rohr:

> The realm of God is right here, right now, in the present tense. The relationship with God's love that sets us free is in our midst. The possibility of freedom, of a whole new world, is already here.

As with "the kingdom of heaven," there are other examples in the "approved" gospels where "the inner path" of the Jesus teachings shines through. Strieber calls out four specific biblical parables that show us how the teachings work. Here are two of them in edited form.

## Parable One. The Parable of the Mustard Seed.

**What Jesus Said:** What is the realm of God like? What shall I compare it to? It is like a mustard seed, which a man took and planted in his garden. It grew and became a tree, and the birds perched in its branches. (Luke 13:18-19)

**What Jesus Meant:** The mustard seed is the self-knowledge that lives within you and grows as you progress along the spiritual path. Once planted in the fertile ground of a seeker, the seed will grow as knowledge grows, no matter how small it is to start. The birds represent the various facets of our true self, including the parts we may not especially like. Once the birds find shelter here (in our soul), we can begin to fully accept ourselves and find inner peace.

## Parable Two. The Parable of the Weeds.

**What Jesus Said:** "The realm of heaven is like a man who sowed good seed in his field. But while everyone was sleeping, his enemy came and sowed weeds among the wheat, and went away. When the wheat sprouted and formed heads, the weeds also appeared. The farmer tells his servants not to pull up the weeds lest they also uproot the wheat. 'Let both grow together until the harvest.' At this time I will tell the harvesters, "First collect the weeds and tie them in bundles to be burned; then gather the wheat and bring it into my barn."' (Matthew 13:24-30):

**What Jesus Meant**: The field is the experience of life and the sower is you, the person living that life. The weeds are the distractions of all kinds that come your way and prevent you from spiritual growth. When Jesus instructs us to let both the weeds and wheat grow, it is because we often cannot separate the good from the bad until we are spiritually mature. We do not want to pull the weeds and mistakenly destroy the wheat, which is the wisdom that grows within us. In time, we learn to recognize the wheat, eliminating the weeds, allowing us to grow closer to God.

# WEEK SEVEN

## Spiritual Lessons from an Eighty-Nine-Year-Old Jazz Icon

As you grow older, do you really begin to figure it all out? Do you start to realize what your purpose is here on Earth and what you need to do before your departure from this life? After years of reading about and talking to elders, I think the answer is mixed. In short, some people just don't figure it out—but the flip side is that some people do.

One person who seems to have a grip on what was and is his purpose is the legendary jazz saxophonist Sonny Rollins who, at the age of eighty-nine, was profiled in the *New York Times Magazine* by David Marchese. Over the previous few years, due to health issues, Rollins had stopped playing live concerts but during this interview he seemed as alive and vibrant as ever.

Rollins is no stranger to spirituality. In an article published in *Yoga Journal*, Rollins says he first began his spiritual quest in the 1950s, when "his yearning for something deeper" led him to the book *Autobiography of a Yogi* by Paramahansa Yogananda. In the 1960s, during a concert tour in Japan, he got into yoga and he has practiced it daily for decades. He says it helps him "find his center" and gives him a clearer understanding of his role in life.

When asked in the *Times* article if he was happy, he replied "Happy is not the word, but I am the most content I've ever been. I have most things figured out." It should be noted that as Rollins was interviewed, he was seated on a couch at home in Woodstock, New York, under a large painting of the Buddha. He commented that he avoids TV and doesn't listen to the radio much, preferring silence. He explains:

**"SILENCE TO ME IS MEDITATIVE. TO GET INTO THAT SILENT SPACE IS A HUGE THING."**

Rollins talked about the several occasions in his life when he sensed the presence of what many of us call God, though he does not use that term. One time, early in his career, he was playing an outdoor show when he looked up into the sky. In his words, "I felt a communication; I felt that I was part of something. Not the crowd. Something bigger."

What follows are edited excerpts from the interview. They show that Rollins, at eighty-nine-years old, is fully in tune with reality and anticipating what is still to come.

- I'm working toward why I'm here — what it's all about. At this point in my life, I don't want to say satisfied, but I feel that I'm closer to an understanding.
- It's always been my idea that the golden rule is a good thing, but I wasn't quite able to understand if the golden rule was possible. [Now] I believe that living by the golden rule is possible. Not only possible but the reason we're here.
- Giving is better than getting and is the proper way to live. Live your life now in a positive way. Help people if you can. Don't hurt people.
- Music is not on the same level as trying to understand life. We're here for eighty-something years. One lifetime is not enough to get it right. I'll be back in another body.
- There's nothing I'll miss about this life. There's a big picture, which is the afterlife, and this life is a little picture. There's also

karma: What you do, you're going to get it back. So this life is a trip, man, and you've got to go through it.

- I know I've done a lot of stupid things and hurt people. I've got a lot of stuff that I'm paying for, and I'm trying to get good karma by not trying to hurt somebody or doing things for my own pleasure or aggrandizement.
- This world is not what it's cracked up to be. This world is just a place to pay off our karma. That's all. There's something huge happening, and it's a matter of feeling. It's different than having book knowledge. The thing I'm talking about is more like intuition. Something is there. I've had experiences which have allowed me to know that.
- I get lonely on occasion. Fortunately, not too often. I like being alone. I have my yoga books. I have my Buddha books. I have a lot of spiritual material that I need to get with. At my age, all my friends are gone. At one time I began to lament that and then I said, "No, this is good that I have nobody to call and waste time talking."
- Understanding is up to you. It's up to me. There's no escape. I got pains and aches all over but spiritually, man, I feel better than I've ever felt. I'm on the right course.
- Dying, it's funny. Everybody is afraid to die because it's the unknown. But my mother died. My father died. My brother died. My sister died. My uncle died. My grandmother died. They're all great people. If they can die, then why can't I die? I'm better than they are? It's ridiculous to feel, oh, gee, I shouldn't die. My body is going to turn into dust. But my soul will live forever.

# The Cure for Loneliness (It's Not What You Think)

You might think the cure for loneliness is a simple one: just get out of the house and spend time with other people. But there's a contrary point-of-view, and it comes from the man who may know more about our collective inner world than anyone around today: Thomas Moore.

Moore has made his name by writing more than a dozen books that deal with the deepest, most complex part of our selves, the soul. In his book, *Ageless Soul: The Lifelong Journey Toward Meaning and Joy*, Moore advises us that when we feel lonely, we need to "go with the symptom." In his words:

> If you are lonely and try to get rid of the loneliness by forcing yourself to be around people, in effect you are repressing an emotion. You are repressing it by fleeing from it. It might be better to acknowledge your loneliness and then give it some attention.

**DON'T RUN FROM THE FEELING OF LONELINESS. IMMERSE YOURSELF IN IT.**

Moore points out that even "a person living in a city teeming with people can be lonely and in need of something other than people." So, the cure for loneliness isn't to force yourself to be around others, but instead to get to the root of the issue.

Moore sees the feeling of loneliness as an inner call for reflection. And the fact is reflection requires you to get comfortable with a degree of solitude, because it calls for "quiet and aloneness." Within this solitude, we then have the space we need to be open to our thoughts and feelings.

Importantly, Moore sees reflection not solely as time spent in passive contemplation. He tells us there are many ways to reflect that involve partaking in activities. Reflection can involve historical or cultural reading (Moore prefers biographies), listening to music, even writing in various forms—journals, essays, fiction. We need to engage with the loneliness within.

Moore believes the cure to loneliness can also be found in greater intimacy with our surroundings. He says that the world itself has a soul and that our relationships are not all human; rather, they can occur with our physical surroundings, including our homes, our neighborhoods, and anyplace we like to visit, be it a church or a nature preserve.

Moore states that "It isn't just companionship that overcomes loneliness but anything that is life giving." And who hasn't had their spirit recharged after a visit to a museum, a walk on the beach or even a few minutes spent gazing at the stars? Moore goes on to say that:

> The best way to deal with loneliness is to pursue vitality even in small things. This means keeping alive your curiosity, wonder, spirit of adventure, love of learning, creative character, interest in people, eccentricity and contemplative lifestyle.

The key is to stay connected to life, to "make sure that you are not closing off a part of yourself." When we open our soul to the wonders of life, loneliness has a way of dissipating or at least is kept at bay. We often discover that what we thought was loneliness was more accurately a need to connect—with our own inner selves and the world immediately around us.

In closing, here are two takes on loneliness that strike similar themes, from two different American authors. Their words express the same unique perspective on loneliness as Moore.

———

*"Loneliness is the human condition. Cultivate it. The way it tunnels into you allows your soul room to grow."*
— *Janet Fitch*

———

*"When I get lonely these days, I think: So BE lonely, Liz. Learn your way around loneliness. Make a map of it. Sit with it, for once in your life. Welcome to the human experience."* — *Elizabeth Gilbert*

———

## WEEK SEVEN/ DAY 3: CHARACTER

# Do You Have the Eleven Traits of a Person with Character?

Who fills the void when leaders don't lead, when those in positions of power and responsibility seem more interested in their own narrow self-interests than the greater good? You and me, of course. It may be our time to step up and display the moral and emotional qualities, like honesty, kindness, and empathy, that are features of people of character.

Why is character important? Because it sets the tone for those around us, whether they be your co-workers, your children, grandchildren, or extended family. What you do and how you act rubs off on others, in positive or negative ways. It's a choice. Do you lead by example? Can you engage in civil discourse with others even when they don't share your point of view?

In *The Road to Character*, David Brooks defines what makes a person of character. It starts with having a certain set of universal traits that include a code of ethics, an inner knowing of what is fair and just. These values have nothing to do with your political affiliation, your social or economic status or your religion. They have everything to do with what makes you tick.

Scanning Brooks's book, I compiled a list of the attributes that help define a person of character and put them into an eleven-point list.

## ELEVEN TRAITS OF PEOPLE WITH CHARACTER (ACCORDING TO DAVID BROOKS)

1. They possess an inner cohesion.
2. They are calm, settled, and rooted.
3. They are not blown off course by storms.
4. They don't crumble in adversity.
5. Their minds are consistent and their hearts are dependable.
6. They answer softly when challenged. They are silent when unfairly criticized, restrained when others try to provoke them.
7. They get things done. They recognize what needs doing and they do it.
8. They make you feel funnier and smarter when you speak with them.
9. They move through different social classes not even aware they are doing so.
10. You've never heard them boast, you've never seen them self-righteous or doggedly certain.
11. They aren't dropping little hints about their own distinctiveness and accomplishments.

Brooks also tells us about the flip side of character, pointing out that those who lack it "never develop inner constancy, the integrity that can withstand popular disapproval or a serious blow. They find themselves doing things that other people approve of, whether these things are right or not. They foolishly judge other people by their abilities, not by their worth."

## THOSE WITH CHARACTER HAVE FOLLOWED A DIFFERENT PATH.

Brooks points out that the person with character has a different set of priorities. They have surrendered "the climb to success" and instead have decided to "deepen the soul" (choosing character over career). They have learned to suppress the ego, or in Brooks's words, "quit the self," and they find it is better to give than to receive.

People with character are humble. They are open to the idea that they don't know everything—and are open to finding answers from anyone at any time. This is important: When you think you know everything, you stop learning and growing as a person. Here's more from Brooks on the value of humility and how the humble person compares to the ego-driven know-it-all:

> The humble person is soothing and gracious, while the self-promoting person is fragile and jarring. Humility is freedom from the need to prove you are superior all the time, but egotism is a ravenous hunger in a small space—self-concerned, competitive and distinction-hungry. Humility is infused with emotions like companionship, love and gratitude.

The act of being humble may require some effort on our parts, especially in a world where boasting and self-congratulation seem baked into our culture, as evidenced everywhere from Washington, DC, to the National Football League. That means we need to become "strong in the weak places" by magnifying what is best in ourselves and suppressing what is unpleasant, including any hints of arrogance or pretentiousness.

Brooks also reminds us that we are not alone in our efforts to be men and women of character. While we must lean heavily on our inner resources, we also can look outside ourselves for help. It is "never a solitary struggle." In his words: "No person can achieve self-mastery on his or her own. We all need assistance from the outside—from family, friends, role models, rules, traditions, institutions, and, for believers, from God."

It is an ongoing process, one that starts at home and extends to the relationships at our workplace and in our community. It involves striving to improve ourselves each day by emulating those we respect and strengthening our moral core. We can be helped by reading the wise words of others or engaging in a regular spiritual practice, at home or through a religious institution. We do whatever it takes to live a life that is an example for others.

**WEEK SEVEN/ DAY 4: CALLING**

# Are the Answers You Seek Already within You?

*"What if what you've been chasing all these years has been in you all along, waiting for the chance to be loved into existence?" — Andrea Balt*

I recently heard *Care of the Soul* author Thomas Moore being interviewed by Oprah Winfrey, where he revealed he no longer sees himself as a "seeker." After a lifetime of intensive spiritual study, including authoring over a dozen books on the soul, Moore said he had discovered all that he needed to know. No more seeking, just knowing.

It reminded me of a tale *The Alchemist* author Paulo Coelho tells that hints at the folly of our endless seeking. You may have heard a version of this story before, but its message is so compelling, it bears repeating here. It goes like this:

> One day the sages were discussing the secret of life and where they should hide it so that men and women could not find it. Bury it under a mountain, one sage suggests. No, the others counter, they will find a way to dig up the mountain and uncover it. Put the secret of life in the depths of the deepest ocean, another sage suggests. No, the others say, one day they will find a way to travel to the depths of the ocean and will find it there. Put the secret inside them, suggests another, they will never think to look for it there. All the sages agreed, and so the secret of life was hidden within us.

## "EVERYTHING IN THE UNIVERSE IS WITHIN YOU. ASK ALL FROM YOURSELF."

The line above is from the renowned thirteenth-century Persian poet and mystic Rumi and merits further inspection. What if the things you were looking for out in the world were dwelling within you? Would that change how you approached life? Would it make you more likely to look within, instead of without, for peace, love and guidance?

———

> *"If those who lead you say to you, 'look, the Kingdom is in the sky,' then the birds will get there first. If they say 'it's in the ocean,' then the fish will get there first. But the Kingdom of God is within you and outside of you. Once you come to know yourselves, you will become known. And you will know that it is you who are the children of the living father."*
> — *Jesus, the Gnostic Gospel of Thomas*

———

Reading this passage from the Gospel of Thomas, you might wonder how you can "come to know yourself." A book could be written (and many have) that attempts to answer this question. But, in a nutshell, you need to look past the thin outer veneer that is the false self, also known as the ego. Then, slow down long enough to connect with the deepest part of yourself, the place where the soul lives.

In a recent Facebook post, the writer and female empowerment virtuoso Andrea Balt tapped into something we all know. It touches on what many of us want, that feeling of being truly alive to the people and events around us. She wrote: "Deep down you're seeking purpose, love, acceptance, intimacy, pleasure, creativity, abundance, bliss - ALIVENESS. You want to feel alive before you die."

We want to feel alive. Connected. Loved. Yet this is a game played from the inside out. When all is right within, when we are calm and centered and at peace with ourselves, we are better able to offer our own unique gifts to the world. Balt explains it this way:

"This love, this freedom you seek, this creativity you need, the pleasure or adventure you crave, all the things you admire in others are already planted in you, waiting for the chance to be watered & trusted & summoned out into the light & bloom through the life you create."

What if Balt, like Paulo Coelho and Rumi and Jesus before her, is correct? What if what you seek is already within you, waiting to be uncovered? Balt reminds us:

> Nothing is missing. It's all already yours. The chase is futile,
> the battle is in vain. By letting go of the specifics & trusting
> the creative god-dess in yourself guiding you from within,
> you have already won.

# The Surrender Experiment: Saying "Yes" to Everything in Life

What if you trusted the flow of life enough to completely let go? What if you stopped making decisions and began saying yes to whatever life brought your way? Would life unfold the way it was supposed to—instead of the way you forced it to happen?

These are the type of questions that led Michael A. Singer to try something he called *The Surrender Experiment*. It's the title of a book he wrote several years ago that details the amazing twists and turns that Singer's life took once he made the following decision:

- To stop analyzing and overthinking every decision he made.
- To start saying yes to everything life brought his way.

Before I get into the details, let me give you some background on Singer. He is probably best known for his first book, *The Untethered Soul*, which landed him a guest spot on the *Oprah Winfrey Show* and became a number-one *New York Times* bestseller in 2007. But his more recent book reveals something even more interesting—his personal story behind the story.

Singer was a self-described "hippie" living near Gainesville, Florida, when he went on a quest to quiet the chattering voice inside his head. It's the voice many of us hear, the one that analyzes and often criticizes our every move. He began a process in which, with help from a daily meditation practice, he learned how to quiet the overanalytical part of his brain. Instead, he went with "the flow," letting things happen rather than trying to steer them to his will.

While in a Radio Shack one day in the late-1970s, Singer took an interest in one of the very first personal computers. He began making trips to the store to "play" with the display model, eventually buying one and teaching himself how to write computer code. He ended up developing a billing program for a doctor's office. Through a series of snowballing synchronistic events, his company became the largest medical software firm in the US.

Singer credits his surrender philosophy for putting him in a position to achieve this success, even though he had never envisioned himself as a businessman. As Singer said yes each step of the way, trusting that life was steering him in the right direction, his small business grew into the market leader.

**HERE'S HOW SINGER EXPLAINS HIS SUCCESS.**

Singer points out that there's a conundrum that most of us face in our daily lives. It's the conflict, or what Singer calls "the battle," between what we want from life and what life gives us. In his words:

"The battle between individual will and the reality of life unfolding around us ends up consuming our lives. When we win the battle, we are happy and relaxed. When we don't, we are disturbed and stressed."

Singer asks himself if life has to be this way. He wonders "if the natural unfolding of the process of life can create and take care of the entire universe, is it really reasonable for us to assume that nothing good will happen unless we force it to?" So instead of doing battle with life, Singer charts another course:

"I decided to just stop listening to all the chatter about my personal preferences, and instead, start the willful practice of accepting what the flow of life was presenting me."

He literally puts life in charge, realizing that "life was asking me to get out of the way and let her do her thing." This is easier said than done because it often means saying yes when the judgmental part of his brain wants to say no. But Singer had spent years readying himself for this task. He had learned to calm his overthinking mind and quiet his ego by meditating for hours each day.

One important point I should mention about Singer's philosophy: Don't confuse "surrender" with passivity or weakness. For Singer, "it required all the strength I had to be brave enough to follow the invisible into the unknown." His will still wanted its way. So, according to Singer, "I let go of myself and allowed what was meant to be—to be."

By accepting "the challenge of serving the energy that came my way," Singer was able to build a large national company. It was not all a bed of roses. At the peak of the company's success, it was brought low by an unscrupulous former employee who falsely implicated Singer in a kickback scheme. An overreaching federal prosecutor pursued Singer in a case that was tied up in the courts for years.

The charges were eventually dropped, and Singer decided to leave the business. He went back to his Gainesville homestead where he had started his meditation sessions forty years earlier. Over the years, his property had grown to more than one hundred acres and several structures, and it hosted daily yoga and meditation services. In his words, "because I had surrendered each step of the way, no scars were left on my psyche." He returned home in peace.

**SINGER BELIEVED HE HAD LEARNED THE MOST IMPORTANT LESSON IN LIFE.**

Singer had learned that by putting life in charge, everything would work out just the way it was supposed to. Singer's parting words summarize his experience and the surrender philosophy:

> Joy and pain, success and failure, praise and blame—they all had pulled at what was deeply rooted within me. **The more I let go, the freer I became.** I realized to the depth of my being that life knew what it was doing. Once you are ready to let

go of yourself, life becomes your friend, your teacher, your secret lover. When life's way becomes your way, all the noise stops, and there is great peace.

# Three Daily Prayers for the Spiritual but Not Religious

D o you believe in a force that is greater than yourself? If yes, how do you engage and connect with this omnipresent force beyond merely recognizing its presence?

**FOR THOSE OF US WHO REFER TO THIS LIFE FORCE AS GOD, ONE WAY TO ENGAGE IS PRAYER.**

I'm not talking about the formalized, ritualistic prayers of the church. I simply mean going into a silent place within yourself and engaging with what John Templeton calls "something wise within us" or what Charles Fillmore refers to as the "the great stillness that pervades our whole being."

Praying on a regular basis can keep us connected with God, offering us solace when facing the everyday challenges of life. As the author David Brooks writes: "You have to draw on something outside yourself to deal with the forces inside yourself." We all need someone (or something) to lean on.

**THE GOOD THING ABOUT PRAYER IS YOU CAN DO IT ANYTIME, ANYWHERE.**

For me, prayer has become an instinctual reflex. Each morning, I give thanks for the good in my life. I also offer silent gratitude for any small blessings that emerge during the day. I sometimes ask for guidance during tough times or patience when I need inner peace. There's no church required; the temple is within.

If prayer is something you don't engage in, or only practice when you're in dire straits, here are three prayers you might consider using on a regular basis.

### PRAYER #1. FOR WHEN THINGS ARE GOING WELL: THE PRAYER OF GRATITUDE.

This may be the single most powerful prayer there is and it's one I use every day. It's a simple prayer of thanks for all the abundance and good in our lives, a thank you to God for all the things that makes life worth living, from the members of your family to a gorgeous sunrise.

In English mystic Reshad Feild's autobiography *The Last Barrier*, the author writes about his spiritual guide who stresses to him the importance of gratitude. He tells Feild he should get up each morning and go to bed each night giving thanks to God. The guide implores:

"How many times a day to you remember to say thank you? You are completely dependent on God and it is to Him that all thanks are due. Until you can be truly grateful, you will always be in separation from God."

In a nutshell, that's the reason for this prayer. It somehow seems to bring us closer to God, because by recognizing God in this way it makes the Divine a real and positive presence in your life. As Oprah Winfrey said, "gratitude can shift your attitude."

> **The prayer:** Start with the words "God, I'm thankful for all the good in my life, including _____, _____ and _____." *Name three things you appreciate most on this day and at this moment.*

## PRAYER #2. FOR WHEN YOU NEED TO MAKE A CHOICE: A PRAYER FOR GUIDANCE.

Can God really help us make a difficult decision? Well, asking certainly can't hurt. When you remember there's a greater power in the universe that can help guide you, it takes some of the weight off your shoulders—and, in time, it can lead you to a decision with the best possible outcome.

John Templeton has written about prayer at length and says that "when we become very still and ask for guidance, we may be directed clearly and unmistakably, with a "yes" or "no." Other times, the best approach is to "release the answer to God and trust the flow of the divine to enter our lives."

In other words, it's sometimes best to give it time. If you don't find the answer you're looking for right away, have patience, and in time the answers will come. Templeton reminds us that as we wait, we are never alone in this process:

"Sometimes, when our prayers seem to be unanswered in the manner we think they should, we may feel that we are not in tune with the timeless, unlimited universal creator called God. But nothing can be separate from God. Everything that touches you, everything that touches each individual in the universe, is a part of God."

> **The prayer:** "Dear God, I ask for your guidance in making this decision. Please lead me to the choice that is best for me, my family, and best suited for my path in life."

## PRAYER #3. FOR WHEN YOU'VE HIT ONE OF LIFE'S POTHOLES: A PRAYER FOR HELP.

Irish New Thought leader Emmet Fox may have gotten it right when he suggested that whenever we find ourselves in a tough situation we should "stop thinking about the difficulty and think about God instead."

Many times, our thoughts are counterproductive when we're troubled or in trouble—we simply don't think straight. So, it makes sense to take a break from our mental struggles and ask for help from a higher power. By putting the focus on God, we take some of the pressure off ourselves. Again, John Templeton provides wise counsel:

"Trials can help us grow and may come into our life to offer a greater realization of God's presence and power. As we maintain trust and peace, our problems are more likely to be solved, and sometimes in a mysterious hour and sometimes even at the eleventh hour."

> **The prayer:** Dear Lord, I trust in your wisdom and know that there is a lesson to be learned from this experience. I ask you to lead me through this difficult time to a better day. *Repeat.*

## WEEK SEVEN/ DAY 7: CONTEMPLATION

# How to Feel Close to God

How would you view the world if you recognized everything as a manifestation of God? If you could see God in all people and all things, might it change the way you viewed those you encountered, and the experiences you had?

My first exposure to religion was through the Catholic church. I attended weekly catechism classes through the seventh grade and Sunday services until I was about seventeen. My perception of God was much like that of another Catholic, Tom Stella, who writes about it in the book *Finding God Beyond Religion*:

The God I encountered was one who judged my every action and who made a judgement about the reward or punishment I would receive beyond this life. I grew up believing that God only loved those who always kept the rules of religion, not those who, like me, did so inconsistently.

One difference between Tom Stella and Tom Rapsas is significant: His Catholic education continued well past mine. While I "dropped out" of the church after high school, Stella went on to become a Roman Catholic priest. He writes that his perception of God didn't change much during his early years in the priesthood. Until he began to realize, with assistance from the writings of Thomas Merton and the Christian mystics, that he had gotten it wrong. God wasn't who he thought he was.

## Tom Stella discovered a God that exists beyond religion.

Father Stella eventually came to a startling conclusion: There is no God looking down upon us. No God with a plan for our lives. No God who would reward or judge you for not living up to his expectations. Stella had not suddenly become an atheist. Far from it. He had begun to view God from a totally new perspective.

What Stella had uncovered was that God could be found not in the heavens, but "in the midst of life." He had come to realize that, to paraphrase Paul Tillich, God was not a being, but being itself. There was no Supreme Being looking down from on high. In fact, God was much closer to home, a part of every person and everything we encounter, a part of each breath we take. He concludes that:

- Every aspect of life is infused with God
- God lives within us as well as within everyone and everything
- God is not apart from creation but one with it, in both good times and bad

Stella had moved on from the distant deity he affectionately now calls "the old guy." He now sees that God is "the spiritual ground of our being," a "compassionate presence" that is with us every step of the way in our daily lives, even in our fear and pain. He believes, no matter our station in life, we are "one with the One we seek."

### CAN YOU SENSE THE PRESENCE OF GOD IN YOU AND AROUND YOU?

The idea that God is present in all things, instead of a presence in the sky, may seem radical to you. It may even cause you to rethink what you thought you knew about God. That can be difficult. But what if Stella is correct? What if God is found in all things? Might we see the world around us, including the people and things in it, in a brilliant new and loving light?

For a moment, consider:

- What if, starting now, you begin sensing that God is present in all things?
- What if you view your friends, neighbors, children, and relatives as having God within them?
- How might this perspective change the way you look at your dog or cat, the artwork and keepsakes in your home, even the way you look at yourself in the mirror?

# WEEK EIGHT

## The Subtle Power of an "Attitude of Gratitude"

*"If the only prayer you ever say is thank you, it will be enough".* — *Meister Eckhart*

What are you thankful for? Chances are, if you stop what you're doing right now, you can come up with a bunch of reasons to give thanks. Think about *everything*, from the people you love to the roof over your head to the ability to read this book. No matter what's wrong in your life right now, you must admit that there is also great good.

According to John Templeton, there's another important and almost magical reason to give thanks. Templeton believed there are fundamental unwritten rules that govern our lives, and one of them is this: offering our gratitude and giving thanks to the universe acts like a magnet. In his words: "The more we are grateful for what we have, the more will be given to us."

Templeton was convinced that as we give our love and appreciation to others, the good we put out into the world reverses course and flows back to us. This chain reaction helps us attract "love, joy, opportunity, health, friends, material good. As we appreciate every blessing, life will open up to us in new and wondrous ways."

As if to prove this point, Templeton began each morning with this simple prayer:

## "THANK YOU, GOD, FOR ALL MY GOOD."

It's a prayer we all might consider beginning each day with, and for me this expression of gratitude starts with the words, "I give thanks (to God) for all the good in my life. I am thankful for …" This mental checklist starts with my family, my home and my health, and continues to my job, my co-workers, the sun greeting the new day, the first signs of spring, whatever!

The gratitude continues throughout my day with the liberal use of the words "thank you." This means being aware of all who assist you, from the person who takes your order at the coffee shop, to anyone who extends you the slightest courtesy, to signing off on each email with the word "Thanks." There is no such thing as too much gratitude.

Psychologist Rick Hanson stresses the importance of a daily gratitude practice in an essay titled "Developing a 'Buddha Brain' Through Gratitude." Hanson, who is Senior Fellow of the Greater Good Science Center at UC Berkeley, writes:

> Gratitude shifts your attention away from resentment, regret, and guilt … and focuses your awareness on positive things, simple good facts such as having enough water to drink, the laughter of children, the kindness of others, or the smell of an orange.

I should point out that Hanson's practice of gratitude also extends beyond a morning prayer. He also recommends taking the time to express gratitude throughout the day and offers the following practical advice:

> To reap the rewards of gratitude, rest your attention on a good fact, noticing details about it, staying with it for at least a few seconds in a row. Then allow a natural emotional response of

gratitude to arise. Continue to pay attention to this feeling of gratitude for another few seconds—or even longer.

The inspirational author James Altucher has had more than his share of tough times. At one point, he lost his home, his wife, and his business, as well as a small fortune. But he rebuilt his life, both spiritually and emotionally, through a regimen he calls "A Simple Daily Practice." A vital part of that practice is what he refers to as "ABG," which stands for Always Be Grateful.

According to Altucher, there are a ton of benefits to Always Being Grateful and practicing ABG on a regular basis. For starters, he says that when you're feeling grateful for all the good things in your life:

- You release dopamine into your brain. This makes you feel uplifted and acts as an anti-depressant.
- You get creative energy. Being grateful for what you have, this second, allows you to start planning the next step in a more creative way.
- You'll better respect and treat the positive things you do have.

Like Hanson, Altucher advises being grateful for more than just a few minutes in the morning. He recommends that we "try to do it all day" and make it a part of our regular spiritual practice. It's something he calls a "Grateful Diet," and he makes the following challenge:

"Be grateful non-stop for the next 21 days. What could it hurt? Be grateful for every object, person, thought, situation, that enters your mind. All of these are deserving of your gratitude. Do this for 21 days. Your life will be completely transformed."

Are you giving thanks each day for the goodness in your life? Could saying "thank you" on a regular basis help you feel better about yourself and also help those around you feel better? Ask yourself those questions. Then, see if an attitude of gratitude doesn't make sense for you as well.

# Why It Pays to Give Life Your Best 95% Effort

What, you say? What happened to giving a 100% effort? Or some of you Type-A types may be wondering why you shouldn't put 110% effort into everything you do. Well, let me explain via an anecdote from entrepreneur Derek Sivers.

Sivers tells the story of living in Santa Monica, California and biking each day on a pathway along the Pacific Ocean that starts in Venice and ends in Malibu. Having run many times on a big chunk of this path, I can vouch for its beauty. It meanders along the beach for miles and features the roaring ocean on one side and a sloping palm-tree-lined hill on the other.

For Sivers, there was just one issue. Being super competitive, each morning he biked the path as fast as he could pedal and it would take him forty-three minutes. He would really try to push it, and the course would still take him forty-three minutes. It got to the point that he was dreading his morning routine, he felt so worn out both physically and mentally.

So he decided to try another approach to his bike ride. He decided to *slow down* just a little. Since he wasn't getting any enjoyment from his "superfast" bike rides, he decided to back off and slowed his ride by two minutes to forty-five minutes, in effect giving less than a 100% effort.

Something amazing happened. Sivers found that by slowing down just a hair, he began to look around more and notice things he hadn't see on his usual rides. He noticed the swaying palm trees and fauna. He saw a flock of pelicans gracefully flying by. He glanced at the ocean and saw two dolphins leaping in the surf. His enjoyment of the ride increased tremendously, and he also felt less stressed about it.

How often do we go buzzing through our own lives at breakneck speed, oblivious to the beauty and small wonders that surround us? Is it possible that our senses become dulled by following the same routine day in and day out?

Let me share a personal story. One night, I got home late from work as I often did and sat down to dinner. My only focus was on the meal in front of me. My wife sat down next to me and asked if I noticed anything new in the room. My eyes quickly scanned my surroundings. I saw nothing new.

She pointed up, and that's when I noticed it. Perched atop the dining room chest was a small wooden statue of a red mermaid. She informed me it had been there for two weeks and she had been waiting for me to notice it but had given up hope.

This incident got me thinking: How many mermaids was I missing? By getting so caught up in my job and spending too much time focusing on work, I was shutting out the small details and moments that enrich our lives and take them beyond the mundane. I pledged to slow down and start paying more attention.

## Is there anything in your life you might better off doing with a 95% effort?

You might consider leaving work thirty minutes earlier each day and devoting that time to connecting with a loved one. Or backing off that morning run just a little to really take in your surroundings. Or maybe even taking the longer, scenic backroad to work, sacrificing a little time for a higher quality experience. You might find that when you stop to notice the details, life becomes a lot more enjoyable.

**WEEK EIGHT/ DAY 3: CHARACTER**

# Making the World a Better Place: One Kind Act at a Time

*"You have not lived today until you have done something for someone who can never repay you."*
— *John Bunyan*

Want to feel better about yourself? There may be no better way than by engaging in a "random act of kindness." It's a gesture that not only makes the recipient feel better but also has a funny way of making the initiator of the act feel good as well. It's a win-win for everyone involved.

There may be no one who better exemplified the spirit of "random acts" than the late Chris Rosati. Out at breakfast one morning, Rosati (who suffered from the neurogenerative disease ALS) gave two girls sitting at the table next to him a $50 bill each. He had one simple request: Do something kind with the money. He forgot all about it until several weeks later when one of the girls sent him an e-mail. It included pictures from a village in Africa with people holding signs that read, "Thanks a lot for spreading kindness Chris Rosati."

It seems the two girls, who were only ten and thirteen-years old, knew about a village in Sierra Leone where the residents had been working to fight Ebola. So, to put their money to good use, the girls paid for a feast so the local community could celebrate being Ebola-free. Rosati referred to this act as having the "butterfly effect," a phenomenon in which a small act in one place can have a large effect somewhere else. He went on to form a kindness initiative, giving out hundreds of $50 "butterfly grants" to "any kid who wants to change the world."

Similar work is done by a group called the Random Acts of Kindness Foundation whose goal it is to "make kindness the norm." They create "RAKtivists," short for Random Acts of Kindness activists. Their website is filled with real-life stories of kindness, like the man who each Valentine's Day visits a local nursing home to give each woman there a red rose. There are also ideas on how to add acts of kindness to your everyday life, with actions as simple as "smile at five strangers today."

I think there are two primary ways we can provide kindness to others, which are listed in bold type below. I didn't have to look far to find recent examples of both, because they came from people close to me—my brother and my wife.

**LOOK FOR OPPORTUNITIES TO SURPRISE AND DELIGHT STRANGERS.**

A few years ago, I traveled with my brother Jim to Florida to catch a few spring training baseball games, and during our last night there we treated ourselves to dinner at the Rose and Crown pub in EPCOT Center. We were enjoying a couple of post-meal pints of Guinness when we noticed something odd.

A girl wearing fuzzy mouse ears had been seated at the two-top table next to us, and as she quietly spoke to the waiter we heard him offer her a hearty "Happy Birthday!" The waiter walked away and we fully expected the girl's mom or dad to appear at any moment and sit down next to her. Only mom or dad never appeared.

We watched as the waiter returned with a glass of ice water, followed by a fish and chips dinner. The girl ate her birthday dinner alone in silence. She looked to be no more than fifteen years old, and we both sat there wondering what events had transpired to cause her to dine solo in such a convivial, family-friendly place.

As we paid our dinner bill, my brother handed the waiter a small wad of cash. He requested that he "please pay the birthday girl's bill for us," and the waiter said he would gladly oblige. We left without saying a word and were long gone before the girl with the mouse ears discovered her birthday dinner had been paid for by someone she did not know.

## LOOK FOR KINDNESS OPPORTUNITIES IN EVERYDAY LIFE.

My wife Laney used to teach fitness classes at a massive local health club where several elderly people had recently become members. They tended to congregate by themselves in a far corner of the main exercise room and appeared to be disconnected from the rest of the gym, out-of-sight and out-of-mind.

Though it wasn't part of her job, Laney decided to go over and talk to the seniors and see how they were doing. She then made it a habit to stop and chat with them each day she was at the club. They appreciated her outreach efforts, and it made her feel good as well. It's further proof that we can derive just as much joy from giving as we can from receiving.

## WEEK EIGHT/ DAY 4: CALLING

# Seven Spiritual Insights from George Harrison's Favorite Guru

Do you remember when the Beatles had a brief fling with Hindu spirituality? In 1968, the group went to India to visit Maharishi

Mahesh Yogi, the leader of the Transcendental Meditation movement. The trip ended abruptly, due to some questionable behavior by the Yogi—but the experience was vital to the spiritual growth and development of one member of the Fab Four, George Harrison.

Disillusioned by money and fame, Harrison had begun seeking deeper meaning in his life. It was a quest that eventually led him to Hindu mysticism and the book *Autobiography of a Yogi* by Paramahansa Yogananda. Though he never met Yogananda (who passed away in 1952), his teachings so impressed Harrison that he used to give away copies of the book to any person he perceived needed a "regrooving." During a visit to the White House in 1977, he even gave a copy to then President Gerald Ford. (Trivia note: Harrison saw to it that the face of Yogananda was included in the sea of people on the Beatles' "*Sergeant Pepper's Lonely Hearts Club Band*" album cover. See if you can locate him.)

When it comes to gurus, Yogananda was somewhat unique in that he wanted people to follow his message, not him personally. His teachings combined Hinduism and Christianity. Yogananda believed in "Christ Consciousness," an awareness of our oneness with God that was achieved by Jesus. He taught that Jesus did not come to Earth to draw people to himself. He came to draw them to the truth, which Jesus said "shall make you free." In Yogananda's words, "Discover who you are, behind your outer trappings, and you will discover who Jesus was."

What follows are insights from *The Essence of Self-Realization, the Wisdom of Paramhansa Yogananda.* The book contains the teachings of Yogananda as recoded and compiled by a direct disciple, Swami Kriyananda (J. Donald Walters), who was with the guru during the final years of his life. When Yogananda spoke or was asked questions, Walters dutifully wrote down his words. The book captures the essence of Yogananda's core teachings.

I have lightly edited and reordered the information from the book below, turning some thoughts into questions. It should give you a sense of Yogananda's life philosophy which many spiritual people, including George Harrison, have found easily relatable.

### SEVEN SPIRITUAL INSIGHTS FROM YOGANANDA

1. **"What is the purpose of life?"** Your purpose is to find God, that is the only reason for your existence. Jobs, friends, material interests—these things in themselves mean nothing. They can never provide you with true happiness, for the simple reason that none of them are complete. Only God encompasses everything.

2. **"Where can I find God?"** It's within your own self that God must be realized. Your own body is the temple of God. Whatever places you visit outwardly, or whatever rituals you perform, the ultimate pilgrimage must be within.

3. **"How do I locate God within?"** Close your eyes and concentrate at the point between your eyebrows. Gaze deeply into the darkness and penetrate the thick veil. In time, you will see the inner light, for it is always there, shining in your forehead. Just like everyone has eyes, everyone has this spiritual eye within their forehead. It is discovered through deep concentration within.

4. **"Can God also be found outside the body?"** Walk outside your door and consider that everything around you is a part of your own awareness of God. Sense the leaves trembling on the trees, the meadow grasses as they wave in the wind. God is present. Listen to the birds singing, feel the sun's rays on your skin. God is present. Imagine the breeze as God's breath, inspiring all things and giving them life.

5. **"How should I pray?"** When you pray to God, pray from your heart. Say what you really feel, not what you think. Be completely sincere. Heartfelt prayer gives power to your thoughts. While it is alright to pray for things, it is better still to ask that God's will be done in your life. God knows what you need and will do much more for you than the best you can imagine for yourself.

6. **"What is the key to happiness?"** When you are right inwardly, all things are right, for you see everything as part of God. You then accept all things as they are, without judgment, and look with kindness and sympathy on everyone. Make up your mind to be happy and no one on Earth can take that happiness from you.

7. **"What is the best religion?"** It is not a religion at all, but self-realization, knowing that your true self is not the ego, but God, the vast ocean of Spirit. It is knowing that in all parts of your body, mind and soul, you are now in possession of the Kingdom of God. You do not have to pray for it to come to you. God's omnipresence is your omnipresence. All you need to do is improve your knowing.

Some final words of advice from Yogananda: "When you are with others, be with them wholeheartedly. But when you are by yourself, be alone with God."

# The "Five Dings a Day" Spiritual Practice

In *Meaningful Work, A Quest to Do Great Business, Find Your Calling and Feed Your Soul*, entrepreneur Shawn Askinosie tells us how he left a soul-killing job as a lawyer and found his true calling, starting Askinosie Chocolate. No ordinary chocolatier, the company sources 100% of its cocoa beans directly from farmers around the globe. (I sampled a bar of chocolate sourced from Tanzania and it was heavenly.)

While Shawn offers valuable lessons in starting a fair-trade business, providing a roadmap to finding your own calling, what interested me most in this book were the author's spiritual pursuits. He tells us about his relationship with a local Trappist monastery (local being Springfield, Missouri) where he becomes an official "Family Brother."

To join the abbey, even as a part-time member, Shawn is required to develop a "Rule of Life." This written document defines his personal spiritual goals and provides structure and direction for how he will get there. This includes the objective of his quest, with the head of the monastery advising him:

"If your objective is to "become a better person" you will fail, but if your objective is to "love God," the qualities you want to develop will naturally follow."

Ultimately, Shawn is instructed to pursue a deepening of "being," a complement to his "abundant doing" which is a product of his Type-A personality. Think about that for a second: Being present, not just doing. As a result, he commits himself to the following rule:

I will walk, rest, pray, work (manual labor of some kind), read, pray—all in God's presence ... my intention is not to receive answers, but to have my heart and mind be open enough to receive them.

## ABBEY LIFE IS VERY REGIMENTED—AND LEADS HIM TO A UNIQUE SPIRITUAL PRACTICE.

Shawn spends a few weeks a year at the abbey and his days start with vigils at 3:30 a.m. He then follows a precise list of activities throughout the day, ending with evening prayers at 7:45 p.m. To maintain this same rhythm when he's away from the abbey, Shawn sets "a series of gentle bells" on his smartphone. The bells ding throughout the workday, a total of five times altogether. In his words:

(The bells) stop me and sometimes even jolt me, which is just what I need. Each time I hear the bells, I stop whatever activity I'm in the middle of and say a tiny prayer. I don't say it out loud ... I just pause briefly, close my eyes, and say it silently to myself.

The "Five Dings a Day" spiritual practice seems similar to the Muslim call to prayer, also known as adhan. Five times a day, mosques around the world summon nearby Muslims for a mandatory prayer session. While the adhan is recited out loud, those gathered will silently reply with phrases like "There is no strength or power except from God."

For Askinose, the prayer he uses are the words "With you, O Christ, I live in hope" and it serves as a reminder of his intentions for the day. As he points out, "you could do the same thing for a short time with any prayer or intention that suits you."

We all could follow Askinose's approach and set our own phones to gently ping us throughout the day. What might you do each time the bell rings? Your personal intentions might include:

- Smiling
- Taking a deep breath and getting centered
- Remembering to be kind/loving to those around you
- Giving thanks for all the good in your life

### A SIMILAR MINDFUL APPROACH IS OFFERED BY THE YOGINI SARA COURTER.

On her blog *Body Karma*, Courter also speaks to the notion of using triggers throughout the day that remind us to set an intention or give a quick blessing. For instance, Courter mentions stopping at a traffic light as a possible prayer cue. Each time we stop at a red light, it serves as a reminder to pray or set an intention. Not driving much these days? Use any cue that suits you, like passing along a silent blessing with the first sip of each fresh cup of coffee or tea or swig from a water bottle.

The cues make it easier to remember to quickly pray or give a blessing and can be worked into your everyday life. The good thing about this approach is there's no planning (or phone) needed, and with a little practice, it can easily be mastered. According to Courter:

> If you wake up one day and decide to say a prayer of gratitude at every red light you hit during your commute, it will take an adjustment period. But, in time, the act will become an art. The new habit awkwardness will steady into skillful execution. There will be a grace and fluidity about it because you will have become it. No longer will you have to think before giving thanks.

It seems like another great way to break through the hectic pace and cacophony of our modern lives—and put us regularly back in touch with what really matters.

# Bedtime Contemplation: Four Steps to a Better Tomorrow

If you live an active life with a full-time job, an endless list of errands to run and possibly kids or grandkids to care for, it can be difficult to stay spiritually-centered. Hours can go by—heck, the whole day can go by—before you realize you're not in touch with your spiritual core, or aware of the beauty and small pleasures found in the seemingly ordinary moments of life.

I've written before about the importance of getting the day off to a good start with a morning routine. Here's an evening practice that can help you stay better tuned into life. In the book *The Ignatian Adventure: Experience the Spiritual Exercises of Saint Ignatius in Daily Life*, Kevin O'Brien writes of a bedtime routine that can help you get prepared for the following day. It's called the Prayer of Awareness.

*"The unexamined life is not worth living."*
*— Socrates*

I've always thought the famous quote above was a bit harsh, but it brings to light the importance of taking stock at the end of each day. With the Prayer of Awareness exercise, we look at what was good in our day and where our efforts or attitude may have come up short. What follows is a slightly reworked version of what appears in the book.

## THE FOUR STEPS OF THE PRAYER OF AWARENESS

1. **Start with a short prayer asking for guidance.** To get in the right frame of mind, take a few focused breaths to clear your head and look within. Open your heart and ask God (or whatever life force you believe in) for guidance. O'Brien reminds us that "there is nothing magical about praying. Prayer is a conversation with God." So keep it simple.

2. **Give thanks for the "gifts" you received that day.** We've already examined the importance of having an "attitude of gratitude." That means giving thanks for any good that happened to you today, even small moments you may have overlooked but upon reflection were special. (Think of a brief exchange with a friend or loved one, a glass of wine at the end of a long day, or, as I write this, the blooming of a Christmas cactus.) O'Brien advises us to: "Review the day and name the blessings, from the most significant and obvious to the more common and ordinary. God (not the devil) is found in the details."

3. **Reflect on the day and contemplate the feelings that arise.** Think about the events and feelings you experienced throughout the day. O'Brien asks us to truly connect with these moments and ask ourselves:

    - Did they draw you closer to God/life? Did they make you more generous with your time and talent? Did they make you feel more alive or more connected to others?
    - Did they lead you away from God/life? Did they make you less hopeful and loving? Did they cause you to become less aware or more self-centered?

    In other words, figure out what worked during the day—and what didn't work. Can the things that worked today be repeated tomorrow? Can the things that didn't work be handled differently or avoided altogether?

4. **Look at your schedule for tomorrow.** What events look to be the most challenging or have the potential to be rewarding? Then, ask God to provide you with the courage/confidence/ patience/peace you need. O'Brien reminds us that God wants to be there with us, but we must keep our hearts open to let God in

The key to making this "prayer" work: repetition. You need to develop a regular rhythm of using this practice for it to truly sink in, so try to use the Prayer of Awareness regularly. If you're like me and often find you're dead tired when you hit the sack, try this simplified four-point version that incorporates the ideas above:

- Connect with God through focused breathing or prayer.
- Think about your low point of the day. Can it be changed?
- Think about your best moment of the day. Can it be repeated?
- Pray for the strength/patience/confidence you need for a better tomorrow.

# The Greatest Thing in the World (as Found in the Bible)

To me, reading the Bible for inspiration can be like panning for gold. I can go hours sifting for insights and meaning only to come up empty. That's why I prefer to have other, wiser souls point out the gold nuggets to me, because if you know where to look, there is wisdom to be found.

I recently uncovered an important Biblical insight in the book *The Greatest Thing in the World*, which draws its message from the Apostle Paul and 1st Corinthians. Not a new release, *The Greatest Thing in the World* was written in 1884 by a Scottish evangelist named Henry Drummond. By 1900, the book had sold twelve million copies, a remarkable figure for the time.

The book's primary message is an interesting one. Drummond preached that while there are many righteous characteristics we might possess, none are more important than love. What Drummond is talking about isn't romantic or maternal love—he means *active* love as in *loving* kindness, *loving* patience, *loving* generosity.

Drummond wrote that love was the truest path to God because "where love is, God is." He wrote that if we lived an actively loving life, others would be attracted to us and influenced by our example. His life philosophy is summed up neatly in the following statement:

> I shall pass through this world but once. Any good thing I can do, or any kindness that I can show to any human being, let me do it now. Let me not defer or neglect it, for I shall not pass this way again.

I won't go into Drummond's detailed interpretation of the thirteenth chapter of 1 Corinthians; better to repeat a version of the original Pauline passage from a letter sent by Paul to the Corinthians. It is as resonant today as it was two thousand years ago.

### PAUL AND THE WAY OF LOVE

> "If I speak in the tongues of men and of angels, but have not love,
>
> I would be like a noisy gong or a clanging cymbal.

If I have prophetic powers, and understand all mysteries and all knowledge,

and if I have faith so strong it could move mountains, but have not love, I am nothing.

If I give away all I have, and am prepared for my own death, but have not love, I gain nothing.

Love is patient and kind; love does not envy or boast; it is not arrogant or rude.

Love does not insist on its own way; it is not irritable or resentful.

Love does not rejoice at wrongdoing but rejoices with the truth.

Love bears all things, believes all things, hopes all things, endures all things.

Love never ends. As for prophecies, they will pass away; as for tongues, they will cease;

as for knowledge, it will pass away. But love will last forever.

Faith, hope, and love, these three abide; but the greatest of these is love."

After analyzing the text, Drummond came away believing that the "spectrum of love" had nine components and were the ingredients of the ideal woman or man. These components, or what might be called rules to live by, are as follows:

**Patience**. Love understands and therefore waits.

**Kindness**. Love causes us to want happiness for those around us.

**Generosity**. Love means giving to others without envy or second thoughts.

**Humility**. Love, but keep our good deeds to ourselves.

**Courtesy**. Love means "not behaving unseemly."

**Unselfishness**. Happiness is found not in getting, but in giving love.

**Good temper**. A symptom of our loving nature.

**Guilelessness**. Love causes us to be honest and open, without underlying motives.

**Sincerity**. Love means being true in our attitudes and intentions.

One important parting message from Henry Drummond has to do with how we will look back on our days when our own end is near. Those who have lived a life of loving activity will have few regrets and an abundance of pleasant memories. In his words: "You will find as you look back upon your life that the moments that stand out, the moments when you have really lived, are the moments when you have done things in a spirit of love."

# WEEK NINE

## Ten Valuable Life Hacks from The Urban Monk

———

*The world is crazy, but you don't need to be.*

———

The words above appear prominently on the website of Pedram Shojai, a man otherwise known as "The Urban Monk." A couple of years ago he published a book, appropriately titled *The Urban Monk*, that serves as a guidebook to remaining calm and focused, even when chaos is breaking out all around you.

Shojai lives in the Los Angeles area and is well acquainted with the stresses and challenges of urban life. He identifies the primary problem as this: "Resting and relaxing are not acceptable in our society … productivity is everything." The solution: we need to get off the hamster wheel of the 9-to-5 world. This means putting together a plan of action that allows us to live in a more chillaxed state.

Shojai's book is chock-full of what are known as "life hacks," tips for making life easier to navigate, including sections on "getting right with food" and dealing with money and spending. But what stands out to me are the tips designed to help keep us calm and relaxed, by simply instituting a few small tweaks to our daily routine.

I've pulled out my favorites below, including a few I had heard about in the past but had forgotten. I've paraphrased Shojai's words, which appear in italics, my own thoughts follow. See if there might be two or three tips you want to add to your life.

## 10 Life Hacks from The Urban Monk

1. **Go barefoot.** *Cutting off the flow of vital qi to your body is a bad idea. This happens as we cut off our contact to the natural world. Take off your shoes and touch the earth.* Shojai also recommends "getting in the dirt" by gardening. Even if you live in an area surrounded by concrete, you can ground yourself by going barefoot at the park or on a beach or even in your house. In my home, we kick off our shoes the moment we walk through the door.

2. **Surround yourself with purity.** *Instead of isolating yourself from nature, honor her and bring her with you everywhere. Silently walk in nature. Communicate with plants. Even though you may be miles away from "nature."* Shojai devotes several pages to the practice of communicating with plants, an interesting concept. But just having greenery in your home can be enough to brighten your surroundings and lighten your mood.

3. **Rest when you're tired.** *A power nap goes a long way. A five-minute meditation break can tap into the same energy. Simply closing your eyes for five to ten minutes can help you power down and recharge in the middle of the day. The goal is to learn to unplug and drop down into a deep, relaxed place.* On days when I can do it, I find there's nothing more revitalizing than a quick afternoon power nap. It's better than a cup of strong coffee.

4. **Follow Pareto's Principle.** *It states that 80% of our positive output comes from 20% of our time and effort, and the flipside is that 80% of your time goes to "bullsh\*t." Find where you're best and engage there.* In other words, eliminate the bullsh\*t. How many minutes or hours did you waste today mindlessly scrolling through your smartphone? We all like to use our phones, me included—just do it less and focus more on what matters.

5. **Try a candlelight meditation.** I've written about meditation many times before, but here Shojai adds an interesting twist. Darken the room and light a candle, and as you meditate stare at the flame. You might also try this while soaking in a nice, warm bath.

6. **Prepare for sleep.** *Have a notebook by your bedside and use it nightly to dump your excess thoughts. Get the "to-dos" out of your head and onto paper.* Do what you need to do to clear your head, including shutting down your devices and TV at least 30 minutes before bedtime.

7. **Slow down on vacation.** *Doing is the disease of modernity. Being is a long-lost art. On vacation, be extra lazy. Nap when tired. Eat when hungry. Ease into a book. Only do things that sound good.* Vacations should be an escape from a regimented schedule. Do less, enjoy more.

8. **Treat Sundays as a micro-sabbatical day**. *Do only what feels natural and try not to make any plans. Give yourself some space to relax and let the day unfold.* Even if you don't attend Sunday church services, you can use Sunday mornings as a time to engage in spiritual activities. Meditate. Read spiritual texts. Contemplate. Take a walk in nature.

9. **Don't stay up late on a Sunday night.** *This is a bad idea.* Enough said. You want your batteries fully-charged for the coming week. Starting a full work-week with a half-a-tank of gas may leave you feeling empty by mid-week.

10. **Remember that everybody has something to teach you**. *When you're interested in information and learning about life, every person you encounter has the potential to offer you something.* That also means the negative encounters. That person who irritates you may be teaching you patience. The person

who whines may be teaching you compassion. The person who hates may be teaching you the importance of tolerance.

## WEEK NINE/ DAY 2: AWARENESS

# How Finding Quietude Can Lead to a Better You

There are two kinds of personal resolutions you can make. One is outward facing, pledging to be a better spouse or parent, boss or employee, or engaging in any behavior that makes the world around you a better place. For instance, by being more kind to everyone you encounter.

The other kind of resolution is inward-facing. While for many of us this can mean a renewed commitment to exercise more or maybe shed a few pounds, what I'm talking about here is an effort to address a part of yourself that can be often overlooked: your spiritual well-being, the "you" that exists at your very core.

Whichever way you choose to engage in spiritual practice, be it through prayer, meditation or spiritual reading, one thing's for certain. You need quietude. Defined as "a state of stillness, calmness and quiet in a person or place," it's not something that happens by accident. We find quietude when we carve out the time and space in our busy schedules to take a temporary leave from our everyday world and ... simply ... be ... still.

There was a time in the not-too-distant past when people devoted an entire day to quietude, spending hour after hour in reflection and solitude. This period is more commonly known as "the Sabbath day" among practitioners of the Abrahamic faiths: Judaism, Christianity, and Islam. In the book *Silence, Simplicity, and Solitude*, Rabbi David A. Cooper tells us that:

> In earlier days, the Sabbath was a time of reflection, inner work, and spiritual revitalization. All details of everyday life were excluded from conversation; all activities of business or future planning were unacceptable.

## ONE MAJOR PROBLEM IS WHAT PASSES FOR RELAXATION THESE DAYS.

For those of us who are not bound to a specific religious faith (and even for many who are), the idea behind the Sabbath has slowly slipped away. Sunday becomes another day to do chores or run errands, to catch a football game or binge-watch your favorite television show. I know because I often fall into the same trap.

This lack of quietude creates a void in our lives. According to Cooper, what is "missing for most people in today's world is the weekly period of solitude and reflection that was an integral part of life for thousands of years." What was once a part of our way of living has been stripped away, our lives filled with the constant glow and buzz of external devices.

## MAYBE WHAT WE NEED IS TO BUILD "POCKETS OF STILLNESS" IN OUR LIVES.

The term "pockets of stillness" was coined by Maria Popova, who writes an email newsletter called *The Marginalian*. She tells us that we need to find ways to escape from our everyday world and locate "places of respite from our everyday struggles." She advises us to: "Meditate. Go for walks. Ride your bike going nowhere in particular."

Popova also suggests we use our downtime to daydream, stressing that "there is a creative purpose to daydreaming, even to boredom."

She says that "the best ideas come to us when we stop actively trying to coax the muse into manifesting and let the fragments of experience float around our unconscious mind in order to click into new combinations."

To do this, we need quietude. We need to ditch our digital devices. No checking messages or scanning social media allowed. We need to separate ourselves from our everyday reality and retreat into a space that is calm and still. By avoiding external stimulation, we are better able to connect to this space.

Returning to David A. Cooper, while it appears to be counter-intuitive, the author tells us that spiritual solitude can better prepare us to engage with the outside world. You come away from these moments of quietude refreshed and recharged, better equipped to handle whatever life sends your way. To quote Cooper:

> When we engage in these moments of reflection and contemplation, we feel commonality and universality with all creation and we dwell in the timeless and spaceless realms, where the soul is at home and the heart is at peace. We develop the light within us and bring it into the world.

**WEEK NINE/ DAY 3: CHARACTER**

# The Dalai Lama and the Amazing Power of a Smile

It's a chicken-and-egg situation. Does the warmth emanating from the Dalai Lama's heart cause him to spontaneously break into a smile? Or does the smile come first, spreading happiness throughout his body and filling his heart with joy?

*"The purpose of our lives is to be happy."*
— *The 14th Dalai Lama*

The Dalai Lama is one of the most revered people in the world. As the spiritual leader of the foremost school of Tibetan Buddhism, it's hard to think of anyone who has done more with their limited amount of time on this earth than Tenzin Gyatso, the 14th Dalai Lama. Yet, if you ask me, the most compelling part of the Dalai Lama has nothing to do with his many accomplishments. It's his ever-present smile.

In virtually every photo you see of the man, the smile is there, conveying warmth and compassion. In fact, it's virtually impossible to find a shot where at least a hint of a smile is not present. It's his natural countenance. Do a Google image search for "Dalai Lama" and you will literally see hundreds of examples.

It's a genuine smile that starts at his mouth and spreads to his cheekbones and eyes. There are many photos where it looks like the Dalai Lama was just told a joke and is enjoying a good belly laugh. But no matter the image, this is one man whose picture says it all. He is at peace with himself. He loves humankind. He lets his love shine through. Which got me thinking:

## WOULDN'T IT BE GREAT IF WE ALL COULD MASTER THE DALAI LAMA SMILE?

Now, I'm not suggesting we put on a fake smile. But the fact is many of us go through life feeling pretty good about ourselves and the world around us. Yet, we often leave this feeling bottled up inside and don't project it outward to those we encounter in our everyday lives.

What I'm recommending is that we take a cue from the Dalai Lama and shine our inner light and love outward. It's easy really, and just involves loosening our face muscles a bit, thinking about all the things we love and are grateful for, and letting our face do the rest.

One person who has tried spreading love through smiling is the humorous, often inspirational blogger James Altucher. I'm sure his mental approach is a little different from that of the Dalai Lama, but he does have a unique way to connect with those who cross his path. In his words:

> I pretend I am everyone's mother or I pretend that everyone who passes me is going to die tomorrow and I care deeply about them … I smile at each person's eyes. I don't stop until they pass me. I love them. They are my babies.

As you might surmise from that passage, James is a bit "out there", but I think his intention is right on. In fact, one day he committed himself to smiling at everyone he passed on the street—not just anywhere, but on the perceived "mean streets" of New York City. And his results were pretty amazing. He not only saw a change in each person who caught his smile, he also saw a change in himself:

> Their faces lightened up. All of them. I could see their faces relax. The tightened cheeks fall a little. The eyes start to smile. Until finally they smiled back as they passed…and for each smile that I gave, it was sent back to me. I felt stronger. Like the rays of a yellow sun hitting Superman. Giving him his superpowers.

Now, James carries no misconceptions that he made the people he smiled at any happier, and he admits this was a somewhat selfish exercise. But it did ultimately seem to have a great effect:

> I traveled for a tiny bit into their lives. And my smile locked with theirs, like a kiss. A small kiss on the forehead. A brush of the lips. A tiny subconscious impulse sending an electric message back and forth between me and each person.

The idea of spreading love around like this is actually based on a very old premise, something the ancient Greeks called agape (pronounced ah-gah-pay). While mentioned in the Bible, John Templeton may have explained it best:

> Agape is a love that's distinctly different from erotic love or romantic love, as it exists on a higher, more spiritual plane. It's the unselfish love you give to everyone and everything around you, while expecting nothing in return. It's love simply for the sake of loving.

With agape, your actions have nothing to do with the actions of someone else. It's all about stepping up and giving love to others around you, even those you don't know. Sound like a worthwhile idea? There's no better way to get the ball rolling than with the Dalai Lama smile. Look in the mirror and try it for yourself. It's easy and will help you, and those around you, feel a little bit better about life.

**WEEK NINE/ DAY 4: CALLING**

---

# 9 Life Tips from Seneca (Circa 45 AD) That Are Truer Than Ever Today

How many more years will you be alive? And what will you do with them? A US government life expectancy calculator gives me a little more than 20 years on this earth; another calculator allots me a more generous 75% chance to live 25.4 additional years.

**YET WE NEVER REALLY KNOW HOW MUCH TIME
WE HAVE LEFT.**

I have written about the business executive who at the age of fifty-three discovered he had terminal cancer and three months to live. (He survived five months.) I have also written about a college buddy of mine, who at the age of fifty-five had a sudden, massive heart attack, dead before his body hit the ground. And while some of us get to live a good long life, like my friend John who passed away at age eighty-six, nothing is promised to us.

The Roman Stoic philosopher Seneca wrote an essay on the specter of death called *The Shortness of Life*. In the first century AD, about the time of Jesus of Nazareth, life expectancy was about thirty-five years of age, though if you survived past the age of ten, you might expect to live to sixty.

For Seneca, time was precious, a resource more valuable than any earthly possession. And the lessons he taught, taking into account our harried 21st-century lifestyles, may be even truer today. I've broken down his thoughts into nine key teachings; Seneca's precise words appear in "quotes."

1. **Life is long if you use your time wisely**. Seneca believed that the biggest enemy of a life well lived is our misuse of time. While we may place high value on money and property, we often don't properly value our time, an asset every bit as important as our 401K retirement account or the home we live in.

   "People are frugal in guarding their personal property; but as soon as it comes to squandering time they are most wasteful of the one thing in which it is right to be stingy."

2. **Live life in the present, one day at a time.** Even more than two thousand years ago, Seneca preached the idea of mindfulness

and living in the present moment. He asks that we live each day as if it were our last.

> "Everyone hustles his life along and is troubled by a longing for the future and weariness of the present. The (person) who organizes every day as though it were his last, neither longs for nor fears the next day."

3. **Procrastination is our biggest enemy. Seize each day.**

> "Putting things off is the biggest waste of life: it snatches away each day as it comes and denies us the present by promising the future. You are arranging what lies in fortune's control and abandoning what lies in yours. The whole future lies in uncertainty: live immediately."

4. **Don't waste time.** Imagine if Seneca could see us today and observed the amount of time we waste watching inane TV programs, mindlessly scrolling on the Internet, and constantly checking and rechecking our social media pages.

> "It is not that we have a short time to live, but that we waste a lot of it. Life is long enough ... but when it is wasted in heedless luxury and spent on no good activity, we are forced at last by death's final constraint to realize that it has passed away before we knew it was passing."

5. **Life is always moving forward. Keep pace or be left behind.**

> "You must match time's swiftness with your speed in using it, and you must drink quickly as though from a rapid stream that will not always flow. (In the) unceasing and extremely fast-moving journey of life—the preoccupied become aware of it only when it is over."

6. **Keep good company.**

"[One needs] friends whose advice he can ask on the most important or the most trivial matters, whom he can consult daily about himself, who will tell him the truth without insulting him and praise him without flattery, who will offer him a pattern on which to model himself."

7. **The quality of our time is important.** Seneca wrote that those who made time for contemplation and the reading of philosophy "are really alive" for they "keep a good watch over their own lifetimes." He also thought that by reading "holy creeds" and books, we are made better people.

> "By the toil of others, we are led into the presence of things which have been brought from darkness into light … Why not turn from this brief and transient spell of time and give ourselves wholeheartedly to the past, which is limitless and eternal."

8. **It's not about living a long life; it's about living a life of value.** What value are you bringing to your time here on Earth?

> "You must not think a man has lived long because he has white hair and wrinkles: he has not lived long, just existed long."

9. **The biggest fear? Looking back at our life with regret.** There's an old adage that says, "No one ever went to their death bed wishing they had spent more time at the office." It's the same with any time-consuming activity that doesn't add value to your life or the lives of those you love.

> "No one will bring back the years … life will follow the path it began to take and will neither reverse nor check its course. It will cause no commotion to remind you of its swiftness, but glide on quietly. As it started out

on its first day, so it will run on, nowhere pausing, or turning aside."

It's all about the precious resource of time and how we use it. Take a moment to pause and reflect: Are you using your time wisely? Are there changes you can make to put your limited time to better use?

# The Six Keys to Caring for Your Soul

Chances are you go for a physical check-up every year. But what about a spiritual check-up? From time to time, it makes sense to take a pause—and evaluate yourself and the world around you to be sure you're living a life that both addresses your spiritual needs and cares for your soul.

While Thomas Moore may be best known for his book *Care of the Soul*, it was in another of his books, *A Life at Work, the Joy of Discovering What You Were Born to Do*, that I came across a passage that talked to the components of a soul-centered life. I counted six in all, and they serve as helpful reminders to the kind of things a spiritually minded person should want in their own life. Moore reminds us:

> The quest for a life work entails creating a soulful style of living. That means living from a deep place ... with an eye toward individual choice rather than unconsciously going with the crowd.

What you'll find below are Moore's words verbatim in bold type; my thoughts follow. As you read the list, consider what you might want to add, or subtract, from your own life. You may find that while you are satisfying some components of a soulful life, some are missing.

## SIX KEYS TO CARING FOR YOUR SOUL

1. **"A soulful life is one of thoughtfulness, care, and engagement—you are present in everything you do, not just going through the motions."** That means being in the moment, as much as possible, each and every day. When you do find yourself caught up in a whirlwind of stress, or mindlessly scanning your smartphone, take a deep breath and come back to the present.

2. **"You take care of your body and health."** The body is a vehicle for the soul and their fates are intertwined. To be healthy and remain healthy, you must engage in a regular exercise program that at minimum gets you moving daily. Jog, walk, bike, swim, take a fitness class—engage in the activity, or activities, that are best suited for you.

3. **"You make your home a place of comfort, welcome, and beauty."** Home should be your refuge from the stresses of the everyday world. Find the photographs, artwork, tchotchkes and icons that speak to you and display them. Care of the soul also means having a comfortable place or two in your home where you can read, meditate, contemplate, pray, or just be.

4. **"You educate yourself throughout your life in values and solid ideas."** Never stop learning or expanding your thinking. If you consider yourself spiritual, this may include a regular diet of spirituality-related books, or if you prefer, podcasts. It will help introduce you to new ideas and philosophies that touch the soul or strengthen the beliefs you already have.

5. **"Your leisure time relaxes you, gives you a rich soulful life, and provides fun and play."** Live a balanced life, disconnecting from work and the 24-hour news cycle from time-to-time. Does your job preclude you from finding time for yourself? It may be time to find a new line of work, because without proper downtime—I'm talking daily, not just while on vacation—the soul cannot flourish.

6. **"Your spirituality is deep as well as visionary, and you incorporate contemplation, discussion, ritual, and prayer into everyday life."** If you're part of an organized religion that meets the needs of your soul, great. But, like many of us, you may find that the way to becoming the best version of yourself is through your own regular spiritual practice. As Oprah Winfrey once said on her SuperSoul podcast, "You must nurture the spirit that is you, to be all you were meant to be."

# The Lazy Person's Guide to Meditation

I've written about meditation many times at *Wake Up Call*. So many times, in fact, that you might get the idea that I meditate on a regular basis. I do not. While I do go through phases where I meditate daily, I often miss a day here and there. As well as the occasional week.

The issue with meditation? It's hard to find time to do the recommended two twenty-minute sessions a day. I know, there's the old saying that if you can't find twenty minutes to meditate, you need to set aside an hour. Call me lazy but I find myself frequently using my spare time elsewhere, including pursuing other activities (like running and engaging in deep contemplation) that provide some of the same benefits.

That's why, for the time-challenged, I'd like to introduce you to two meditation-like techniques that only take a few minutes. You can do them whenever you feel like. And in both cases, they have a way of calming and centering you, offering a taste of the benefits of meditation without the work.

Both approaches are pulled from the Sam Harris Waking Up app, which also features a bevy of standard meditations. Each represents a way to get "out of your head," giving the over-thinking, ego-driven mind a break. They also help us become aware that the world is vaster and more awe-inspiring than our little brains ever imagined.

### First, let's take a look at two different types of consciousness.

The English philosopher Alan Watts once talked about two types of consciousness. He called one type "spotlight consciousness," which is the ego-based, "me" consciousness. It's the focus most of us bring to daily life. The other type of consciousness he coined is "floodlight consciousness." It's a state of mind in which we have a total awareness of our surroundings and the vastness of life.

Watts cites an example when we use both types of consciousness at once. When we're driving a car and having a conversation with a passenger, we employ our spotlight consciousness to engage with the person next to us. But even though we are not thinking about it, we are also engaging our floodlight consciousness. We are totally aware of our surroundings as we safely motor down the road.

The two meditative approaches that follow are all about engaging the floodlight form of consciousness, the total awareness that is always present, even when we don't recognize it. As meditation teacher Loch Kelly says, to find this awareness, there's no manager or thought process required. The awareness exists by itself, so it's just a matter of getting the "small mind" out of the way and realizing it is there.

## LAZY TECHNIQUE #1: THE DIRECT APPROACH

This mindfulness practice comes from Stephan Bodian, who describes it as "more spontaneous and less laborious" than regular meditation. Author of the landmark 1998 book *Meditation for Dummies*, Bodian says that we already have the wisdom and compassion we're looking for. We just need to locate it by parting the clouds that hide it and tuning into the awareness that is always present. When we do this, we arrive at a natural state of "inner spaciousness" where we can be at peace. Here's how it works:

1. As you begin this exercise, remember to have no expectations. There is no need to strive for anything. Just sit in a comfortable chair.
2. Take a few moments to shift your focus from your thinking mind to your breath. Allow both your body and mind to settle in.
3. Sit quietly and let everything be as it is. Don't follow your breathing, just let everything be.
4. Let any sense of boundaries dissolve between you and the world around you. Move beyond the mind and the body and rest in this open awareness. There's no need to look for it, it is already there.
5. Consider the sky. It doesn't have to do anything. This innate openness is your natural state.
6. Thoughts are like birds or clouds. They are just passing through. If you find yourself fixated on people or events, let them pass. Return to the field of awareness.

7. Let go of any judgements. There's no doing, no manipulation, just rest. Sink back into the awareness that is the source of all that is.

8. When you're ready, go about your day, remembering this awareness that is always there.

### Lazy Technique #2: Glimpsing

This second technique, called "glimpsing," comes from Loch Kelly and represents another way to get out of the head and enjoy "the pervasive, spaciousness of awareness." His goal is to get the ego to "let go, to semi-retire." To do this, he focuses on our vision to help calm us and tamper down our internal monologue. (Sounds crazy, but it works.)

1. Sit comfortably and settle in, keeping your eyes open. Feel your body resting on a chair or cushion.

2. Focus your eyes on a specific object in the awareness field in front of you for a moment. Move to another object. Then to a third object.

3. Now, soften your gaze away from individual objects and with your eyes open, begin "receiving" the world around you. Keep your vision as open as possible, without focusing on anything.

4. Breathe. And smile.

5. Now, open the awareness to each side of your body, using your peripheral vision, on both the left and right. Become cognizant of the field of awareness that is on both sides of you.

6. Move this awareness into your head and then allow it to move through you. Recognize the field of awareness that is now behind your back.

7. There is no effort involved. The awareness exists by itself. Let go. Just be.

8. Stand up. Stretch. Move with this open-hearted presence. It is still with you and around you.

# Ten Surprising Truths about Jesus (You Won't Hear in Church)

Once a year, I'll pick up a new book about Jesus in search of fresh insights on the man and his mission. My personal preference is that these books are not tied to any specific dogma or religion but explore the many mysteries and myths that surround Jesus and his life. I found just such a book in *Jesus, the Human Face of God* by scholar Jay Parini.

The author identifies himself as a Christian and a regular church-goer, so he does not have a hidden agenda—but it's clear that Parini does not take everything in the Bible at face value. He reinterprets some Bible passages and reveals their hidden meaning, while also using Gnostic and historical texts to look at misconceptions and lit-tle-known truths about Jesus. Below are ten of his key points, some of which you may already know and others that may surprise you.

1. **Jesus never set out to create a new religion.** He considered himself a devout Jew with his own ideas on how to reform Judaism, not someone who planned to start his own religion. Even his earliest followers, who called him Rabbi or Teacher, mainly saw themselves as Jews who wanted to modify Judaic practices, not create a brand-new religion. Christianity did not

become an official religion until about three hundred years after Jesus lived.

2. **According to Jesus, he didn't perform miracles**. Those around him did. Jesus emphasized that he wasn't the reason miracles of healing occurred, what really mattered was the faith of the person being healed. Jesus thought of himself as an instrument of God—who enabled people to be healed through their own belief. For instance, in Luke 17:19, Jesus heals ten lepers and proclaims, "Rise and go, your faith has made you whole." Personal faith is what matters most.

3. **Jesus told us how to access heaven on Earth.** Parini reminds us that in the Beatitudes (Matthew 5:3-11), Jesus emphasized that the kingdom of heaven was immediately available to those who practiced the same virtues he did. These include humility, mercy, peacefulness and, of course, love. If you live your life with these qualities, Jesus says that you too can open the doors of heaven—right here on Earth.

4. **Post-resurrection, even his closest followers didn't recognize Jesus.** After the death of Jesus, Mary Magdalene arrived at his tomb—but didn't recognize the resurrected Jesus, mistaking him for a gardener. Neither did several of his other disciples, including two who saw him at the shore (John 21:4). Parini says there is a subtle teaching here: "We should not expect to recognize Jesus at first, even as he wakens within us."

5. **His family members may have thought he was nuts.** The family of Jesus appeared to have regarded him as somewhat volatile, even mad, and thought his ideas were strange. When he was preaching to a large crowd one unidentified family member even yelled out, "He's out of his mind" (Mark 3:21).

6. **Like Presidents' Day, the birthday of Jesus was combined with another holiday.** Christians didn't settle on December

25 as Christmas Day until the fourth century. This choice probably had something to do with its proximity to the winter solstice—and the fact that it was near a "feast day" celebrating Sol Invictus, the official sun god of the Roman Empire.

7. **Did Jesus really raise Lazarus from the dead? Maybe, maybe not.** Parini sees the meaning of the raising of Lazarus as potentially symbolic, not a literal raising of the dead, but a figurative one. It ties into an early-Christian belief that many of the teachings of the Bible were not meant to be taken literally. Lazarus stands in for everyone who follows Jesus and finds himself raised from the "living dead" to a new life.

8. **Jesus believed you can find God inside you.** "Wake up to God … his kingdom is inside you, within your grasp." The bold line above is Parini's take on the true meaning of Matthew 3:2, which usually reads: "Repent ye, for the kingdom of heaven is at hand." He posits that the original translators inserted the word "repent" for an Aramaic word that has a very different meaning. Additionally, as several early Christian texts point out, the kingdom of heaven is found not above, but here within our reach, available to us all.

9. **The letters of Paul come second in the Bible, but were historically first.** While the letters of Paul appear after the four gospels in the Bible, they represent the earliest Christian documents. The gospels were written after Paul's letters. What's curious is that Paul makes no mention of either the life or death of Jesus, only his teachings.

10. **To be a follower of Jesus, you don't have to go to church.** To quote Parini: "Jesus never meant to found a formal church with rituals and organized practices, to ordain priests, or to issue doctrinaire statements that formed a rigid program for salvation. Other than 'follow me,' his only commandment was

'to love one another as I have loved you.'" In other words, you can follow Jesus and his message without attending church. It's something that Jesus never requested or required.

# WEEK TEN

## A Short Fifteen-Point Guide to a Happy Life

Sometimes inspiration finds you. Other times you find it. The key is knowing where to look, and for me one of the easiest places to locate a little spiritual stimulation is on one of the bookcases in our home. It was there, under a thin layer of dust, that I stumbled upon *A Short Guide to a Happy Life* by Anna Quindlen.

Do you remember this book? It was an instant bestseller when it first came out, to my surprise, more than twenty years ago in the year 2000. It's a quick read, perhaps the thinnest hardcover in my library. There are black-and-white photos interspersed with the text, and even if you stop to take in the images, you can finish this book in about twenty minutes.

I dismissed *A Short Guide to a Happy Life* the first time I read it as trite, more of an essay than a real book—but on a belated second glance, I see its value. It captures one wise woman's take on life, what's important and what should be ignored, and at least some of its insights are sure to speak to you. Here are eight of my favorite passages, lightly edited. Read them slowly.

1. You are the only person alive who has responsibility for your life. No one else.

2. Remember that you are still a student, still learning every day how to become human.

3. Life is made up of moments, small pieces of glittering mica in a long stretch of gray cement. Look for them.

4. All of us want to do well. But if we do not do good, too, then doing well will never be enough.

5. Be generous. Send an email. Write a letter. Kiss your mom. Hug your dad.

6. Get a life in which you are not alone. Find people you love, and who love you.

7. School never ends. The classroom is everywhere. The exam comes at the very end.

8. This is not a dress rehearsal; today is the only guarantee you get.

Those are the book's first eight points. What follows are seven additional keys to happiness from another stumbled-upon source, a file of old Xeroxed clippings I found in a box in my attic. The stapled pages I uncovered had no title and no author was credited. I believe it came from a blog I can no longer identify, but judging from the other pages around it, it's about fifteen years old.

1. When you say "I love you," say it truthfully. When you say "I'm sorry" say it with eye contact.

2. Remember that sometimes silence is the best answer.

3. When you find you've made a mistake, take the appropriate steps to correct it.

4. Remember that sometimes not getting what you want is lucky.

5. Believe and trust God, whoever or whatever you conceive God to be. (But always lock your car.)

6. Marry or be with the person you love talking to the most. When you get old, conversation will be more important than anything else.

7. Share your knowledge. It's a way to live forever.

# West vs. East: Did We Get Happiness Wrong?

*Start chipping away.*

That's both a chapter heading and advice from Arthur C. Brooks' recent book *From Strength to Strength, Finding Success, Happiness and Deep Purpose in the Second Half of Life.* "Chipping away," one of many compelling ideas forwarded by Brooks, is a way to increase happiness as we grow older.

Brooks explains that the way we view the world is often dictated by society or more specifically by the cultural norms we live within and may have unconsciously accepted. In his words:

**In the West:** We believe success and happiness come by accumulating more stuff. More money, more accomplishments, more relationships, more experiences, more possessions.

**In the East:** They believe accumulating more stuff leads to materialism and vanity. This derails the search for happiness by cluttering our lives and by clouding our true nature.

This is where the concept of "chipping away" comes in. Brooks tells us that most Eastern philosophies believe we need to "chip away" the excess in our lives until we find our true selves. (Think of a sculptor chipping away at a block of stone to reveal the art inside.) We shouldn't "accumulate more to represent ourselves but rather strip things away to find our true selves." This is the opposite of Western thinking where we believe we should have a lot to show for our lives, collecting "trophies" along the way.

The good news is that it's within our powers to turn things around. We can start chipping away right now—at our possessions, at our insatiable quest for new experiences and accomplishments, at our hunger for more money and recognition. Only then can we discover a new meaning of success, true peace, and contentment.

### THE PROBLEM MAY BE OUR FLAWED FORMULA FOR SUCCESS.

According to Brooks, for most of us in the West, our satisfaction in life has always been determined by a simple equation:

*Satisfaction = Getting what I want*

This is a flawed formula. Because "while we know more or less how to meet our desire for satisfaction, we are terrible at making it last." We have fleeting moments where all is right with the world, but the moments dissipate. We then begin our pursuit of the next experience/relationship/possession we want.

Social scientists call it the "hedonic treadmill" and it works like this: You need constant success to enhance your feelings of self-worth and not feel like a failure. So, you run and run and run, capturing small successes along the way—but making no progress toward a lasting happiness. As Brooks points out, our equation ought to be rewritten to read:

*Satisfaction = Continually getting what I want*

Many people hope that "at some point they will finally feel truly successful and happy." But it does not happen. After getting a promotion, the businessperson looks to the next step on the corporate ladder. The new homeowner begins eyeing a bigger, pricier house.

The millionaire seeks even more riches. To paraphrase the Rolling Stones, we can't get no satisfaction.

To illustrate this point, Brooks mentions a cartoon he saw years ago of a man on his deathbed. The man whispers to the loved one at his bedside, "I wish I'd bought more crap." (Said no one, ever.) And inherently, it's something we all know: More stuff doesn't equal more happiness.

## MAYBE WE NEED A NEW EQUATION FOR A HAPPY LIFE.

Brooks believes the true equation for a simple life should be rewritten as follows:

$$\text{Satisfaction} = \overline{\text{What I have}} \div \overline{\text{What I want}}$$

Your satisfaction is determined by what you have, divided by what you want. Ideally, your "haves" and "wants" are closely aligned. If you find your wants are greatly outnumbering your haves, then it may be a time for a re-evaluation of your goals in life. Will that new "thing" really bring lasting happiness. Or just a fleeting feeling of joy?

The key to true happiness? Brooks quotes the bestselling author Simon Sinek who asks people to find their "why" in life if they ever want to achieve contentment and unlock their true potential. To paraphrase Sinek, you need to articulate your deep purpose in life and shed any activities that are not in service of that purpose.

In Brooks's case, he stopped to consider the forces in the future that would be most responsible for his happiness. He made a list of the things he wanted, eliminating anything that would bring only a momentary burst of satisfaction. His list boiled down to four items:

- Faith
- Family

- Friendships
- Work that is satisfying and serves others

Everything else is extraneous. Brooks is now aligned with a primarily Eastern way of thinking that "satisfaction comes not from chasing bigger and bigger things but paying attention to smaller and smaller things." This raises the questions: Are you paying attention to the right stuff? Is there anything you can start "chipping away" in your life? I, for one, am cutting down my "want" list right now.

## WEEK TEN/ DAY 3: CHARACTER

# The Hidden Meaning of Zen

During his storied life, the religious scholar Huston Smith researched virtually all the world's religions. But Smith was no ordinary scholar—he not only studied each religion, he became a hands-on participant, engaging in the religious practices and customs of each one.

In a story he tells in his autobiography *Tales of Wonder,* the most difficult religion to grasp may have been Zen. Smith studied for a grueling week at a Zen Buddhist monastery in Japan. During day-and-night meditation sessions, he had to try and decipher koans like "Does a dog have Buddha-nature?" and "What is the sound of one hand clapping?"

As hard as he tried, Smith couldn't find the proper answers to the koans. At least not from the perspective of the monk who was supervising Smith. Each of Smith's answers was quickly dismissed as incorrect. The stern taskmaster prodded and literally poked Smith (in the ribs, with a stick) to keep him awake and alert as he tried, and failed, to solve the koans time and time again.

Now the truth is that koans have no pat answers nor are they supposed to. They're meant to demonstrate how our normal ways of reasoning don't work, opening our minds to a new way of thinking. By dwelling on the koan, the student (in this case Smith) learns to be present in the moment. He starts to simply be instead of getting stuck intellectually trying to figure things out. So, the real "answer" is found not in the response to the koan, but in the change to the student's mental state.

By the end of his seven-day stint, an exhausted and despondent Smith was no closer to finding the answers. He felt as if he had just wasted a week of his life. He went to see the monk with the intent of releasing his frustrations by chewing the man out—only to have the monk greet him with a warm smile and invite him into his humble home.

Smith was taken aback by the monk's now kind and friendly demeanor and proceeded to ask him a few simple questions. The answers taught him more in a few minutes than what he had learned from a week of trying to unravel the meaning of the koans. Smith's first question:

### "WHAT IS ZEN?"

The monk told Smith that while koans are helpful, they are not Zen. And while meditation is helpful, it is not Zen. He then went silent. "Then what the hell is Zen?" asked Smith incredulously. The monk replied "Simple, simple, so simple." He told Smith that Zen is:
- Infinite gratitude toward all things past
- Infinite service to all things present
- Infinite responsibility to all things future

The monk told Smith when he traveled home the following day to not overlook all those who would help him get there: the taxi driver, the gate agent, the flight attendant, the pilot. Give thanks to everyone. The monk then brought Smith to the present moment. He looked above him and gave thanks for the roof over their heads, then bowed to Smith to thank him for his presence. The monk's final words of advice:

**"Make your whole life unceasing gratitude."**

Zen, like most of the world's religions, places a premium on gratitude, encouraging us to give thanks for all the good that is in our lives. If we follow the lead of Smith's Zen master, we can go a step further and fill every day with "unceasing gratitude." This simple act can better connect us with our environment. It also helps us realize that at any given moment we have reasons to be thankful.

**WEEK TEN/ DAY 4: CALLING**

# Will You Live "Your Own Damn Life" Before You Die?

*"The role of a fully realized human being is to arrive at the door of death having become oneself."*
*— Michael Meade*

In an old issue of *Sun* magazine, I ran across an article that featured the author Michael Meade. A natural storyteller, Meade tells us about an African proverb with the following moral: "When death finds you, may it find you alive."

At first glance, the words don't seem to make sense. Of course, death will find you alive. You've got to first be alive in order to die. But Meade goes on to explain the proverb's meaning like this:

> Alive means living your own damn life, not the life that your parents wanted, or the life some cultural group or political party wanted, but the life that your own soul wants to live. That's the way to evaluate whether you're an authentic person or not.

### ARE YOU LIVING AN AUTHENTIC LIFE?

It all comes back to purpose and a question we need to ask of ourselves: Am I being true to my inner compass, following the life my soul wants, doing the things I was put on this planet to do? Or am I living in a sort of suspended animation, waiting for the right time to make a move, while living a life of unfulfilled potential and quiet discontent?

These questions are important because time is something we can't stop or even slow down. Before we know it, days, weeks, years have slipped by. (Can it really be the 2020s?) I'm reminded of the words of my friend Jim McMullan, who died a few years ago: "One day you wake up and look in the mirror and you realize you're an old person—and you wonder, where did the time go?"

For a while I thought I understood what Jim told me but could not totally relate to it. Now I can. I have reached the third and final phase of my life. I look in the mirror and see the age lines growing more distinct. I awaken in the morning and my body is just a little stiffer; it takes a little longer to get out of bed.

That's no reason for despair. If anything, our advancing age gives us a little more freedom. We have put in our time, paid our dues, and can follow Meade's lead to "live our own damn life" with fewer consequences. Sure, we can pursue an authentic life for our own self-centered reasons—but it also represents an opportunity to give back to our family, our community, the world. The reason:

## We're not just growing older. We're becoming "elders."

Michael Meade instructs us that there is a difference between being "older" and being an "elder." The first happens to us without us lifting a finger. We naturally grow older. But becoming an elder requires our active involvement. It involves living authentically and with purpose. Meade explains:

> When older people become elders, they act not out of fear, but out of wisdom and understanding. They're not sitting at death's door still trying to check their portfolios online. Elders feel inspired to give back the wisdom they've extracted from life and not simply be receiving material benefits.

Give back the wisdom we took from life? But how? Deli owner and life philosopher Ari Weinzweig reminds us to think one step at a time: "Simply being purposeful, can, in itself, be a powerful purpose." Consider what small step you can take each day to add a little more knowledge, or more joy, or more love, to those around you. In Meade's words, our goal should be to:

————

*"Live a passionate, imaginative, meaningful life right up to the last moment."*

————

You are never too old (or too young) to take this step and it can happen with your next action. Make a list of the things you want to do. The people you want to connect to. The steps you need to take to live your most authentic life. For inspiration, remember these words of encouragement offered by Mahatma Gandhi while in his seventies:

> It is nonsense for you to talk of old age so long as you out-run young men in the race for service, fill rooms with your laughter, and inspire youth with hope when they are on the brink of despair.

It's time. Let's go for it. Let's be the people we are meant to be.

# Seven Ways to Relieve Stress

How do you hold up when life gets especially stressful? A *New York Times* article titled "I Am Going to Physically Explode: Moms Rage in a Pandemic" captured the angst many of us occasionally feel. Writer Minna Dubin explained "Mom rage" as "the colloquial term for the unrestrained anger many women experience during pregnancy, postpartum and beyond" and called it part of to-day's landscape. During the worst days of the coronavirus pandemic, Dubin wrote:

> Between stay-at-home orders, COVID-19 health concerns, financial instability (or fear of it), and police violence against Black people, it is no surprise that mothers are experiencing intensified rage above the surface, and feelings of grief, fear, and loneliness below.

Don't these feelings extend to many of us, female or male, mom or not? Watch the news for thirty minutes today, or simply scan a few major news sites, and it's enough to set your internal world on fire with a dizzying array of feelings—concern, disgust, bewilderment, anger, alarm—not necessarily in that order.

A friend of mine recently told me he stopped watching the news, hadn't seen it in more than a week, either on the tube or online. But if you're like me, it's hard to sit with your head in the sand as the earth is shaking around you. At minimum, you need to keep up-to-speed on the news and how the latest local and world events are affecting your community. And to stay sane:

**WHAT WE NEED DURING THESE CRAZY TIMES IS A LITTLE SELF-CARE.**

You and I need to find a way to relieve stress that doesn't involve escaping to the beach or the mountains for a week. (Though that's nice if you can swing it.) So what follows are seven small acts that can help you de-stress immediately. Most of these tactics take only a few seconds, though they require a little practice—and by practice, I mean remembering to use them.

Think of these seven suggestions as a part of your stress relief toolbox. You can use them one at a time or in any combination. For instance, you might find that numbers one, two, and five can snap you out of any momentary funk you might be in.

**SEVEN WAYS TO RELIEVE STRESS**

1. **Breathe.** When people are in stressful situations, they often engage in shallow breathing. What you need to do is take a deep breath. *Innnnnnnnnnn. Outtttttttttt.* Repeat. The increased oxygen intake has a way of clearing your head and calming your nerves. It's something you might try repeatedly throughout the day.

2. **Smile**. I'm not talking about a big, goofy grin, but a slight up-turn of the lips at each corner. Try it now. There's something

about a smile that can help lighten a tense moment, like a muscle memory that somehow takes us back to a happier time.

3. **Repeat a mantra.** I've written about meditation before and finding a key phrase, or mantra, that works for you. While it can be hard to find time to meditate, a quick interior repetition of a personal mantra has a way of reminding you of the meditative state, relaxing the mind. Think phrases like "God gives me strength" or "Everything is going to be alright."

4. **Go for a walk.** Stress has a way of tightening our muscles including the one inside our heads. Take five or ten minutes to go for a short but brisk walk, even if it's just around the block. There's something about putting the body in motion that makes the mind feel better. In the words of Terri Guillemets: "Walking is good for solving problems—it's like the feet are little psychiatrists."

5. **Eat good food.** We all like a little junk food now and then. I personally have a soft spot for potato chips. Yet we must balance our cravings for sweets and salts with healthy foods including fruit and vegetables. They're not only good for you. You'll feel better after eating them.

6. **Carve out some alone time.** One mom says that when she needs alone time, she "listens to music or a podcast, reads or just sit in silence." Another woman with three children has another solution: find the time to take a shower. Whatever, however, you can do it, find some time for solitude.

7. **Remind yourself: "I'm doing the best I can."** Don't be too hard on yourself. These times can be tough and you may slip up now and then, saying or doing something you later regret. Forgive yourself. The next moment is a chance to get back on track.

# Two Prayers You Probably Don't Say (But Maybe Should)

When you pray, what do you pray for? Do you pray for specific things to happen: say a promotion at work, the attention of a person you're romantically interested in, or winning the Powerball lottery? Do you pray for the well-being and happiness of others, perhaps for a close friend or one of your children or grandchildren?

I was thinking about the nature of prayer recently, during the final days of my father-in-law's life. I ran into a neighbor and explained to him the dire situation. The man we called Grandad had terminal cancer, was in at-home hospice, and probably only had a few days left to live. My neighbor responded, "I will pray for him."

At the time I wondered what he might be praying for. Was it a prayer that the cancer would go into remission, and he would make a miraculous recovery? A few days later, when I informed the neighbor of Grandad's serene passing, he expressed his condolences and his gratitude that he had passed in peace. That was just what my neighbor had been praying for.

### PRAYER #1. THE PRAYER FOR THE BEST POSSIBLE OUTCOME

We often pray for specific things or for a specific outcome. We pray that we'll get that new job or promotion, or that big home across town. We might even pray that a loved one will emerge from a serious injury or illness unscathed. Yet, the truth is, we do not have a crystal ball and cannot see the future. We do not know if our prayers will really make our lives, or the lives of those we pray for, better or more rewarding. For instance:

- We may pray for a troubled relationship to work out when it's best that both parties move on to new, more meaningful relationships.
- We may pray to get a job we applied for, not realizing it will require late nights and weekend work, costing us precious family time.
- We may pray to get a home we put a bid on, even though it may ultimately put us in over our heads financially.
- We may pray for the recovery of a loved one who is near death's door, only to prolong their suffering.

What if instead of praying for a specific outcome, we prayed for the best possible outcome? This means praying for what is best for us or for those we pray for—without judgement or the desire for a preconceived result. It takes the decision making of what is fair and right out of our hands and puts it in the hands of a higher power, call it fate, the source of all life or God. Why? Because fate/the life source/God knows best.

The American spiritual philosopher Ralph Waldo Emerson shared a similar belief in this method of prayer. Emerson asserted there was "a higher power" that regulated our daily events and trying to change our circumstances was "unnecessary and fruitless." Instead, we should turn inward to the part of ourselves where we can find God. Prayer then becomes "the contemplation of the facts of life from the highest point of view."

## PRAYER #2. THE PRAYER FOR YOUR ENEMIES

It may surprise you to learn that that according to a 2014 report published in *Vox*, the two most common prayers people engage in are prayers for "people who mistreat you" and prayers for "your enemies." This type of prayer may seem as foreign to you as it does to me, but it follows the lead of Jesus, who famously said: "But I say to you, love your enemies, bless those who curse you, do good to those who hate you, and pray for those who spitefully use you and persecute you." (Mark 5:44)

Pray for those who use me and persecute me? If this sounds difficult, it might help to hear what Martin Luther King, Jr. said about this practice. King reminded us that in the passage above Jesus was talking about the love called agape. This is not romantic love but the unconditional love that God gives to us. Think of it as a mirror, in which we receive love from God then reflect it outward to the world. In Dr. King's famous words:

> Why should we love our enemies? The first reason is fairly obvious. Returning hate for hate multiplies hate, adding deeper darkness to a night already devoid of stars. Darkness cannot drive out darkness; only light can do that. Hate cannot drive out hate; only love can do that. Hate multiplies hate, violence multiplies violence and toughness multiples toughness in a descending spiral of destruction.

Praying for those who spite or slight us can be tough, but as author Wendy Merron pointed out, "Being angry is like holding a piece of burning coal in your hand and hoping the other person feels pain." A prayer for our "enemies" helps us release any negative feelings we may be holding onto. What's more, when we pray that the hearts of others be softened, it also has a way of softening our own hearts. In the long run, love always wins.

# This May Be the Best Description of God (Ever)

If someone asked you "Who is God?" or "What is God?" how would you answer the question? I gave it my best shot several years ago and can tell you it is no easy task. It is, as the saying goes, like trying to define the undefinable.

That's why, when listening to an episode of the National Public Radio show Fresh Air, my ears opened wide when I heard the host Terry Gross put the question to Barbara Brown Taylor, a guest on the show. Taylor is a former ordained priest in the Episcopal Church, who went on to become a college professor and author.

Her response just might be the best definition of God I have ever heard or read. For starters, it recognizes that the concept of God is very personal and is different from person to person. There is no single correct answer. From there, it goes on to define a God as more of a presence than a person:

> When I use the word God, I am so aware I'm using a code word and that everyone who hears that word and probably everyone who uses it imagines something different, imagines a different posture in front of that being, that presence. I suppose my own image, my own idea of God, as imperfect and as evolving as it is, right now would be the glue that hooks everything together, the consciousness that moves between all living things.

> When I use the word God, I do not envision a large person with two arms, two legs and nose and two eyes. I envision, instead, some presence so beyond my being, a presence that both knows the stars by name and knows me by name, as

well, that is not here to be useful to me, that is not here to give me things as much as to ask me to give myself away for love. I, of course, get a great deal of what I mean by God from the tradition in which I stand—the Christian tradition. But when I say I believe in God, I mean I trust. I trust in the goodness of life, of being. I trust that beyond all reason. I trust that with my life. And that's what I mean by God.

For me, the key line here is "the glue that hooks everything together, the consciousness that moves between all living things." It matches what I've always thought was the best short definition of God, which comes from the theologian Paul Tillich, who passed away in 1965. It goes like this:

### GOD IS NOT A BEING; IT IS BEING ITSELF.

This notion of God also compares to a definition put forth by John Templeton who, along with Thomas Moore, Mirabai Starr, and Richard Rohr, has probably done the most to shape my spiritual point-of-view. Templeton is better known as a legendary Wall Street figure, but his greatest contribution may have been his books on spiritual philosophy and the world's religions. In his book *Worldwide Laws of Life*, he wrote:

> The wonderful substance of God flows in and through us and extends in every direction. Truly, there is no place we can go where we are not bathed in the infinite sea of this substance of the universe.

Templeton equates the "wonderful substance" of God to love. God is love and love is God. And if we are open to receiving this love from God, love can also flow from us. We give and we receive in an endless cycle. Templeton goes on to explain:

Love is more than affection. It is that magnetic, attractive force that binds families, friends, states, and countries together. Love has been called the "harmonizing glue of the universe." It is an inner quality that beholds good everywhere and in everyone.

This idea of a "harmonizing glue" matches Taylor's description of "the glue that hooks everything together." An interesting and thought-provoking concept, isn't it?

# WEEK ELEVEN

## My Wise Eighty-Six-Year-Old Friend Just Passed Away. Here are His Final Words.

I first met John Gray in early 2014. He was a reader of my *Wake Up Call* column and we began a regular exchange of ideas via e-mail. I soon found myself collecting some of his choicest sayings and, to his great enjoyment, wrote a story about him titled "Musings on God and Life from an 85-Year Old Expat Living in France."

Over the past several months, his once lengthy e-mails grew shorter, his responses more clipped. He had been in the hospital, receiving some sort of medical treatment--and then the messages stopped altogether. Last week, I received a note from his daughter that John had passed away.

I had saved several of John's more recent e-mails—and when I cut-and-pasted the best parts into a single document, I realized they read like a complete letter. With a little editing, I pieced together the parting message that John would have surely liked to share with others, had we been able to discuss it.

One of the more interesting parts of John's backstory is that he left Los Angeles in the 1960s and moved to a small village in France, never to return to the US. But rather than escape from the world, it turns out that John ended up embracing it. I'll let his words speak for him, as I bid my friend a fond farewell.

For some context, the letter begins with John encouraging me to enjoy an upcoming vacation after a tough stretch at work. We had previous conversations on the nature of God, and he continues that dialog here:

Hello my dear friend,

Take some time off, you're not missing anything. Or have you forgotten what that was? Do you have time like Thoreau or Burroughs to know all the different bird calls, to listen to the silence? Are those days gone forever?

As for me, I live my life as best I can, helping my neighbors and friends in my simple way. I believe that God resides in my own being and manifests itself in my acts of kindness, my simple sincerity, trying to respect each person I meet just as they are—prying smiles, tenderness and love out of them; softening their hatreds, their prejudices, their frustrations of the moment.

How I do this is simple. I smile, shake their hands and cheer them up! It is my contribution to humanity and it costs nothing. I try to live each day, in spite of the ugliness I see in our world, with friendship and kindness to all I encounter. I love showing affection to all and my being kind to the hobo on the bench, my complimenting a friend, my feeding the animals and birds, all of these things are the beauty in me that I am sharing.

I do not know where this love and tenderness, compassion and caring, and these other wonderful instincts that perhaps all of us have comes from. Perhaps we accumulate it throughout our lives, each and every one of us; and with time it penetrates and reaches our souls.

So many times, joy and happiness swell up inside me, especially when I see a gentle gesture from one toward another.

I feel it when I am looking at beautiful paintings, scenes in Nature, a happy couple holding hands walking in the park. I wonder about even the trees who must dread the tornados and dry spells. This idea is not absurd, for even plants seem to react to the love and care of the human hand.

But if God is within us, why is it just in some of us? It is not religion that instills this in us, it comes from within and why some have it and not others, we do not know. Were the great painters and writers and romantics like us given something special or is it just a quirk of Nature? Is it God or an omni-scient power?

This, I cannot answer. But it is an instinct within me that has prevailed my whole life. Whatever its origin, it exists in me. My Dad also had it within him, so this sense of a divine presence may well be part of our genes. And along with all the other positive and beautiful human instincts, it needs to be encouraged and fed.

The spirit is indeed within us. How it flowered in me or you and the millions of others that radiate with this light will remain our mystery. I have accumulated my beliefs from Lao Tzu and our great writers throughout history whose wisdom was wise and positive. What more do we need to guide us in being good to our fellow Man?

Relax now and enjoy your freedom! Enjoy your family in depth and quiet!

Love, happiness and a big hug for all,

John

WEEK ELEVEN/ DAY 2: AWARENESS

# Follow Your Bliss—By Answering These Three Questions

What is the secret to a happy and contented life? We've all heard the aphorism made famous by the American author and mythologist Joseph Campbell that you should "follow your bliss." It sounds like a brilliant idea, one that most of us can get behind—but what exactly does it mean?

Campbell's remarks on bliss occurred during a discussion with journalist Bill Moyers on a popular PBS series titled *The Power of Myth* that first aired in 1988. He expanded on the notion of what it means to follow your bliss with this thought:

> If you follow your bliss, you put yourself on a kind of track that has been there all the while, waiting for you, and the life that you ought to be living is the one you are living. Wherever you are — if you are following your bliss, you are enjoying that refreshment, that life within you, all the time.

The hard part, of course, is determining "the life you ought to be living." Campbell went on to say that "a little intuition" can help you find your path—but ultimately what constitutes "bliss" is very personal. Your idea of bliss may be different from mine, and your next-door neighbor may have a totally different take on what bliss means to her or him.

## LOOKING FOR YOUR BLISS? ANSWERING THESE THREE QUESTIONS MAY HELP.

According to my trusty laptop dictionary, bliss is defined as "perfect happiness," "great joy" and "a state of spiritual blessedness." You may be in this blessed head space right now. If you are, that's fantastic, you have been graced with a wonderful gift. But for many of us, a little digging is needed to determine what bliss might look like in our own lives.

The three questions that follow might help you pursue your bliss. They can help you determine what you really want from life and help gauge where you are right now. So, ask yourself:

- Who do I want to be with?
- What do I want to be doing?
- Where do I want to be living?

Next, let's take a deeper dive into each question posed by who?/what?/where? Use the additional questions below as thought starters to help you figure out where you are today and where you ideally might like to be.

**Who do I want to be with?** Do I have loving, caring people in my life? Do those around me share my beliefs and values? Is my relationship with my significant other in a good place? If not, can it be improved and how? What other relationships can be strengthened? Do I need to end any relationships that are toxic or take the steps necessary to embark on new ones?

**What do I want to be doing?** Am I in a line of work that I enjoy? Does it make the most of my tools and strengths? Am I making a contribution to the people and world around me? Do I feel valued? Is there something I could be doing that I might enjoy more and that would make greater use of my knowledge and abilities?

**Where do I want to be living?** Am I in the apartment or house I want to be in? Do I like my neighborhood and community? Am I living close enough to my friends and loved ones? Geographically, am I in the climate I want to be in? Am I near the things I appreciate most, whether it's the woods, the coastline or a city environment?

If you're not happy with your answers to all three questions, that's okay. The fact is often one or two of these factors may be in a state of flux. You may be engaged in a fulfilling line of work but surrounded by a toxic group of friends. You may live in a wonderful home and community but be less than happy with your current job situation. The key is to identify the one area that needs the most work and begin making the necessary changes to bring you closer to living a blissful life.

### Spiritual guidance on finding your bliss.

If you've dwelled on the three questions above and still feel lost, it may be time to connect with a higher authority. Dutch writer and theologian Henri Nouwen offers guidance on discerning our best path in life in his aptly titled book *Discernment*. Nouwen reminds us that "each of us has a mission in life" yet we often don't believe it or think about our purpose long enough to become aware of it. In his words:

> We seldom fully realize that we are sent to fulfill God-given tasks. We act as if we have to choose how, where, and with whom to live. But we were sent into the world by God. Once we start living our lives with that conviction, we will soon know what we were sent to do.

When determining what we were put on this earth for, we often mistakenly believe that we are here to complete some grand task or accomplish some amazing feat. Nouwen tells us that while our individual tasks can be very specialized, "they may be the general task of loving one another in everyday life." In other words: in what way can you bring more love to those in your life?

To determine what he needed to do each day, Nouwen would spend an hour in quiet prayer, meditation, or contemplation every morning. He felt he could sense God at these moments, a presence that was "often subtle, small, quiet and hidden." He said that by doing this, he was able to experience each day not just as a series of random incidents but as "divine appointments and encounters."

The bottom line: If you still feel lost after asking yourself the three questions, start living one question at a time, one hour at a time. Ask for guidance. Then, take the small, incremental steps that are necessary to find and lead a blissful life. It's your birthright.

# The Field of Honor: Nine Keys to Being a Person of Integrity

What do you do when the world isn't right around you? When you see a friend or stranger being mistreated or a person in authority behaving badly? Do you assist and defend those being persecuted or fall silent? Do you call out the person in power and try to hold them accountable or close your eyes to any wrongdoing?

**BE THE CHANGE YOU WANT TO SEE IN THE WORLD.**

While there are many national and global problems that are seemingly out of our control, there are things we can do on a local level—in our homes, workplaces and communities. This means that, as the quote attributed to Gandhi above suggests, **we need to be agents for**

**good**. We need to be the beacons of moral character we want to see in the world.

I was reminded of this point the other day, when my wife showed me a passage in the book *City of Girls* by Elizbeth Gilbert. It has to do with "the field of honor." A character named Olive explains the concept this way to her partner Peg:

> The field of honor is a painful field. That's what my father taught me when I was young. He taught me that the field of honor is not a place where children can play. Children don't have honor, you see, they aren't expected to because it's too difficult for them. It's too painful. But **to become an adult, one must step into the field of honor.** Everything will be expected of you now. You will need to be vigilant in your principles. Sacrifices will be demanded. You will be judged. If you make mistakes, you must account for them. There will be instances when you must cast aside your impulses and take a higher stance than another person—a person without honor—might take. Such instances may hurt, but that's why honor is a painful field.

Olive then reminds Peg, and all of us, that we have a choice—the option to step up or step back, as we encounter problems and difficulties in life. We can choose to be people of action and do something or choose to be silent and do nothing, even though our hearts tell us to act. Olive continues:

> Of course, nobody is required to stand in the field of honor. If you find it too challenging, you may always exit, and then you can remain a child. But if you wish to be a person of character, I'm afraid this is the only way.

While it may be "the only way," Olive goes on to say that while she regularly tries to apply this idea to her own life, she is not always successful. But importantly, she makes the effort, even though it may cause personal discomfort or inconvenience. You have to do what you believe in and there are just some ideas, and some people, that are worth fighting for.

**"COURAGE IS NOT THE ABSENCE OF FEAR, BUT THE CAPACITY TO ACT DESPITE OUR FEARS."**

The quote above comes from a person known for courage, the late US Senator and former POW John McCain. It underscores the notion that if we want to stand in the field of honor, we must overcome our fears, sometimes of retribution, sometimes of venturing into the unknown.

There's a stirring passage in McCain's book *Character is Destiny,* where he quotes the Shawnee Indian leader Tecumseh. It reads like guidance for the woman or man who has decided to live his or her life with honor and moral integrity. I've broken the passage into the nine key points below:

**NINE KEYS TO BEING A PERSON OF HONOR AND INTEGRITY**

1. Trouble no one about their religion.
2. Respect others in their views, and demand that they respect yours.
3. Love your life, perfect your life, beautify all things in your life.
4. Seek to make your life long and its purpose in the service of your people.
5. If in a lonely place, always give a word or a sign of salute when meeting or passing a friend, even a stranger.
6. Show respect to all people and grovel to none.
7. When you arise in the morning, give thanks for the morning light, for your life and strength. Give thanks for your food, and the joy of living.

8. Abuse no one and no thing, for abuse turns the wise ones to fools and robs the spirit of vision.

9. Be not like those whose hearts are filled with fear, so that when their time comes they weep and pray for a little more time to live their lives over.

To avoid becoming like those in point nine above, we have a choice. We can meander through life directionless, moving from one distraction to the next, until the clock runs out and our time is up. Or we can commit ourselves to a life of character and honor, and a beneficial purpose that adds to the lives of others and gives our own lives true meaning. It is only then that we'll be able to look back at our time on earth without regret.

**WEEK ELEVEN/ DAY 4: CALLING**

# How to Overcome a Midlife Crisis — at Any Age

A mid-life crisis is described as "a psychological crisis brought about by events that highlight a person's growing age, inevitable mortality, and possibly shortcomings of accomplishments in life … produc[ing] depression, remorse and high levels of anxiety."

The description above (via Wikipedia) says a mid-life crisis can happen between the ages of forty and sixty, while another source narrows it to ages forty-five to fifty-five. But the fact is, a mid-life crisis can happen at any time and is not restricted to this ten- or twenty-year span. You can have a "crisis of calling" at thirty years of age. You can also have one at sixty-five or seventy.

The crisis is the sudden and intense realization that your life is not where it is supposed to be, that at some point in your past you zigged when you should have zagged. And at this juncture you have a choice. You can continue to muddle through life, burying the feeling that you should really be on another path. Or you can take action and pursue your true calling.

———

*There comes a time in life when you hear the Great Calling. When we hear this inner voice, it is our summons, a holy message that we're at a crossroads and a new chapter of life is about to begin.*

———

The passage above is from *A Fierce Heart: Finding Strength, Courage, and Wisdom in Any Moment*, by Spring Washam, a disciple of Jack Kornfield. Washam, an African-American meditation teacher who hails from Oakland, California, advises us that it's our primary task in life to pursue this "great calling." She compares it to "the hero's journey," where an ordinary human being "goes on an adventure, faces a challenge or crisis, and comes out a changed person."

The idea of the hero's journey was first popularized by the great American mythologist Joseph Campbell, who explained it in similar terms:

> A hero ventures forth from the world of common day into a region of supernatural wonder: fabulous forces are encountered and a decisive victory is won: the hero comes back from this mysterious adventure with the power to bestow boons on his fellow man.

Washam calls the "great calling" an invitation to adventure and a beckoning to a higher path. In her words, "We go inside ourselves and reflect on who we are and why we are here." The issue for many of us is that while we hear the call loud and clear, it comes without any real instructions. We know something isn't right—we just don't know how to address it.

This is the time for introspection. Washam advises us that "If we listen carefully, we can hear a voice trying to get our attention and wake us up. The first sign, or messenger, comes when our lives are no longer satisfying. We lose interest in the things that used to make us happy. The winds of change are blowing, and an unbearable restlessness grips our soul. The call speaks to us in questions: Who am I? What is my purpose? What am I doing with my life?"

Yet the fact is no book can tell you what *your* specific calling might be. You need to discover that for yourself, which requires a little soul-searching. While Washam tells us that the inner voice can be frightening, we need to step up and "pay attention to this calling, or the voice will get louder and even more disruptive." She goes on to say: "When what has been comfortable isn't working anymore, it is a prompt to move you toward what you're being called to do. Life is shifting. You are changing."

It is at this point in life that we need to "discover our deepest truths." This can mean taking up "artistic pursuits like dancing or singing, joining a spiritual community" or I would add developing new and stronger personal relationships, pursing a new vocation or perhaps moving to a new city or small town. "It's a process of self-discovery as we move toward a deeper understanding of our lives."

As Washam points out, the journey is not always easy. "The call to awaken is powerful and can be shocking and confusing, especially to those accustomed to our behaving in predictable ways." In other words, our friends and family might get a little freaked out by our actions and the new path (or paths) we are pursuing. Yet, for our own sanity and well-being, we must pursue this new direction.

Washam reminds us that at the end of the hero's journey "The hero or heroine returns to their community to bring back the newfound knowledge and wisdom they have bravely acquired. Most significantly of all, they return transformed and ready to begin a life of service." Ultimately, we return a better person. By satisfying our calling, we find greater contentment within ourselves—and are better able to assist those around us.

# Five Fresh Spiritual Practices for Crazy Times

How do you stay sane when the world around you is going nuts? In his book *Spiritual Practices for Crazy Times*, the noted interfaith author Philip Goldberg has some answers. He discusses our current plight—and the seemingly daily adverse events that can take the wind out of your sails or momentarily knock you off the spiritual path. Goldberg tells us: "In crazy times like ours, we need prayer, meditation, mindfulness, and other spiritual practices more than ever. They are not luxury items like a vacation, they're more akin to necessity."

Goldberg mentions a 2018 Gallup poll that revealed "the level of stress, anger, and worry in America was the highest it had been in a decade." Now, consider that in 2018 the COVID-19 pandemic had not yet materialized, and deeply embedded issues around racial injustice in the US had not fully come to light. If Gallup held that poll today, it would be no surprise if our levels of worry, stress, and anger hadn't reached new, unmatched heights.

It's during times like these that we need to stay spiritually active, digging deep into our spiritual toolboxes to maintain our own sanity. We need actions and activities that can both ground us and give our unsettled mind a rest. There's just one issue: to paraphrase a line from the movie Jaws: "We're gonna need a bigger toolbox."

That's where *Spiritual Practices for Crazy Times* comes in. Goldberg has a plethora of suggestions, including meditation, prayer, yoga and breath work. The aim is "not the absence of outrageous slings and arrows," which are often out of our control "but the presence of peace, perhaps even joy." Our ultimate goal should be to:

## Maintain calmness, clarity, and courage amid crazy times.

While we've previously discussed the importance of spiritual practice, Goldberg introduces new ideas that can help strengthen your practice and buoy you when you feel yourself slipping beneath stressful waters. Here are five of my favorites, which represent a sliver of the practices in *Spiritual Practices for Crazy Times*. The words in italics below are Goldberg's (lightly edited), followed by my thoughts.

### Five Fresh Spiritual Practices

1. **Lean on a spiritual buddy.** *Your informal community of friends, family, and others is indispensable. People you trust and respect, with whom you share history and mutual concern, can add solace, support, and wisdom to your path. They can help you locate your inner strength, resiliency and courage when you need it most.* As the old Bill Withers song goes, we all need somebody to lean on. Goldberg points out it's worth trying to make these connections in person, as opposed to on the Internet or via text.

2. **Find safe harbor in a sacred space.** *Sacred spaces are vital habitats for the soul. A park bench can be sacred space. Go to them often. Sit. Breathe. Be fully present.* I'm going to separate this from the idea that follows by asking you to find a sacred space in your own home. It can be a cozy chair in the den or a win-

dow seat that looks out at a tall tree or maybe a folding chair on the back porch. It's a place where you can read, contemplate, or just simply be. And no matter where you live, consider adding plants to your sacred space to add life to your surroundings.

3. **Place yourself in nature's cathedrals.** *Whether you access nature in the woods, on beaches, or in a city park, treat every opportunity as a sacrament. No agenda, no expectations, no earphones. If you're accustomed to an energetic jog or hike, enjoy your workout, but at some point slow down and linger.* As a runner, this idea rings especially true to me. Sometimes you just have to slow down in order to really take it all in. Look, really look, at your surroundings, taking in the beauty of nature with all your senses.

4. **Soothe the soul with art**. *Go to a museum when it's least crowded, and if a particular piece lifts your spirit, give it the time you need to soak it in fully. Literature, music and cinema can also be sanctuaries. Don't ignore the spiritually transformative power of stories and songs.* Can't or don't want to visit a museum in person? These days, you can visit the world's best museums online. (Google "best virtual museums.") It's the next best thing. Goldberg also tells us that "music that expresses how you actually feel can be more healing than music that expresses how you want to heal."

5. **Smile**. "Sometimes your joy is the source of you smile, but sometimes the smile can be the source of your joy." This inspirational quote is from Thich Nhat Hanh and reminds us that smiling has the power to cause a subtle shift in our emotional state. Think of the Buddha and his "half smile of unshakeable contentment." Put the Buddha smile on your face and see if it doesn't, in some curious way, lighten your load.

Some parting advice from Philip Goldberg: "Go easy on yourself." During stressful times, we're all more likely to act in ways that don't reflect our true character. If that happens, simply catch yourself and start all over again. In Goldberg's words:

"Give yourself the kindness and compassion you'd give your neighbor. You're an imperfect human like the rest of us, so lighten up. Make radical self-acceptance a spiritual practice of its own."

## WEEK ELEVEN/ DAY 6: INNER WORK

# Spirituality for the Time-Challenged: The Ten-Second Happiness Exercise

Think you don't have time for spiritual practice in your life? Well, Chade-Meng Tan, the former Google "Jolly Good Fellow" (yes, that was his title) begs to differ. He has an exercise that can enhance your sense of happiness and well-being and it takes only ten seconds. In fact, I've done it in seven seconds, so I can guarantee you it won't take much time out of your busy life.

The exercise is called "The Joy of Loving-Kindness" and its inventor, who goes by the name Meng, has taught and preached its benefits to businesses and corporations around the world. The amazing thing is, for all its simplicity, it seems to work. For example, one woman who tried it at work claims it led to her best day on the job in her seven years there.

**THE JOY OF LOVING-KINDNESS WORKS LIKE THIS:**

- **Step 1.** When you're out in a public situation, whether it's at work, a social event or anywhere people might gather, identify a person in the room or your environment and just think: "I wish this person to be happy."
- **Step 2.** Find a second person and repeat Step 1. That's it!

For maximum effectiveness, Meng recommends repeating this thought up to eight times per person, secretly wishing for their happiness. When you do this, you may find a funny thing happens: You'll find yourself feeling happier, too.

**YOU CAN ALSO CONDUCT THE JOY OF LOVING-KINDNESS EXERCISE AT HOME.**

The home version of this exercise takes all of two minutes and lets you spread warmth and good cheer to family members and friends, even those you may not have seen for a while. Again, there are just two simple steps:

- **Step 1.** Sit down and get comfortable, in a way that "allows you to be alert and relaxed at the same time." Your eyes can be opened or closed.
- **Step 2.** Bring to mind someone you wish to be happy. Feel the joy and love in your own heart. Focus your attention on spreading this joy and love to the person you're thinking about and silently say: "I wish this person to be happy."

Rubbish, some of you may be thinking. Does this really work? I can't say for sure that it has any effect on the person you're thinking about, nor can Meng. But time after time, the ex-Googler reports it has a way of making those who engage in this simple practice feel better about themselves.

## It may have something to do with focusing outward instead of looking inward.

Tim Ferriss, who has tried Meng's exercise, reports that he does a three-to-five minute Joy of Loving-Kindness session every night and reports that it makes him a happier person. He can't put his finger on why this happens, but surmises:

> I think it's effective because meditation is normally a very me-focused activity, and you easily get caught in the whirlpool of thinking about yourself. This loving-kindness drill takes the focus off of you entirely—which, for me, immediately resolves at least 90% of the mental chatter.

## Here's a bonus ten-second exercise that may help you if you're stressed.

Another exercise for the time challenged comes from the Catholic monk and author John Michael Talbot. It can be used anytime you're feeling stressed or tense and is based around a simple-breathing exercise. I've edited his description of the practice down to a five-step process.

1. Start with a prayer: "God, give me peace."
2. Calm your heart. Still your mind. Begin breathing slowly as you pray for peace.
3. Make each breath a prayer. As you inhale and exhale, meditate on the grace and love of God.
4. Next, take a deep breath in and silently say "the grace of God."
5. Take a deep breath out and think "the love of God."

Repeat as needed. Five or six times seems to work best.

# The One Vital Lesson That All Religions Teach

Karen Armstrong is a former Catholic nun who left the church and became one of the world's leading writers on spirituality and faith. She has penned books on the Bible, Buddhism and Islam, as well as *A History of God*. In a recent interview, Oprah Winfrey asked Armstrong the following question:

### IS THERE A COMMON THREAD THAT TIES TOGETHER ALL RELIGIONS?

Leaning on a lifetime of religious study and writing, Armstrong said there was one theme she found in all religions. She then stated that if you got this one thing right, nothing else mattered. That one thing is compassion.

Armstrong tells us that all religions stress the Golden Rule, some variation of this thought: Always treat others the same way you would like to be treated yourself.

In the Bible, this is stated in Matthew 7:12 as "Do unto others as you would have them do unto you." In the Jewish Talmud, it reads "That which is hateful to you, do not do to your fellow man." In Buddhism, it is stated "Hurt not others with that which pains yourself."

---

"Compassion is something really worthwhile. It is not
just a religious or spiritual subject. It is not
a luxury, it is a necessity."
— *Dalai Lama*

---

Armstrong advises us to follow the lead of Buddhism and have compassion for all living things. This starts by realizing that every

231

human being, no matter how fortunate or happy they may seem, has some level of pain within. By honestly looking into our own hearts, we can sense our own pain, and realize that this pain and suffering exists in others as well.

We all endure hardships. We must realize we are not alone. The rest of humanity is on the same often difficult journey through life and deserves the same compassion we often only reserve for ourselves. I was reminded of this fact the other day, while reading a late-night tweet by *Hamilton* creator Lin-Manuel Miranda. He wrote: "Goodnight to all your mistakes and deleted tweets and frayed nerves and broken hearts and nervous tics. I am aching just like you and I am learning just like you."

That's a universal truth: Life is one big learning experience, and we are all in it together. We need to treat and respect others like we want to be respected, without petty meanness or copping attitudes for minor transgressions. We also need to start living not just for ourselves, but for others.

We can do this by being involved and active in our own personal universe. We can offer others a haven of peace of which we are the center. Start looking around you, family first. Is there someone you know who is distressed or needs a kind word? Do you see an opening for a heartfelt conversation? Next, move outward to your workplace and community. As Armstrong says: "Try being a light to the people you meet every day."

This extends to the strangers you see on the bus, walking down the street, or in line at the bank or coffee shop. Each person you encounter may be enduring their own personal tribulations. Smile at them. Silently wish them well. When appropriate, encourage them or offer a kind word. Do your part to make the world a better, more compassionate place.

## Twelve Steps to a Compassionate Life

The following steps are from Karen Armstrong and are an edited version of a list that appears at Oprah.com. For a complete explanation of each step, see Armstrong's book by the same name—though this should be enough to get you started on living a more compassionate life.

Step 1. **Learn about compassion.** Know the Golden Rule.

Step 2. **Look at your own world.** Start with your immediate family.

Step 3. **Show compassion to yourself.** It's the first step toward compassion for others.

Step 4. **Be empathetic.** Know the pain you feel is felt by those around you.

Step 5. **Be mindful.** Be fully present in life.

Step 6. **Take action.** Engage in small acts of kindness.

Step 7. **Realize how little you know.** Be humble.

Step 8. **Connect with others.** Listening is as important as speaking.

Step 9. **Show concern for everybody.** This includes people of different races and cultures.

Step 10. **Increase your knowledge.** Never stop looking and learning.

Step 11. **Recognize those in need.** Identify the people who need your help.

Step 12. **Love your enemies.** Perhaps the hardest step of them all.

# WEEK TWELVE

## Eight Life-Affirming Benefits of Growing Older

If you've passed the half-century mark, I probably don't have to tell you there can be a downside to getting older. It's a little tougher to get out of bed in the morning and get moving. Aches and pains begin announcing themselves more frequently. You might occasionally have trouble recalling a name or place or thing you once knew.

Yet, with the negatives of growing older, there also comes an upside. We begin to realize that there's some truth in the adage "as we grow older, we grow wiser." We make fewer "stupid" mistakes and know how to correct them when we do. We learn to choose our battles. We're more apt to issue an apology when warranted, or to express our gratitude.

In the book *On the Brink of Everything: Grace, Gravity and Getting Old*, Quaker teacher Parker J. Palmer does a fine job illustrating the benefits that come out of our aging minds and bodies. Parker, who wrote this book just after he turned eighty, sees aging as a time of discovery and engagement. In his words, "Age itself is no excuse to wade in the shadows. It's a reason to dive deep."

To Palmer's way of thinking, "old is just another word for nothing left to lose, a time in life to take bigger risks." In other words, a time to continue growing. What follows are his words in bold type, my thoughts follow. No matter your age, see which aspects of growing older you're now enjoying and what benefits are still to come.

1. **You lose the capacity for multitasking but rediscover the joys of doing one thing at a time.** This allows you to give the task at hand, or the person in front of you, your full and undivided attention.

2. **Your thinking slows a bit, but experience makes it deeper and richer.** You learn how to better appreciate the moments, like this one, that make up your life.

3. **You become more aware of the satisfaction found in simple things: a talk with a friend, a walk in the woods, sunsets and sunrises, a night of good sleep.** You come to realize that the possessions of life, the big home, expensive car, fancy shoes, are not where true happiness is found.

4. **Things you once lamented doing, now become part of "a larger weave, without which the fabric of life would be less resilient."** You realize that past mistakes were learning lessons and without them, you would not be the person you are today.

5. **You become more grateful for those who have helped you.** You also learn the joy found in expressing thanks to all who have helped you, past and present.

6. **You no longer feel the need to prove anything to anyone.** You begin to realize it doesn't really matter what other people think, that you are the best judge of you.

7. **It's easier to say no to anything that's not "life-giving."** You learn it's better to turn down a job you don't want to do or remove yourself from an unhealthy relationship.

8. **It's more about "who you are" than "what you do."** In Palmer's words, "you get to show up to life as your true, God-given self." You're able to more fully realize your own potential and become the person you were meant to be.

WEEK TWELVE/ DAY 2: AWARENESS

# Is Your Intuition Influenced by Your Spirit Guide?

To navigate through life, most people rely on their five senses: sight, smell, hearing, taste and touch. But if you're like a lot of spiritual people, you sometimes find yourself relying on a way of knowing that exists beyond the physical senses. It's a sixth sense known as intuition.

### YOU'VE PROBABLY FELT THE PUSH OR PULL OF INTUITION. WHERE DOES IT COME FROM?

If you listen to two prominent names in the world of spirituality, author and frequent *Oprah Winfrey Show* guest Gary Zukav, and the modern-day channeler Paul Selig, they will both tell you intuition comes from a non-physical source: spirit guides.

In his landmark book *Seat of the Soul*, Zukav explains that many of us are "multisensory personalities" who rely on "impulses, hunches and sudden and subtle insights" for guidance. These different strands of intuition originate in our soul and are informed by "advanced intelligences that assist the soul on its evolutionary journey."

Zukav states these "nonphysical teachers" produce a level of truth we would be hard-pressed to uncover on our own. He explains it this way:

> Other intelligences inhabit other ranges of frequency. They coexist with us but are invisible to us. In the place that you now sit exist many different beings, each active in its own reality. These realities comingle with yours ... but are undetectable to the human eye.

237

While the five-sensory person may receive the same insights, he or she believes they originate from the psyche and gives them short shrift. On the other hand, the multisensory personality strives to increase his or her awareness of this guidance and interacts with it. According to Zukav, when faced with a decisions or challenge, you should:

> Ask the Universe to 'help me to see.' The answers may not always come in the ways that you expect, but they always come. Sometimes in the form of a feeling—a yes or no feeling—sometimes in the form of a memory, or a thought or a dream, and sometimes in the form of a realization that is prompted by an experience that will occur the next day.

Zukav believes we can ask for and receive this guidance from a spirit guide at any time. It starts with "approaching the questions in your life with a sense of faith that there is a reason for all that is happening" and that what is happening is for your own good. He writes of the rich rewards of accessing this wisdom:

> The ability to draw consciously upon your nonphysical guidance and assistance, to communicate consciously with a non-physical Teacher, is a treasure that cannot be described, a treasure beyond words and value.

Have you heard of Paul Selig? Over the past few years, he has produced a number of channeled books dictated to him by a spiritual guide. If like most people, even those with a spiritual bent, you question whether this is too "woo-woo," I recommend you listen to a podcast or watch a video where this channeling takes place. If Selig is a fraudster, he has put together one fantastic act. With repeated exposure, I've decided to take Selig at his word.

Writing in his first book *I Am The Word*, Selig compares our head to a radio that is constantly being bombarded by various frequencies.

(Zukav uses a similar radio analogy.) Often lost in all the noise is the guidance we receive. If you're determined to hear this guidance, you must decide that you are aligned to a higher frequency and that's what your radio is playing. This is the place where your spirit guides communicate with you, offering guidance and support.

Selig writes that we already hear these guides on a regular basis but literally tune them out. The key is to "trust that you have a spirit guide or an angel or guardian or a personal teacher" and believe that these guides are working with you to support your growth. Once you do this, you'll be better able to tune in to your own higher knowing. This can result in intuitive hunches, feelings and, in some cases, a clear inner voice that tells you precisely what you need to do in any situation.

In *I Am The Word*, Selig (through his spirit guide) provides a number of invocations for us to recite to get the ball rolling. They are declarations of our intent to tune into this higher frequency and put it to use, a signal to our spirit guides that we're open to their assistance. Here's a portion of one:

> I have wisdom now available to me and I will ask myself what
> I need to know. I have understanding available to me, and I
> will consciously connect to my understanding in a way that
> will give me the information and knowing that I require.

Are spirit guides real? Are they here all the time but we just can't see them because they exist in another dimension? If we believe in them, can we better access their wisdom? Do they work in our lives like proverbial guardian angels? Maybe, but you'll never know until you try to make the connection for yourself.

## WEEK TWELVE/ DAY 3: CHARACTER

# The Dark Days of Winter: A Time for Spiritual Growth

Does January put you in a winter funk? It sure does for me. Once the Christmas decorations have been packed up, and the initial cheer of "Happy New Year" has dissipated, I'm ready for spring. And why not? Right now, where I live, it's uncomfortably cold with "feels like" temperatures in the twenties. The trees are bare having dropped the last of their leaves. The skies are gray, with overcast days far outnumbering the sunny ones. And the winter blues are settling in.

**SOME SEE BLUE PERIODS AS AN OPPORTUNITY FOR SPIRITUAL GROWTH.**

In the sixteenth century, the mystic Saint John of the Cross was imprisoned for not obeying an order from the Roman Catholic Church. His incarceration was hellish and included regular beatings and solitary confinement. But John used the time to write an epic poem called *Dark Night of the Soul.* John saw it as the "start of a journey" that would lead him to "the blessed place of perfection," one in which there would be a divine union between his soul and God.

Kudos to John—but it's hard to imagine connecting with God when the dog days of winter have set in and you're merely trying to stay afloat in a sea of melancholy. During our blue periods, it can seem as if God has disappeared altogether, leaving us to fend for ourselves. The religious scholar Mirabai Starr, in her modern translation of "Dark Night of the Soul," describes this state of mind vividly:

> The soul is left baffled and bereft. The soul sits helpless ... and simply breathes into the darkness. There is nothing else to do.

The seeker in this state may be shy about disclosing his inner struggle to anyone for fear it will reveal nothing but his own deadly doubts and spiritual failures.

So, what do you do when you feel like a spiritual ne'er-do-well, abandoned by the divine spirit, left to fight off the bullying emotions of doubt and despair all by yourself? Starr says there is only one course of action, just one thing you can do: "All the seeker can do is surrender to the darkness and take humble refuge in the ineffable stillness … we have nowhere to go but into the silence."

To find solace in the silence, Starr says we must be fully present in "the tender, wounded emptiness of our own souls." That means not hiding from or ignoring the darkness, even though this may be our impulse, but immersing ourselves in it. Think of lowering yourself into a warm bath in a darkened room. She explains:

> It's about not turning away from the pain but learning to rest in it. Rather than distracting ourselves from the simple darkness at our core, we sit with it, paying close attention, and opening our hearts to all that is left, which is love.

Similar wise advice on dealing with the winter doldrums comes from the spiritual writer and psychologist Thomas Moore. In his book *Dark Nights of the Soul, A Guide to Finding Your Way through Life's Ordeals*, Moore advises us that the best way to proceed during times of melancholy is not to fight the blues, but instead to "live in, and with, the darkness":

> Go with developments, rather than against them. If you feel empty, empty out your life where it needs it. If you feel sad, let sadness be your dominant feeling. Being in tune with your deep mood is a way of clarifying yourself. Speak for it. Show it. Honor it.

Thomas Moore argues that when we feel sad for extended periods, it is best not to treat these moods with pharmaceuticals. Unless one is clinically and chronically depressed, he suggests we try to ride out these periods as best we can without medicating them away. Especially when the symptoms can be lessened through exercise, proper diet and sleep, meditation, or prayer. Moore warns:

> Ours is still a therapeutic society that values the removal of symptoms over the soul's sparkle and shine ... broaden your imagination of what is happening to you. If your only idea is that you're depressed, you will be at the mercy of the depression industry, which will treat you as one among millions, for whom there is only one approved story.

The dark night is a time for soul work, for strengthening and deepening our character, and for discovering "what it is to live religiously." Moore explains what happens during this period, when you experience the world from the point-of-view of the soul:

> It is the deep, dark discovery of roots and cellars, the opposite of enlightenment, but equally important and equally divine. Letting your spark light up a dark and dangerous world is a way of healing both you and your world.

Moore sees the dark nights of the soul as indispensable to our spiritual growth. While he recognizes the difficulties and challenges they pose, he tells us the darkness can add "character and color and capacity" to our lives and is a gift to be appreciated. In his words:

> Nothing could be more precious than a dark night of the soul, the very darkness of which allows your lunar light to shine. It may be painful, discouraging, and challenging, but it is nevertheless an important revelation of what your life is about. In that darkness, you see things you couldn't see in the daylight.

**WEEK TWELVE/ DAY 4: CALLING**

# How to Make the Most of "The Second Half" of Life

*Every once in a while, I meet a person who radiates joy.*
*These are people who seem to glow with an inner light.*
*They are kind, tranquil, delighted by small pleasures, and*
*grateful for the large ones ... they live for others, and not*
*for themselves. They know why they were put on this earth*
*and derive a deep satisfaction from doing what they have*
*been called to do. — David Brooks*

Did you read the quote above and think, hey, I'd like to be that person? I know I did. It's how David Brooks begins his book *The Second Mountain* and it describes how we too might reach the same deep-seated level of contentment and get the most out of our second half of life.

What's the "second mountain"? Brooks sees life as comprised of two different stages or journeys. He refers to them as the first mountain, the place we all start in life, and the second mountain. Let's start by looking at his take on the first mountain and what it entails:

"The goals on the first mountain are the normal goals that our culture endures—to be a success, to be well thought of, to get invited into the right social circles, and to experience personal happiness. It's all the normal stuff: nice home, nice family, nice vacations, good food, good friends, and so on."

Brooks reminds us that traversing the first mountain can be a difficult journey. Along the way, we may get knocked off course by some real or perceived failure. Our marriage may fall apart, we may lose our job, suffer a blow to our reputation, or go broke. We may also grow bitter as we grow older, feeling the world has slighted us in some way, and simply close our eyes to what life has to offer us in our later years.

But for some of us, when our journey is complete on the first mountain, we look at the horizon and see a second mountain. It's marked by the realization that there is something more important than our personal happiness and own self-interests.

Brooks points out that in our culture we often get caught up in pursuits that feed the ego, like the quest for money, power, and fame. But for those who reach the base of the second mountain, those things no longer really matter. Instead, in his words, "we want the things that are truly worth wanting." We come to realize: "Oh, that first mountain wasn't my mountain after all. There's another, bigger mountain out there that is actually my mountain."

The second mountain is not the opposite of the first mountain, and to climb it doesn't mean you're rejecting the first mountain. It just means you've realized that there's more to your life than the pursuit of personal success, that there's actually a "more generous and satisfying phase of life" out there. You trade ambition and independence for kindness and relationships. In Brooks's words:

> If the first mountain is about building up the ego and defining the self, the second mountain is about shedding the ego and losing the self. If the first mountain is about acquisition, the second mountain is about contribution. If the first mountain is about moving up, the second mountain is about planting yourself amidst those who need and walking arm in arm with them.

You make commitments to the well-being of others. You refashion who you are, and do things like performing spontaneous acts of kindness, "making generosity part of your daily routine." That doesn't mean rejecting things you achieved on the first mountain but changing your values and philosophy so that your idea of a good life does not stop there.

When we change our focus from ourselves to those outside the self, we elevate our own level of contentment and happiness. According to Brooks: "The people who radiate a permanent joy have given themselves over to lives of deep and loving commitment. What flows from their spirit is mostly gratitude, delight, and kindness."

Brooks concludes that the things we thought were most important—achievement, affirmation, intelligence—are actually less important, and the things we had undervalued—heart and soul—are actually more important. In other words: You stop asking, "What do I want from life?" and start asking, "What can I offer life?"

**WEEK TWELVE/ DAY 5: PRACTICE**

# Twenty-One Simple Rules to Live by (from Mahatma Gandhi)

Do you have a code or set of rules you live by? I often resort to my favorite authors and books for guidance, but I recently came across a short but compelling twenty-one-point list from a legendary figure that has earned a prominent spot in my spiritual arsenal. It comes from Mahatma Gandhi.

First, some background: Gandhi was the leader of the Indian independence movement that challenged British rule during the 1930s and '40s. Through nonviolent civil disobedience, Gandhi helped lead India to independence, inspiring civil rights movements around the world. He later worked to bridge the divide between Hindus and Muslims, an act that would lead to his assassination at the age of seventy-eight.

More than a political leader, Gandhi was also recognized as his country's spiritual leader. He wrote that his way of thinking was inspired by the Hindu holy book the *Bhagavad Gita*. He first became acquainted with "the Gita" in 1888 and said it taught him how "a perfected man is to be known." These teachings were in effect, his rules to live by.

Gandhi believed that all reality is "an incarnation of God." There was no higher goal in life than to become like God. It was the only way one can truly be at peace and "the only ambition worth having." To reach this state of self-realization, it required "desireless action … by dedicating all activities to God, by surrendering oneself to Him body and soul."

This idea of "desireless action" means that as you go through life, you must act but not be tied to outcomes. It's a philosophy perhaps best encapsulated by the line from the Rudyard Kipling poem "If," which encourages us to "meet with Triumph and Disaster, and treat those two impostors just the same." Gandhi phrased the sentiment like this: "Do your allotted work but renounce its fruit—be detached and act—have no desire for reward, and act. He who gives up action, falls. He who gives up only the reward, rises."

In the following passage, Gandhi addresses what it means to be a true devotee of the Gita—though I think you'll find its message is pertinent to people of all faiths, and something we can all aspire to. While it appears in his writings as a complete paragraph, I have taken the liberty of breaking it down line by line.

## TWENTY-ONE SIMPLE RULES TO LIVE BY, FROM MAHATMA GANDHI

A true devotee lives his life as one:

1. Who is jealous of no one,

2.  Who is a fount of mercy,
3.  Who is without egotism,
4.  Who is selfless,
5.  Who treats alike cold and heat, happiness and misery,
6.  Who is always forgiving,
7.  Who is always contented,
8.  Whose resolutions are firm,
9.  Who has dedicated mind and soul to God,
10. Who causes no dread,
11. Who is not afraid of others,
12. Who is free from exultation, sorrow, and fear,
13. Who is pure,
14. Who is versed in action and yet remains unaffected by it,
15. Who renounces all fruits of action, good or bad,
16. Who treats friend and enemy alike,
17. Who is untouched by respect or disrespect,
18. Who is not puffed up by praise,
19. Who does not go under when people speak ill of him,
20. Who loves silence and solitude,
21. Who has a disciplined mind.

# A Four-Step Guide to the Prayer Many Believe is "Better than Meditation"

Let's take another look at a method of prayer that comes from an ancient Christian contemplative tradition. It dates all the way back to a fourteenth-century text titled *The Cloud of Unknowing*. For over five hundred years, it fell out of favor until it resurfaced in the 1970s thanks to Trappist monk Father Thomas Keating. It's called centering prayer.

Keating (who passed away in 2018 at age ninety-five) saw that the church was losing many of its young members to Eastern religions, drawn by the allure of meditation. He was aware that the church once had its own form of meditation, now largely relegated to monastic settings. So, with help from two fellow Trappist monks, he set out to develop a form of Christian meditation that would be accessible to all. He spread the word far and wide through lectures and books like *Intimacy with God: An Introduction to Centering Prayer*.

### How does centering prayer, which is also known as contemplative prayer, work?

While earlier in this book I featured a guide created by Keating disciple David Frenette, this method comes directly from Thomas Keating himself. Much like other forms of meditation, it's recommended that you practice centering prayer for about twenty minutes a session, twice a day. And like meditation, a short session is better than no session.

### The Four Steps of Centering Prayer

1. Choose a sacred word as the symbol of your intention to consent to God's presence. Invite God within.
2. Sitting comfortably with eyes closed, settle briefly and silently introduce the sacred word as the symbol of your consent to God's presence.
3. When you become aware of thoughts, silently return ever so gently to the sacred word.

4. At the end of the prayer period, remain in silence with eyes closed for a couple of minutes.

Now as a practitioner of centering prayer, I want to let you in on a few additional pointers that come from both me and the writings of Keating:

- While meditation has the mantra, centering prayer has "the sacred word." I admit I cheat a little and use three words: *Rest in God*. It's a constant reminder of the action I want to take.
- You don't have to repeat the sacred word or phrase continuously, it's merely a way to maintain your intention of faith and bypass the thinking process.
- Let your thoughts go by "like boats on the surface of a river." Pay no attention to them, "it's like noise in the street or music in the supermarket."

## WHAT MAKES CENTERING PRAYER A BETTER VERSION OF MEDITATION?

According to Keating, the Eastern traditions put a great emphasis on what the self can do and as a result "contain the innate hazard of identifying the true self with God. The Christian tradition, on the other hand, recognizes God as present but distinct from the true self."

In other words, centering prayer adds God to the equation. Keating points out that it can be easy to forget the presence of God. What centering prayer does is allow us to "sense God's presence and eliminate the feeling that God is absent." He notes that this act "furthers our spiritual journey" as it makes us aware of the Divine indwelling at the core of our being. This Divine force is available to us anytime, anywhere, twenty-four hours a day.

Keating believes that when we practice centering prayer on a regular basis, "a different kind of knowledge rooted in love emerges, in which the awareness of God's presence supplants the awareness of our own presence." He sums up the effects of centering prayer this way:

> [Centering prayer] is the opening of mind and heart—our whole being—to God beyond thoughts, words and emotions. We open our awareness to God, who we know by faith is within us, closer than breathing, closer than thinking—closer than consciousness itself.

# Jesus and the Lost Messages

What if there's more to the story of Jesus and God than what's found in the Bible? What if the Bible is only telling part of the story—and if you dug a little deeper you could find a rich trove of knowledge that could both better inform and enlighten you?

During a conversation I had with the Christian theologian Matthew Fox, he made a simple but profound statement: "God did not stop speaking to us after the Bible was written." Think about that for a moment. Did God impart the knowledge found in the Bible, then suddenly stop talking? Or, as Fox asserts, did God continue to speak to us throughout history, through mystics like Julian of Norwich, even continuing to speak to us today?

It's an idea that is reinforced by religious scholar Elaine Pagels in her book *Why Religion? A Personal Story*. Pagels finds that "Christianity's traditional exclusion of anything outside its boundaries is too confining." It wasn't always this way. In the early days of Christianity, monks played a vital role in collecting a variety of spiritual texts in monastery libraries, including the early Christian books knows as the Gnostic Gospels.

In a recent study, Hugo Lundhaug, a theologist at the University of Oslo, reported that "a far greater diversity of thought existed amongst people who considered themselves Christian than we previously thought." Some of the Gnostic texts were reproduced and read by Christian monks well into the fourth and fifth centuries. But "in time, the reading of such unusual texts would have become less acceptable until finally the command came to discard them completely."

## WHAT MATTERED MOST TO EARLY CHRISTIANS WAS DEEPENING THEIR SPIRITUALITY.

Pagels, who is a professor of religion at Princeton, is the author of the seminal book on the early Christian texts, *The Gnostic Gospels*. She points out that the early Christians were a much more open-minded bunch than those who followed, as they were not totally beholden to the Bible. In her words:

> What mattered to these monks wasn't dogma. They weren't judging the value of sacred writings by whether or not they conform to Christian doctrine. They were open to exploring other traditions along with their own ... apparently less concerned with what to believe than with deepening their spiritual practice.

That's what we'll be doing now: exploring sacred writings that were lost to time and deepening our spiritual practice. What follows are three examples from the Gnostic texts called out by Pagels. The first two provide additional enlightenment on the true message of Jesus, even though it may contradict what's found in the Bible. The third message is more general in nature, but one we might all take to heart.

## Message #1. The Kingdom of God Is a Place on Earth.

Pagels points out that in the *Gospel of Mark*, Jesus announces that "the kingdom of God is coming soon." But what does Jesus mean by that? Some take it to mean that a catastrophic, world-ending event will ensue, and that Earth will be replaced by something closer to heaven. But the Gnostic *Gospel of Thomas* suggests that Jesus was merely speaking in metaphor:

> Jesus says: If those who lead you say to you, "The kingdom is in the sky," then the birds will get there first. If they say, "It is in the sea," then the fish will get there first. Rather, the kingdom of God is within you, and outside of you. When you come to know yourselves then … you will know that you are the children of God.

The core message: The kingdom of God is not a place in the sky; it's actually a state of being! When we enter this state, we "come to know who we are and come to know God as the source of our being." With this realization, we can experience the essence of God within us at the present moment, even today.

## Message #2. The Light of God Is Within Us.

Pagels tells us that a primary theme in Jewish mystical tradition is that the "image of God," a divine light, is hidden deep within each of us. Our goal is to find this light which also serves to connect each of us with one another. As the *Gospel of Thomas* says: "Within a person of light, there is a light. If illuminated, it lights up the whole world; if not, everything is dark."

Another passage in the *Gospel of Thomas* suggests that in searching for this light, we can find what we're seeking right where we are.

Jesus says: "Recognize what is before your eyes and the mysteries will be revealed to you." It's the equivalent of having "a secret door within us" that if we open it, will reveal all that is known and all we need to know.

This idea is expanded on in another Gnostic text titled *The Revelation of Zostrianos* where the author writes: "If you seek with everything you have, you shall come to know the good that is within you; and you will know yourself as one who comes from the God who truly exists."

## MESSAGE #3. WE ARE CONNECTED TO ALL BEINGS.

The Gnostic text *The Gospel of Truth* expands on the idea that "when we come to know ourselves, simultaneously we come to know God." Pagels informs us that this is "not intellectual knowledge, but knowledge of the heart." We are intimately connected with the Divine, since "in him we live and move and have our being."

This book also talks to how we are connected "with one another and with all beings" because in each of us "dwells the light that does not fail." Because of this connection we should:

1. Speak the truth with those who search for it.
2. Support those who have stumbled.
3. Extend your hand to those who are ill.
4. Feed those who are hungry.
5. Give rest to the weary.
6. Strengthen those who wish to rise.
7. Awaken those who are asleep.

# WEEK THIRTEEN

WEEK THIRTEEN/ DAY 1: INSPIRATION

## Seven Life Lessons from the Boy and the Mole

Have you heard of the book *The Boy, the Mole, the Fox and the Horse*? It topped the bestseller list in the *Publisher's Weekly* comics category for more than a year, selling more than a million copies. It has also been made into an animated film. But to label this book a "comic" is a misnomer.

Written and illustrated by Charlie Mackesy, *The Boy, the Mole, the Fox and the Horse* is a fable that eavesdrops on a conversation between the four characters in the title. The pages are sparsely worded and interspersed with sketches. Yet, for all its brevity, the book is packed with inspirational thoughts covering themes like love, courage, and kindness, and ultimately the realization of why we are all here.

What follows below are seven key thoughts from *The Boy, the Mole, the Fox and the Horse*. These ideas appear in bold type, followed by my take on each one. For additional insights, I suggest you pick up this enchanting little book. You'll find that what at first glance appears to be a children's book has wisdom for those of all ages.

1. **What is the biggest waste of time? Comparing yourself to others.** In our times, this might be labeled as "Instagram disease." It involves looking at others and wishing you had a better, more exciting life. Know that what you see is only a highlight reel featuring the very best parts. Feeling envious? Change the

focus to your own life including your own personal strengths, all you have to be thankful for, and the good things to come in the future.

2. **As you get older, you may wish you had listened less to your fears and more to your dreams.** Fears can be tamped down, but dreams have a way of sticking with you. If you feel you've spent too much of your life listening to your fears and not doing what you really want, know this—it's never too late to pursue at least some aspect of a dream that's been delayed. Did you once dream of moving to France? Start planning an extended stay there. Figure out what part of your dream you can still realize.

3. **One of our greatest freedoms is how we react to things.** No event or other person has the power to do us harm—unless we let it happen. In any situation, we have the ability to control our reaction to it. Practice taking everything in stride knowing that all things must pass. Adversity can be overcome, and we often come out of a bad situation stronger, wiser, and better prepared for what the future brings.

4. **Asking for help isn't giving up.** It's refusing to give up. Sometimes we need to lean on others, be it our significant other, a group of friends, an outside organization or God. Asking for help is not a sign of weakness. It's a sign of inner resolve and strength to find solutions to whatever problems have come your way. The sooner you ask, the sooner any problems you may be facing can be resolved.

5. **The greatest illusion is that life should be perfect.** The truth is life is messy at times. It's just the way things are. For virtually every one of us, there are rough edges in our jobs, with our friends and with our relationships with the people we love the most. A better way to view life is put it on a scale and ask your-

self: Does the good in my life outweigh the bad? Life does not have to be perfect to be immensely rewarding.

6. **When the big things feel out of control, focus on what you love.** Between extreme weather events, political crises, and the ongoing violence of war, it can sometimes seem like the world is spinning out of control. That's when you've got to stop looking outward, via social media and twenty-four-hour news channels, and focus on the good around you. This might include the loved one in the room next to you, the dog resting at your feet, the hot cup of coffee in your hands. What you really love is often found right under your nose.

7. **The best discovery is that you are enough.** It can seem like we're all on an endless quest to become better people, to lose weight, to get more physically fit, to be kinder, to become more spiritually enlightened. Kudos to all of us for making these and other efforts. But the fact is, you are good as you are right now. You always have been. You always will be.

# Finding Magic in Everyday Life

*"The universe is full of magical things patiently
waiting for our wits to grow sharper."*
— *Eden Phillpotts*

What if there is magic in the world that is just out of our view? What if by honing our instincts, by taking the time to look at life a little more closely, it revealed itself? The magic I'm talking about here has nothing to do with sleight of hand or pulling a bunny out of a hat. It's about the magical realization that there's more to life than what meets the eye.

On the National Public Radio show *Fresh Air,* author Amber Scorah was recently discussing her new memoir *Leaving The Witness.* It's about her life as a Jehovah's Witness, a religion she left as a young adult. During her conversation with host Terry Gross, she was asked about her current spiritual beliefs now that she is no longer moored to a religion. Her response was thought-provoking:

> My spirituality is related to this kind of a spiritual feeling I think I've had my whole life, which I used to chalk up to being a religious experience. I think of it more now of as a spiritual experience. It's just that there's the magical all around us, and life is made up of these moments where, if you choose to notice them, they're around you. And because those things, like the love I saw in my son's eyes for me when he was a baby, are so inexplicable and transcendent, I think that they feel magical. If you think about them that way, you can in some way appreciate the magic of it.

If we don't see magic in our own lives, it may be due to the fact that we don't slow down long enough to notice what's going on around us. It may be our human conditioning that we sit back and wait for magic to happen *to* us, instead of realizing that we must be an active participant and part of the process. Writing in *The Universal Christ,* Franciscan friar Richard Rohr gives us his take on magic:

> I think humans prefer magical religion, which keeps all the responsibility on God performing or not performing. Whereas mature and transformational religion asks us to participate, cooperate, and change.

This lack of "participation" on our part comes at a huge cost. Thomas Moore, writing in *The Re-Enchantment of Everyday Life,* says that: "Those of us who have been brought up in a secular culture don't realize how much our lives have been impoverished by the lack of magic."

What is missing according to Moore is our inability to see "the penetrating experience of every experience that rises out of a world that is alive and that has deep and mysterious roots." He tells us that to live in a magical world, "we have to assume the role of magician in our everyday lives." When we live by magic, "we don't try to understand everything that is happening and everything we're doing. We allow nature to remain mysterious, but we tap into it to share its hidden powers."

For you and me, this means stopping to take notice of the magical moments around us, the small wonders that are part of our daily landscape. Our senses are often dulled by habit and routine, so we can tend to overlook them. In his own case, Moore mentions the following places where he finds magic around his own home:

- The road near my house appears as a true friend when I've been away on a trip.
- The tree just outside my kitchen window is a good companion as I wash dishes.
- The birds with their outrageous colors and habits, their cries and swoops, the acrobatic way of animating the sky, their songs, and chants.

The magic may already be there in your own life, waiting to be discovered. It may just involve looking at the world with new eyes, actively seeking the magical instead of waiting for it to find you. We sometimes must seek before we can find.

# Humility: What the Ego Doesn't Want You to Know

*Being humble doesn't make you weak. It actually makes you a better person.*

I wrote those words several years ago and from time to time I'm inspired to revisit them. It happens each time I meet a man or woman whose ego seems to have outpaced their humanity, whose preoccupation with themselves supersedes their concern for those around them.

They are not alone. I admit there are times when my ego gets a little too big for its britches and needs to be taken down a notch or two. And what's the best way to counterbalance an overstimulated ego? A good place to start is remembering the important role humility can play in our lives.

By definition, humility is a modest view of one's own importance. John Templeton described it as "a virtue, a character trait that allows one to think and reason well. It is related to open-mindedness, a sense of one's own fallibility, and a healthy recognition of one's intellectual debts to others." Compare that to the ego which is prone to display "arrogance, closed-mindedness, and overconfidence in one's own opinions and intellectual powers."

### BEING HUMBLE MEANS KEEPING THE EGO IN CHECK.

Templeton believed that the biggest barrier to you and I becoming the people we are meant to be is our ego. It's the part of us that wants to be in control, make a good impression, prove a point, show our

260

superiority. Yet for all its self-certainty, this aspect of our selves is often flawed and lives a rather shallow existence. Templeton explains:

> The personal ego identifies with our appearance, our achievements, our possessions. It is this self that is inclined to compete with others, and to feel hurt or angry if it doesn't get what it wants. It is this self that wants to feel important, to always be right and in control.

Templeton goes on to tell us that within each of us is a part separate from the ego, a "higher self," that contains "a spark of the divine." In many people, this higher self is hidden by the personal ego, which can dominate and overpower it. We don't see the powerful, greater part of ourselves because "we are blinded by our identification with the personal."

Yet, solely identifying with the ego can be a mistake, because our higher self "is infinitely more loving and wise and is always there for us." The ego may not like it, but if we put it aside and identify with this higher, more humble part of our being, we come to recognize that "this is our real, essential self." Templeton goes on to say:

> To truly express greatness in our lives, we must learn to be humble. It is not our own personal greatness we should express, but a power far greater than ourselves. When we are willing to put aside the whims and demands of our personal selves (or ego) and listen to the guidance of the greater self within, we gain access to an infinite source of power.

As the philosopher Jacob Needleman points out, when we escape the "day-to-day self" known as the ego, we realize there is something greater out there that lives both outside us and within us. Diminishing our ego helps us to realize our true potential and contribute to a greater good. In Needleman's words:

Everything the ego always wanted—safety, security, happiness, the ability to give and receive love—is granted by this great thing outside me. Yet it is given to me within. In that moment the ego submits, because it realizes that this great gift is not of its own making. This gift comes from God, and anyone can have it.

## CAN GREATER HUMILITY LEAD TO GREATER LOVE?

In a blog post titled "Having Humbleness in All We Do," deli owner and life philosopher Ari Weinzweig gives us his take on the importance of humility. He says that "an increase in humility would lead us all to more love, more care, more kindness and, I'm pretty sure, peace and dignity." He explains humility this way:

> Mozart once said, "The music is not in the notes, but in the silence between." Humility fits that frame. It's the space between the sounds. The whisper between the words. The energy between the egos. Humility is both ethereal and essential. Like great music, it's hard to measure—and often goes past unnoticed by casual listeners. But if we pay close attention, we can begin to benefit from the beauty and grace that humility brings to the world.

Weinzweig concedes there is a place for the ego as it "helps us to stand up for what's right, to speak our minds, to put our art out into the world." But he goes on to say that "on its own, the ego creates all kinds of problems. Humility is the counter-rhythm. It balances out the ego, brings us back to ourselves."

The key to increasing humility? Weinzweig tells us it's "regular reflection." This can include "journaling, intentional mindfulness, talking about your struggles with friends who are themselves grounded in humility." It might also include an honest assessment of your relationships to those closest to you, including neighbors, co-workers and family members.

Are you leading your life led by the ego—or through the humbler, higher self? It's a question we might ask ourselves daily.

# A "Friend" Dies at Forty-Nine and Leaves Me Asking Three Questions

I'm not on Facebook much, but recently I stumbled upon a startling post on my feed. It was from a Facebook friend, a woman named Jolie, who was announcing her own death and memorial service. Upon closer inspection, I realized Jolie had given the keys to her account to someone else. She had passed away at the age of forty-nine.

Like a lot of Facebook friends, I didn't really know her, though we had been friends since 2012. We shared only one mutual friend, Andrea Balt, the force-of-nature behind the provocative and inspiring Rebelle Society. I imagine Jolie had read a *Wake Up Call* column at some point, something I wrote caught her eye, she followed me and I followed her back.

I began looking at what she had been posting. Just a month prior to her death, with the advent of warm weather near her northern Michigan home, she wrote about how she wished it could be summer all year. She posted inspirational videos and quotes. She shared funny videos. She posted stories from a local café that looked like it served a mean breakfast. But she also wrote this three months ago:

Can't sleep with this cough. Hoping it is the bronchitis and not the tumor on my lung. Times like this I tell myself don't worry about money, just seize the day tomorrow. Just live, trust myself, trust life.

I looked up Jolie's obituary and discovered she had been diagnosed with advanced ovarian cancer three years earlier. She fought the good fight, encouraging others with the disease, as she struggled with it herself. She travelled three times to Tijuana, Mexico for experimental treatments.

This past Fourth of July, she wrote and shared a few posts, thanking a local restaurant for taking good care of a visiting relative. She wrote of hearing the first fireworks "boom!" of the night.

On July 5, she shared a video of a pretty cabin in the woods with stained-glass windows. Then there is nothing until July 10, when her death is announced by a close friend.

I have written about death before. But this death, at such an early age (the death of anyone younger than I am feels early), sticks with me. I wonder if Jolie had read my story last year, about a cancer survivor, titled "Three Questions to Ask Yourself Before You Die." The questions were:

- **What do I still have to give?**
- **What do I still have to learn?**
- **What do I still have to experience?**

I don't know how Jolie would have answered these questions. Would she have felt short-changed? Was there not enough time, were there not enough healthy years, to do all she was meant to do? But, after reading the many Facebook responses to her death (see below), I think I at least know the answer to the first question.

> "After a lifetime of giving, loving and caring...she is finally at peace. We will all miss you, and will remember you as a giver, a loving person and a fighter."

"Regardless of her condition, Jolie always put on a bright smile and seemed happy-go-lucky even though I know she struggled with her illness."

"Her love of life, her gratitude, her enormous quiet power, her love, her awesome hugs, her free spirit, joy and humor carry on through all of us who loved her."

"The light that shines in our community is less today as Jolie walked on but will remain forever in the hearts and memories of all whose lives she touched."

"This is not a goodbye Jolie, simply a so long. I know I will see you again, I love you dearly, always have and always will. Thank you for always living life with such a great giving heart."

"A true warrior and a great friend, always positive in life and always smiling. You give others hope to fight and remind us that life is precious, and we should cherish it each and every day."

As becomes obvious from these comments, Jolie was beloved. In the forty-nine years she was here on Earth, she gave life her all right to the end, touching the lives of so many others. Since none of us know when death will strike, it raises a few questions I'm also asking myself:

- If you died today, how would others remember you?
- Have you lived your life for the benefit of others, or simply for your own self interests?
- Have you taught others the things you're supposed to teach?
- Will you be able to say you gave, learned, experienced, all you were supposed to in this lifetime?

# Six Ways to Wake Up and Reconnect with Life

Do you ever find yourself disconnected from life, more concerned with your to-do list or personal issues than the people and environment around you? Or perhaps you find yourself mindlessly scrolling through your smartphone just a little too often, tuning out the real world in the process?

There's an exercise to cure that—or make that six exercises. Think of them as ways to wake up your consciousness and stay better connected to the world around you. I stumbled upon them while reading the companion journal to *Falling Upward: A Spirituality for the Two Halves of Life* by Richard Rohr.

While the book is set up to help readers navigate the second half of life by answering a series of probing questions (with blank pages provided for answers), more compelling were the experiential exercises at the end of each chapter. Here are the ones I found most helpful, with Rohr's lightly edited words appearing in italics.

### Six Ways to Wake Up and Reconnect with Life

1. **Take a Slow Walk.** *Treat yourself to a slow walk in the neighborhood. Take the time to think about your breathing as you go. Notice things of beauty that might never have appeared beautiful to you in the past.* Rohr mentions picking up a stone or stick to take a close look at it. You can also simply take in the majestic beauty of a tree swaying in the breeze or the unique architectural feature of a building or home you're walking by. Take it all in.

2. **Really Observe.** *Notice how people treat each other and how you treat others. When you're waiting in line, watch for the presence or absence of patience or understanding around you. Look for signs of compassion and empathy.* Once you go through a few hours in this hyper-aware state, Rohr advises us to consider how these observations might lead to greater compassion and maturity in our own lives.

3. **Listen to Inspiring Music.** *Dance if you are inclined, even the most subtle of movements will do. Experience the places in your body where you are holding on to things that keep you from embracing a thriving existence. Breathe into these places.* You might also consider listening to classical music, if you don't have a favorite composer, any concerto by Mozart will do. You may find that music reaches a pleasure point in your brain that other activities can't touch.

4. **Just Sit.** *Seek out a quiet, sacred place in your home or outside where you are able to sit undisturbed. Be fully present in this space for a set period of time each day. Repeat a word or phrase that holds meaning for you to settle your mind. If thoughts intrude, use your word or phrase to bring you back to quiet.* The preceding passage reads like a non-fussy version of meditation and may be the most valuable tip here. We all need time to clear the head and settle into an inner peace. Do you have a sacred space in or around your home? If not, look for a place of quiet where you might have a glimpse of nature or greenery.

5. **Reach Out.** *Jesus had no problem with the exceptions, whether they were drunkards, Samaritans, lepers, Gentiles, tax collectors or wayward sheep. Look for the "exceptions" in your everyday life. Consider how you might reach out to such a person.* This can include the homeless person down the street, a cantankerous neighbor, or a bitter co-worker. Assume they are dealing with

issues you don't know about and see if a smile, friendly word, or a kind gesture might ease their burden.

6. **Pay Attention to Life.** *Use all your attention as you observe people and events with new eyes. Pay attention to things that you may have never noticed before. Look especially at faces and read what they say. As you touch others, perhaps as you shake hands, truly feel the person's grasp.* As we pay more attention, Rohr also asks us to speak gently and with more humility. Soften your expression and make eye contact. As the poet Maya Angelou and others have written, "people may not remember what you said, but they will remember how you made them feel."

## WEEK THIRTEEN/ DAY 6: INNER WORK

# The Ten-Minute Thinking Person's Meditation

While I make a noble effort to meditate most days, I often go through periods where my chattering monkey mind makes it close to impossible. And quite frankly, there are spans of time when I feel so calm and centered from my other morning activities (like running and spiritual reading) that I don't feel the need to meditate.

So, it was with great interest I recently read about a unique approach to meditation that actually involves a little thinking over the course of the practice—and it only takes ten minutes to complete. It comes courtesy of Tony Robbins via the Tim Ferriss book *Tools for Titans.*

Now most meditations are all about clearing the mind, or some might say going beyond the mind, to establish a sense of peace, contentment, and even happiness. However, this meditation puts the mind to work in a constructive fashion and, for me, achieves the same goals.

Granted, this is not a typical meditation practice, but it's a great way to obtain the clarity and confidence you need to meet the day ahead. Please note that I've altered this meditation just a bit by adding some focus on the breath and expanding on some of the descriptions.

## THE TEN-MINUTE THINKING PERSON'S MEDITATION

**Minute 0-1. Focus on Your Breath.** This means paying attention to the air coming into your lungs on the inhale and out your nose on the exhale. Take deep, l-o-n-g breaths. It's amazing how the simple act of paying attention to the breath has a way of quieting the mind.

**Minutes 1-4. Give Thanks for Three Things.** Consider anyone and anything that brings happiness to your life. Having trouble coming up with three things? Keep it simple. Be thankful for the sun streaming through the windows, the roof over your head, your good health. It's impossible to be angry when you're expressing gratitude.

**Minutes 4-7. Feel the Presence of God.** Not a God believer? This still works. The idea is to look within and sense the vast compassion and benevolence that emanates from your heart. For me, this is where I feel the presence of God. For you, it might be a warm feeling inside. Again, focus on the breath and let this sense of goodness move outward from the heart to your arms, your legs, your mind.

**Minutes 7-10. Visualize Three Things You Want to Happen This Day.** This is especially productive for the Type-A personalities out there. It is what it sounds like, looking at what the day ahead has in store and visualizing positive outcomes for three things you want to accomplish. In the words of Robbins, "See it as though it's already been done, feel the emotions, etc."

Not sure of the timing of each activity? Use your best judgment—or if you need to, use your phone or a watch. Again, this is not a standard meditation practice. But if you're looking for a quick practice that mimics meditation's calming, centering effects, it's definitely worth a try.

## WEEK THIRTEEN/ DAY 7: CONTEMPLATION

# Is Jesus "The Way" to God? Or in the Way?

I read a lot of religious books and it's rare to come across one that changes the way I view Christianity. I now have two such books on my bookshelf: *The Universal Christ* by Richard Rohr and *Finding God Beyond Religion* from Tom Stella. By chance, both authors emerged from the world of Roman Catholicism. Rohr is a Franciscan friar, while Stella is a former Catholic priest.

---

*"Having grown up a Catholic, I put Jesus on a pedestal."*

---

The quote above is from Stella, and it mirrors my own upbringing as a Catholic. I saw Jesus as separate from myself, either as God incarnate or as the gatekeeper to God. But what if Jesus was just like us—a flesh and blood human being, with a special connection to God that we too could achieve?

Like many Christians, Stella no longer believes Jesus is the only way to connect with God—but just one of many ways. As reported by the Christian Broadcasting Network, a 2020 Probe study showed that even among evangelicals, 60% of those surveyed believe that "Jesus, Buddha, and Muhammad are all equal in regard to a path to salvation." Among other Christians, the percentage who agree is likely much higher.

Stella goes on to point out what he believes is a common misconception about Jesus: that he is the only child of God. But the truth is we are all the offspring of God. Stella calls out how in Luke 11:1, Jesus didn't say to pray to "my" father but to "our" father. He was a son of God just like we are all sons and daughters of God. This leads Stella to the following conclusion:

"Perhaps what is needed is not to take Jesus off the pedestal, but to come to the realization that there is a place on it for us as well. We have the capacity to share the same intimate relationship with God that he did."

---

**"God is not apart from us, but at the heart of us."**
— *Tom Stella*

---

Stella believes that for many Christians, Jesus has gotten in the way of the awareness of our own intimate relationship with God. In his words, "We have hailed him, but we have failed to see him in our own likeness." He wonders if we might "embrace Jesus as a human being who reveals the incarnate presence of God in all beings."

"Jesus saw the sacredness in all of us," no matter our faults or past transgressions, regardless of our station in life. We are all worthy. Perhaps Jesus was merely illustrating the relationship all of us could have with the Divine, proof that we can achieve the same intimate relationship with God. As religious scholar Elaine Pagels points out in the following passage from *Beyond Belief*:

> God's light shines not only in Jesus, but potentially in everyone. The Gospel of Thomas encourages the hearer not so much to believe in Jesus ... as to seek to know God through

one's own divinely given capacity, since we are all created in the image of God.

## A SIMILAR TAKE ON JESUS COMES FROM RICHARD ROHR.

Writing in *The Universal Christ*, the Franciscan priest and author Richard Rohr writes that "in Christianity, we have made the mistake of limiting the Creator's presence to just one human manifestation, Jesus." Because of this, we have spent our time following Jesus, when our time might be better spent following his message.

Rohr wonders if God needed us to focus our attention on someone and that someone was Jesus. But there was just one problem: We went too far. We spend our precious time here on Earth worshipping Jesus the messenger and trying to get other people to do the same. This obsession often becomes "a pious substitute for actually *following* what he taught."

Rohr points out that most Christians believe that "God's presence was poured into a single human being," Jesus. But maybe Jesus simply realized what was already there—a world saturated by the presence of God. So like Jesus, we are not separate from God. We are, in fact, immersed in God who is present in every particle of life. It's a presence we too can immerse ourselves in!

## WHAT JESUS REALLY WANTED WAS FOR US TO "SEE THE WORLD WITH HIS EYES."

What if we were able to see the world with the same love and compassion as Jesus? Wouldn't our own world grow richer, more compassionate, and more loving? Like Jesus, could we also become representatives of God here on Earth?

Rohr reminds us that God is the DNA that was within Jesus and is within all of us. "The Divine Presence is here, in us and in all of creation, and not 'over there' in some far-off realm." God's presence can be found in the material world all around us. And when we realize that God is in and of all things, we view the world differently.

Jesus showed us what a complete human might look like if we lived to our highest potential—and wanted us to achieve this potential in our own lives. When we come to realize that what's known as Christ consciousness is possible for us to experience too, it "has the power to radically alter what we believe, how we see others and relate to them, and our sense of how big God might be." We become the fully realized humans we were meant to be.

Rohr tells us that when we "stand in solidarity with everything and everyone else," we see the Divine in literally everything and everyone. When we learn to see God in all things, we see the world and ourselves "in wholeness, not just in parts." Accepting this fact can cause a radical change in our perspective:

> Once we know that the entire physical world around us, all of creation, is both the hiding place and the revelation place for God, this world becomes home, safe, enchanted, offering grace to anyone who looks deeply.

# WEEK FOURTEEN

## You've Reached a Spiritual Dead End. Now What?

Have you been in a spiritual rut lately? The definition of being in a rut is getting stuck in "a habit or a pattern of behavior that has become dull and unproductive." And just like we can get stuck in a rut at our job or in our home life, we can also get stuck in our spiritual practice.

The problem may be our routine, doing the same things over and over. We read books by the same handful of spiritual authors. We peruse the same set of Bible passages. We use the same meditation technique or rote method of prayer. And we find that what once stirred our souls and opened our hearts, no longer has the same effect.

**MAYBE IT'S TIME TO TRY A DIFFERENT APPROACH.**

What follows are four ways to shake things up and breathe some new life into your spiritual routine. That's important because when we're refreshed and recharged spiritually, we feel better inside and out—and show up in the world as the best and truest version of ourselves.

**Idea #1. Fall in love with three new things.** This idea comes from the former Dominican priest, activist and author Matthew Fox and his book *Essential Writings on Creation Spirituality*. Now an Episcopal priest, Fox writes about the four paths of creation spirituality, one of them being the need to "fall in love at least three times a day." This starts by engaging with life with open eyes and an open heart.

Now, Fox is not talking about romantic love but our ability to "fall in love with a star, a wildflower, a bird, a tree, an animal." It could also be platonic love, or *agape*, for "another human-being—preferably one different from oneself," be they of a different race, religion, or sexual persuasion than we are. He continues:

> We could fall in love with music, poetry, paintings, dance. If we could fall in love with one of Mozart's works each week, we would have seven years of joy. How could we ever be bored?

**Idea #2. Spend more time in the natural world.** In his book *On the Brink of Everything*, Quaker teacher Parker J. Palmer advises us to "spend time in the natural world, as much time as you can." We should observe the amazing creations of Mother Nature, paying special attention to the parts of the natural world that speak to us, even if it's the silence.

Of course, to do this you've got to get outside! If you're fortunate enough, you might find nature right outside your door, in a park or natural setting in your neighborhood, or a short drive away. One thing you might try tonight: instead of mindlessly watching the television set or burying yourself in your phone, take a moment to step outside and look up at the stars.

What's the importance of being outside? As Steven Rinella recently wrote in the *Wall Street Journal*:

> As creatures of the earth, we are inherently connected to the natural world. A relationship with nature fulfills our yearning to belong to something bigger than ourselves that will outlast us all.

**Idea #3. Find sanctuary.** Palmer thinks of finding sanctuary as "a largely silent, solitary process of reflection that helps us reclaim the ground of our being and root ourselves in something larger and truer than our own egos." You might find this sanctuary during the early morning hours or before you retire at night. Palmer explains its importance in his own life:

> Sanctuary is where I find safe space to regain my bearings, reclaim my soul, heal my wounds, and return to the world as a wounded healer. It's not merely about finding shelter from the storm—it's about spiritual survival and the capacity to carry on.

**Idea #4. Get out of your comfort zone.** It may be time to expand your thinking. Try a new book, a new podcast, a new place of worship. It's important to read or hear the ideas of other voices in the spiritual community. You might just come across a fresh way of thinking that causes you to look at the world in a new way or that reignites a spark deep within. You'll never know what you might be missing, until you take that first step and try something new.

How about you: What changes can you make to your spiritual life? What new disciplines can you explore? How will you shake up your status quo and rekindle your spiritual flame?

# "The Last Time": A Unique Way to Look at Life

I recently came across a five-minute audio clip that forced me to look at life from a fresh perspective. It can be found on Sam Harris' *Waking Up* meditation app, which also includes a number of "lessons." As I write this, during the time of the COVID-19 quarantine, there's one that has special resonance. It's called "The Last Time" and it starts like this:

> I want you to take a moment to think about all the things in this life that you will experience for the last time. Of course, there will come a day when you die, and then everything will be done for the last time. But long before you die, you will cease to have certain experiences. Experiences that you surely take for granted now.

The subject matter may seem gloomy but think about this for a moment. Harris asks us,

> If you are a parent (or grandparent), when is the last time your child (or grandchild) will sit on your lap as you read them a bedtime story? When is the last time you will tuck her or him into bed?" There is always a last time for events like this, and we never know when it will be.

The funny thing is we often do things for the last time and it's beyond our cognitive abilities to realize it. Harris talks about the last time he skied fifteen years ago. On that day, when he took off his skis, he was "not even dimly aware of the possibility" it could be the last time he ever skied. Yet now, it's not certain. I can tell a similar tale about kayaking and I'm sure you have a similar story.

Of course, when discussing the "last time" concept, one has to consider the millions of people struck down by pandemics like COVID-19. Many were healthy one moment, then a few weeks or even days later they were dead, with no advance knowledge that their end was near. If they knew a year or even a month ahead of time, would they have lived their lives differently? Would they have been kinder, more loving, less concerned with the mundane worries of everyday life?

It might make sense to follow the lead of Onnit founder Aubrey Marcus who recently cited an ancient stoic wisdom called Memento Mori. Translation: Remember you are going to die. This is the only thing certain about our collective futures. And while most people reading this will certainly live to see another day, the fact is, one day we're going to die and we don't know when. Marcus points out, "This makes time our most precious resource. When we take a moment to look at how we spend it, something profound emerges."

Harris echoes this sentiment, reminding us that "we have no assurance we will be here next year, next week, even tomorrow." Yet we still often overlook the precious moments of our lives, even things as simple as our family gathering for dinner at the kitchen table. So how do we live our lives to their fullest knowing that we may not receive a clear signal that our end is near?

**ALL WE CAN DO IS BE IN EACH MOMENT, RIGHT HERE, RIGHT NOW, STARTING TODAY.**

To paraphrase Harris, "when you know you do everything a finite number of times, it adds a specialness to the moments." You begin to realize you never know when the "last time" of any activity or event that has special meaning to you will occur. Harris suggests: "Paying more attention can make everything seem more special. Attention is your true source of wealth, so pay a little more attention."

Let's look at how this might play out in our own homes now and in the coming weeks. Are there certain daily happenings that you are taking for granted? Do you need to be more in the moment? Can you take the following three actions?

- When you talk with someone, be fully present and really listen.
- Notice small acts like washing the dishes or doing the laundry and respond with gratitude.
- Be patient and kind even when others are not.

In Harris's words, "Connect with your life." There's no better time to do this than now, when our worlds have grown smaller and, in most cases, our ability to connect with those closest to us has never been easier—or more comforting for everyone involved.

## WEEK FOURTEEN/ DAY 3: CHARACTER

# "Sorry About Your Can." Proof That When We Give, We Also Receive.

Imagine opening your mailbox one day and finding an unmarked, sealed plain white envelope. You open it and inside you find an unsigned note and $250 in cash. Here's the surprising story behind this act of generosity.

Good friends of my family live in a rural section of Maryland, where the houses are few and far between and the roads are narrow. On a windy trash collection day, one friend (Matt) went to bring in the garbage can from the curb only to find the lid had been blown into the center of the road—and had been run over by a car.

While the heavy plastic lid was bent in the middle, it was still usable. Matt wasn't overly concerned and brought the trash can back to its resting place on the side of the house. Which should have been the end of the story—but it wasn't.

A few days later, Matt went to retrieve his mail and found the previously mentioned plain white envelope, with no name or address on it, inside his box. He opened it and found it contained a handwritten note and $250 in cash. Here's what was written on the note verbatim:

*Hello,*

*On my way home, I accidentally ran over your trash can lid.*
*I'm not sure if it did any damage, but I wanted to do the right*
*thing. I hope this pays for a new one. Sorry about your can.*
*Have a nice day!*

Now while it was a sturdy trash can, its actual value was closer to $50. So why leave $250 in restitution? Maybe the extra money was for any perceived inconvenience that was caused. Or perhaps the reason that the $250 was left transcends the rational dollar-value of the trash can—and was a gesture of good will. Either way, it's an act of generosity that reminds me of the following adage often attributed to St. Francis of Assisi:

**FOR IT IS IN GIVING THAT WE RECEIVE.**

Like the thirteenth-century Italian monk, John Templeton believed that "we receive freely when we give freely." Templeton wrote that abundance and prosperity need an inflow and an outflow, "just like any body of water, if it is to remain fresh, clean and moving." (And interestingly the human body is comprised of 60% water.) He wonders:

> Do we keep the energy of abundance flowing by circulating part of what we have received by giving to others? Then, miracle of miracles, the more we give away, the more we have! This is the joy of allowing the energy of the universe to flow uninterrupted through us.

Templeton's notion is that to experience the joy of receiving, we must experience the joy of giving. We give and we receive. It's a cosmic quid pro quo. The only caveat is that we must give willingly, while expecting nothing in return. Which, in our busy lives, is often easier said than done. Life blogger Seth Godin sums up the issue this way:

Generosity takes effort. It requires the space to take your mind off your own problems long enough to see someone else's. It requires the confidence to share when a big part of you wants to hoard. And it requires the emotional labor of empathy.

Think about it. The person who ran over the trash can lid could have continued on their way. Certainly, no one would have been the wiser. But he or she decided to come back. And not just with a note of apology, but with a gift that far exceeded the value of any damage done.

It's enough to, at least temporarily, restore your faith in humanity—and make you wonder if there wasn't something bigger at play here. Was the giver paying it forward? Or simply aware of the rewards of giving for both the giver and the receiver?

## WEEK FOURTEEN/ DAY 4: CALLING

# Your Soul Is Calling.
# Will You Answer?

Are you becoming more aware of the passage of time? Ever wonder if you're making the most of your life? Or do you fear that something integral may be missing? If you can relate to these questions, then Thomas Moore's book *Ageless Soul* is required reading.

As you may know, Moore has written for decades on various facets of the soul. In this book, he has turned his attention to how aging impacts this deepest part of our selves. He reminds us that "the soul is not a technical or scientific term. It's an ancient one, rooted in the idea of breathing and being alive. It lies deeper than personality, ego, consciousness and the knowable." The soul is who we are at our very core.

---

**"The first taste of getting old can be unsettling."**
*— Thomas Moore*

---

Amen to that, Thomas! You're cruising through life, one day blending into the next, when suddenly you receive a series of unmistakable signs: You're not as young as you think you are. Here are just a few of the signals that time is catching up to you:

- You notice an unfamiliar stiffness and soreness upon awakening and after you exercise.
- You observe new wrinkles on your face or spots or creases on your body.
- You walk into a room in your home—and forget the reason you entered it.
- You find yourself holding printed materials further and further away from your body, at an arm's length, to read them.
- You notice that people are treating you differently, asking if you need assistance, or addressing you in a more formal way.

### MOORE CALLS THESE "SMALL SHOCKS." I CALL THEM "WAKE-UP CALLS."

These events snap us out of our illusion of eternal youthfulness and force us to confront an uncomfortable fact: We're getting older. The "wake-up calls" that come with aging may be unsettling—but they are also necessary. Without them, we might go through life without reflecting on the subtle but significant changes that remind us that our time here on this earth has an expiration date.

### IT'S YOUR CHOICE: YOU CAN AGE GRACEFULLY OR GROW OLD.

Moore tells us there's a difference between aging and growing old and it works like this:

- **Growing old** is a passive state where you sit back and let life happen to you.
- **Aging** is an active state, "a process by which you become somebody real and alive...more spiritually and culturally complex."

Active aging requires your full attention and participation. No putting on blinders to the changes that are happening to you or making excuses that you're "too old" for this or that. You'll need to start thinking about what steps you can take to continue to grow and thrive and become the complete person you were meant to be.

One approach suggested by Moore is to "stay young from the inside out." Everyone has the flicker of youth inside them and "that youthfulness needs only to be freed." That means keeping the old person who craves order and tradition in check and letting "the youthful attributes of energy and ideas come to the forefront."

### AS YOU AGE, YOUR SOUL WANTS YOUR ATTENTION.

Moore points out that for those of us who have had a long career, our priorities may have been focused on things like meeting the expectations of our boss or customers, getting promotions, and increasing our salary. The soul doesn't care about this stuff. In Moore's words, "the soul lives on a different set of values."

So how do we ensure we're living the fullest, richest life possible and making the most of what Mary Oliver calls our "one wild and precious life"? Thomas Moore offers us a few clues via the seven-point checklist below. The words in bold are from Moore. I have added my own thoughts that follow each word or phrase.

**YOUR SOUL MAY WANT:**

1. **Beauty**. Regularly expose yourself to the things that are beautiful to you. This may be art or music or spending time with nature, be it walking in the woods, jogging on the beach, or simply being fully present as you gaze out at your backyard.

2. **Contemplation**. Spend time alone in silent thought, at least fifteen minutes a day. If needed, use meditation or centering prayer to cleanse the mind.

3. **Deeply felt experiences.** What really speaks to your soul? It may be watching the sunrise, skiing down a snow-covered hill or having a romantic candlelit dinner at home.

4. **Meaningful relationships.** Stay engaged and in touch (physically) with your spouse or significant other. Converse regularly with the friends and family members that matter most.

5. **Knowledge.** Keep your mind active by reading, listening to podcasts, and watching TV shows, on the subjects that interest you.

6. **A sense of home.** As the saying goes, home is where the heart is. Find it in the place you live or a place you visit often. Spend quality time there.

7. **Art.** It speaks to our soul in ways words cannot. Display the art that speaks to you in your home; make regular visits to art museums and galleries.

I'd like to add an eighth point to the list:

8. **Movement.** The body is a vehicle for the soul and as we move through life, we need to stay active, helping to care for and

strengthen the soul's home. I run several times a week, but you might choose to walk or swim or bike or attend fitness classes.

**WEEK FOURTEEN/ DAY 5: PRACTICE**

# Five Ways to Hear What God Is Telling You

God is always speaking to us at different times and in different ways. That's the basic premise of the book *Discernment* by the late Henri Nouwen, who was a Roman Catholic priest and author of thirty-nine books who taught at Yale, Harvard, and Notre Dame. Of course, the idea that God is in constant contact with us may cause you to ask:

*"If God is talking, why don't I hear him?"*

Nouwen says the way to hear God is through the process of discernment, which put simply is spiritual judgement and understanding. It's a way of making decisions that relies not on the intellect alone but involves "a regular discipline of listening to the still, small voice beneath the rush of the whirlwind, a prayerful practice of reading the subtle signs in daily life."

Before we go further, you might be wondering about Nouwen's definition of God. Nouwen tells us that he shares the views of his fellow Catholic Thomas Merton, the notion that "God is the foundation of all life and source of all existence, not just a grandfatherly figure in the sky." God is the substance of life.

Nouwen writes that the key to discernment is "responding to that place deep within us where our deepest desires align with God's desire." When we make that connection deep within, it allows us to "sift through our impulses, motives and opinions," so we can make decisions that bring us closer to God. In turn, we are able to bring more love, joy, and peace into our lives and our ability to show love and compassion to those around us in enhanced.

## THE KEY TO DISCERNMENT IS "LISTENING TO A DEEPER SOUND."

According to Nouwen, "when we are truly listening, we come to know that God is speaking to us, pointing the way, showing the direction." When we can detect how God is guiding us, we "know when to act, when to wait, and when to be led." As the musician and author Robert A. Jonas points out in the foreword to Nouwen's book:

> When we use discernment, we notice our lives become less chaotic and less filled with drama. We notice that we are less anxious and fearful. We notice that we feel more comfortable with solitude and with accepting mystery and uncertainty. We discover a deep inner peace.

**How do we hear God?** How do we become versed at "listening to a deeper sound and marching to a different beat," engaging in a life in which we become "all ears"? Nouwen has several suggestions, ways in which "God's presence can be detected in the ordinary activities and routines of the every day." Here are my favorites.

## FIVE WAYS TO HEAR WHAT GOD IS TELLING YOU.

1. **Prayer and Contemplation.** Nouwen notes that our spiritual lens is sharpened when we engage in daily prayer and contemplation. He mentions no specific prayer, only that we ask God for guidance, an act that can be combined with quiet contem-

plation. Nouwen says that "the most interesting things in life often remain invisible to our ordinary senses yet are visible to our spiritual perception." Prayer and contemplation bring them to the surface.

2. **"Reading the Book of Nature."** The phrase above is from Nouwen, who tells us that "God's first language is nature." (An interesting parallel to the idea that God's primary language is silence.) Nouwen believes that "nature makes you more attentive to divine guidance." He mentions taking long walks amongst tall trees and how they spoke of "peace, stability, harmony, rest, life and death, coming and going, staying and leaving." Natural surroundings put us in a mental space in which the Divine can be heard.

3. **Paying Attention to People in Your Path.** Nouwen counsels us that God speaks through the people we meet in daily life, primarily through "family members and close friends with whom we have a primary relationship" though even complete strangers can sometimes deliver important messages. According to Nouwen, people are "human vehicles of divine presence and direction" and "living signs pointing the way to home, vocation, or a new direction." By paying attention to the people God puts on your path, you can discern God's direction for your life.

4. **Analyzing the Events of the Day.** Nouwen sees God as present in the activities and encounters that happen each day and that these events represent "signposts" and "continuing occasions to change the heart." These signs and signals offer us daily guidance. In his words, "Whatever happens—good things or bad, pleasant or problematic—ask, 'What might God be doing here?'"

5. **Looking at What You Are Drawn to Read.** This is an interesting idea, that what we are drawn to read during any given period can be another way God is offering us guidance. Nouwen makes it clear that he is not talking about just the Bible, but any spiritual reading and all types of "good books and human literature." They become "vehicles of divine communication" joining our will and the will of God as one.

# Six Portable Spiritual Practices—from a Spiritual Master

Q: Any advice for the spiritual practitioner who may be stuck or who needs to dust off their practice?

A: Keep your practice simple and portable. Travel lightly.

I asked the question above of Matthew Fox while talking to him about his latest book, *Essential Writings on Creation Spirituality*. Fox is one of the most acclaimed living spiritual practitioners and academics of our time, with a robust CV that includes writing a total of thirty-seven religion and spirituality books, gender and ecological activism, and a leading role as a priest within the Episcopal church.

Fox's answer to my question, to keep it "simple and portable," is telling. It shows how often we tend to complicate matters, especially when it comes to our spiritual practice. The author went on to offer several pointers, techniques that are both easy to do and can be done anywhere. No special rituals or exertion required. And you can engage in any of these practices right here, right now.

The first bits of advice center around meditation, which Fox sees as "vacationing time, time off for the soul." In his current book, Fox discusses two different types of meditation, an "emptying" kind and a "filling" kind. They both have merit. Here's a breakdown of each:

- **Filling Meditation**. You fill your soul by focusing on something of beauty. You might gaze out at the beauty of the ocean, for example, or look in awe at a colorful sunset. Whatever lights your fire. In these moments, "your senses blossom" as you move into a state of silent awareness and appreciation.
- **Emptying Meditation.** You empty your mind and yourself, letting go of all images, distractions, and personal goals. It's the equivalent of a mental cleansing of the palate. Once complete, this emptying then allows for a greater appreciation of the world around you.

Fox points out that in the West, with our hectic lives and busy schedules, we "are more drawn to the emptying kinds of meditation." But whichever type of meditation you choose, Fox tells us they have the same effect: to "see reality as it is in all its clarity and radiance and truth." He continues:

> Jesus called it recognizing that the domain of God is among us. (Buddhist monk) Thich Nhat Hanh describes it as developing our capacities for deep looking, listening, and awareness of the present state of things beginning with ourselves. Quoting Nhat Hanh, "When we are mindful, touching deeply the present moment, we can see and listen deeply and the fruits are always understanding, acceptance, love, and the desire to relieve suffering and bring joy."

During our conversation, Fox added a few additional "no fuss, no muss" spiritual practice techniques. What they have in common is their ease of use. You can use any of them right now or as soon as you get to the bottom of the page.

- **Recite a mantra.** Like meditation, this practice helps stop the overanalyzing mind from thinking so much, "numbing the left brain, allowing the right brain to prosper." A mantra is a word or phrase that is repeated over and over. Fox advises us to "think bumper sticker: shorty pithy statements like 'the Kingdom of God is within you' (Jesus) or 'All shall be well' (Julian of Norwich). My personal favorite: 'God is Good.'

- **Use breath work.** It's as easy as focusing your attention on the breath. Breathe in. Breathe out. Once your attention is focused on the breath, try this: *Breathe in joy, breathe out sadness. Breathe in hope, breathe out despair. Breathe in peace, breathe out conflict.* Repeat.

- **Discover the sacred.** No research required. Fox points out that "holiness and beauty can be found all around us": in the tall trees outside your window or in your neighborhood park or by simply looking up into a star-filled night sky. The sacred also can be found in art, in music, in architecture—any environment or setting that soothes the soul.

I'll add one additional tip that was provided by contemplative teacher and clinical psychologist James Finley. You can think of contemplation as sort of a wordless meditation, in which we allow ourselves to be fully in the present moment. Finley suggests we regularly:

- **Engage in contemplation.** To paraphrase Finley: Don't think of anything. Wordlessly rest in the presence of God. It is a presence beyond all thoughts and images. Allow it to intimately access your heart as you intimately access it. Rest in the oneness that ties all of life together.

# What is God's Gender? Let's Ask Mirabai Starr.

When you picture God, do you conjure up an image of a fatherly figure with long white hair and a beard? If you answer yes, there's a pretty good reason for that. Attend a religious service at any church, synagogue, or mosque and, more often than not, you'll find God referred to in strictly male terms.

You may be surprised to learn that in the three Abrahamic religions, Christianity, Judaism and Islam, God is not defined as a man or woman—but as a spirit with no physical substance, neither male nor female. Yet, our understanding of the Divine can include both masculine and feminine characteristics.

When talking about God, the Reverend Phillip A. Carl of Reston, Virginia, points out the conundrum in designating God's gender. When delivering his sermons, he'll often use the female pronoun as in: "Thanks be to God! She has blessed us with gifts too numerous to count." But Carl writes that when he uses *She* to speak of God, he sometimes feels like there's a "speed bump" between his listener and his intended message. He can sense his congregants thinking:

> She? Why'd he say "she"? And then our minds go to remembering that God is neither male nor female and the only reason we think of her as a him is because, in antiquity, males were thought to be superior and, since God is superior, God must be male. Then our minds eye goes to Michelangelo's portrait of God on the ceiling of the Sistine Chapel where "he" is a macho old white guy with fierce eyes and a very male beard.

## I'VE MET GOD. SHE'S BLACK.

You may have seen this provocative message on a T-shirt, social media post or on posters plastered around Manhattan. (If you haven't, do a quick Google search and you'll see it's ubiquitous.) I've got to say that the first time I saw it, it stopped me in my tracks.

To say, "I've met God, she's Black" challenges preconceived conceptions about who and what God is—something Mirabai Starr does masterfully in her book *Wild Mercy: Living the Fierce and Tender Wisdom of the Women Mystics.*

Starr pokes one hole after another in the notion that God should be thought of in masculine terms as she underscores the feminine side of the spiritual story. After all, if God has no gender, couldn't God be represented by the image of a woman just as suitably as by the image of a man? Starr suggests it's time to adjust our thinking: "Pretending God's a dude hasn't exactly worked out for the vast majority of the human family, let alone the animal and plant communities or the air or the waters."

Starr speaks out against "the toxicity of unbalanced masculine rule," enlightening us to the female presence that can be found in all faiths and religions, across cultures and throughout history. In many ways, Starr's *Wild Mercy* reads like a spiritual clarion call, not only to women who embody God's feminine side, but to a growing number of men who are ready for a new and deeper experience of God. Starr invites us to recognize God as seen through the eyes of women, and, in so doing, to find ourselves in a new intimacy with God. In her words:

> We are no longer willing to wait for invitations from men's ancient elite clubs; we do not believe true spiritual experience is limited to these privileged spaces. Instead, we find the face of the Holy One in the faces of our babies and our lovers, our elders and our coworkers, the dirty dishes and the deep quiet

that falls over our homes when everyone else is sleeping and we stand at the window, looking at the moon.

## STARR SHOWS US THE POWER AND LOVE OF THE DIVINE FEMININE.

She tells us about Sophia, the feminine goddess of wisdom found in ancient Greek philosophy and in Christian mysticism. She introduces us to the living Earth goddess Gaia. She teaches us about Julian of Norwich, a fourteenth-century anchoress who declared that "just as God is our Father, so God is also our Mother." According to Starr, Julian experienced Jesus as one who took "a personal interest in every single being, like a loving Mother, forgiving us when we screw up and rejoicing when we return to love."

From Mother Mary to her own mother, Starr weaves a tapestry of her favorite teachings from women of wisdom past and present. This diverse line up includes Teresa of Ávila, Quan Lin, Kali, White Buffalo Calf Woman, and Our Lady of Guadalupe, to name just a few.

Starr also details her personal religious practices, including how she celebrates the Jewish day of rest, Shabbat. While the Christian Sabbath is observed on Sunday, Shabbat is observed from a few minutes before sunset on Friday until nightfall on Saturday. Shabbat invites, welcomes and embodies the presence of the divine feminine here on Earth:

> In the Jewish tradition, the holiest of holy days—holier than the High Holidays themselves—is Shabbat, and she is female. Yes, the Sabbath itself is a feminine being. The Shekinah is the indwelling feminine presence of the Divine. She resides in exile during the rest of the week and on Shabbat she comes home.

Starr reveals that "on Shabbat, I slow down and remember to praise her (Shekinah) with my footsteps. I caress her with my breath.

I thank her." She suggests all of us set aside a regular day—once a week, a day a month, a weekend—as a personal Sabbath or Shabbat. We need to find our own way to put aside our daily concerns and let ourselves rest. "Read, write poetry, color in a coloring book, take a hike, make a beautiful meal—anything that reconnects you with your soul."

Starr suggests that the key to making these rituals have meaning in our own lives is repetition. In that way, they become a continuing reminder of who we are. She instructs us to "enact this ritual again and again, week after week." We might think of "all spiritual practices, all rituals and ceremonies and creative arts, as bells designed to wake us from the slumber of our separateness."

Once we awaken, we will be better able to "engage in the very feminine values that have been missing from our religious and political institutions: the willingness to be present, to listen, and, most of all, to allow our hearts to be moved by the suffering of the world." She invites us to join her in a contemplative adventure as "contemporary mystics masquerading as ordinary people."

Starr reminds us that "we are all born with a particular task we are meant to contribute to the healing of the world, and we are precisely and perfectly designed to do it." And the good news: "it is probably something you are already good at and is almost definitely something you love doing." She asks us to consider: "What is the unique task imprinted on your soul?"

# WEEK FIFTEEN

## The Ten-Point Self Improvement Plan—from Jack LaLanne

*"It is a religion with me. It's a way of life.*
*A religion is a way of life, isn't it?"*
*— Jack LaLanne on "keeping fit"*

My wife sometimes tells me "You're too much in your head" and I know what she means. At any one time, I'm usually reading or listening to several spirituality-related books and podcasts. Most recently, my head has been swirling with notions of good and evil spirits, Eckhart Tolle and communicating with the dead.

It's at these times I remind myself: You need balance between the mind and body. So, I rededicate myself to a fitness regimen that includes stretching, running, and lifting light weights. Which got me thinking about a story I wrote several years ago about an early poster boy for balanced living, Jack LaLanne.

### Do you remember the Jack LaLanne Show?

As a child, I recall my mother watching "The Jack LaLanne Show" on our black-and-white television set. LaLanne was a fitness expert before there was such a thing, and I remember him as a man in constant motion. Wearing his trademark jumpsuit, he took viewers through exercise routines that could be done right at home, using props like a kitchen chair and a broomstick.

A few years ago, there was an online video clip of LaLanne (since taken down due to copyright issues), and if you looked over his shoulder you could make out a list of ten words handwritten on a whiteboard. He was promoting a "Ten-Point Self-improvement Plan" and I found his ideas as relevant today as they were fifty-plus years ago.

For those who don't remember Jack LaLanne, he's regarded as "the founder of the modern fitness movement." He declared that his life mission was to "help people help themselves" and he meant all people. LaLanne insisted that exercise was for everyone, regardless of your age or physical condition and that you could engage in it anytime, anywhere, no gym required.

Importantly, what made Jack LaLanne different from other early exercise gurus, was that he took a 360-degree view of life. While he preached the benefits of regular exercise, he also spoke of the importance of a proper diet, having the right attitude, and the need for faith. He wanted to improve his viewers' well-being, body, mind, and spirit.

Jack called his ten-point list "little secrets to help improve yourself from the bottom of your feet to the top of your head." And he promised that if you tried it each day for a week, you would begin to see "an amazing change in the way you feel and look." Check out the list and Jack's advice in italics below, followed by a few of my own comments.

## JACK LaLANNE'S TEN-POINT SELF IMPROVEMENT PLAN

1. **Exercise.** *It's the key to everything. If you don't exercise you will look and feel old.* Jack exercised daily right through his ninety-sixth year of life. The key is movement, we need to move to keep our minds and body healthy.

2. **Nutrition.** *Eat more fruits and vegetables, and more lean meats. Cut out white flour, sugar and fried food. Be conscious of what you're putting in your body.* Jack was ahead of his time in asking us to remove processed foods from our diet. They weren't good for us then, they're not good for us now.

3. **Positive Thinking.** *Think wonderful thoughts. Count your blessings. Appreciate what you have and don't focus on what you don't.* In other words, be grateful. Instead of yearning for things you don't have, give thanks for all you do have.

4. **Good Habits.** *Replace a bad habit with a good one.* Jack would have been puzzled by our mindless devotion to our smartphones. Instead of scanning your social feed for the umpteenth time, try a quick meditation session or take a walk around the block.

5. **Grooming.** *Be aware of your personal appearance, the way you look, how you dress. Be a lovelier you.* We live in very casual time, but it feels good to "dress up" every now and then.

6. **Smile.** *Keep a pleasant look on your face. Smiles are infectious.* It's amazing how having a smile on your face can change the way others react to you.

7. **Posture.** *Whether you're walking, standing or sitting, pull the tummy in and keep the shoulders back.* No leaning on countertops, walls or chairs and no slouching. Remember to sit or stand tall.

8. **Help Others.** *It is more blessed to give than to receive. Help others have a better life.* When you help others, you also help yourself have a happier life. Giving has its own rewards.

9. **Relaxation.** *Spare five to ten minutes each afternoon to lie down in a dark room, completely relaxed. Recharge the human battery.* Can't lie down in a dark room? Find a quiet place to escape to and simply breathe. Working in Manhattan, I would

occasionally retreat to a local church. Now that I work from home, I take a brief "cat nap" many days.

10. **Faith**. *You can't do it all by yourself, have faith in Nature and God above. Put forth some effort and you'll find that God helps those who help themselves.* Amen.

It sounds like an easy-to-follow plan, doesn't it? Read these ten points again. Consider printing them for easy access and try them tomorrow, and the next day and the day after that for a full seven days. See if the result isn't a happier, healthier you. A final reminder from Jack: "Try to eat better, including more fresh vegetables and fruit. Get more exercise. Let's get back to the way nature intended us to be—happy, with a big smile on our face."

**WEEK FIFTEEN/ DAY 2: AWARENESS**

# Is God "Closer Than Your Own Breath"?

*"God is indwelling; and because God is indwelling, I do not have to seek God so much as I have to remember my connection with God." — Karen Brailsford*

Remembering our connection to God—that's the hard part, isn't it? The words above come from journalist Karen Brailsford and her book *Sacred Landscapes of the Soul.* Comprised of a series of short essays that she calls "landscapes," her stories have a common thread: the idea that God is everywhere and with us always, just waiting for our acknowledgment.

Brailsford has a unique spiritual background in that she was raised in the South Bronx and attended a Baptist church as a youth. Today, she resides in Los Angeles, where she is a member of the Agape International Spiritual Center led by the New Thought leader Michael Bernard Beckwith. She writes for the center's monthly magazine, *Inner Visions.*

Brailsford's notion that the spirit of God is always with us, closer than we can possibly imagine, can be found in many religions and spiritual philosophies. For instance, this reference is found in the Bible in 1 Corinthians 3:16: "Don't you know that you yourselves are God's temple and that God's Spirit dwells in your midst?"

A similar sentiment appears in this passage from a very different source, the great Sufi poet and mystic Rumi:

"Why look for God?

Look for the one looking for God...

but then Why look at all?

He is not lost ... He is right here ... Closer than your own breath!"

The problem is, while we may be able to sense God in this present moment, it is often hard to retain this knowledge as we live our lives. Our minds often seem incapable of going about our daily business while remembering our connection to God. The key may be constant triggers that remind us of the divine presence.

We need reminders that God is always there, like the Muslim call to prayer five times a day, or the sound of church bells ringing in the distance. I think Brailsford's short essays do just that—remind us of the presence of the Divine—and can be a valuable tool when read in small batches or one story at a time each day.

What I found most compelling in *Sacred Landscapes of the Soul* were the first-person essays that appear in italics every few pages in the book. They appear to have been channeled or as Brailsford explains: "The words flowed through me as if they were being communicated directly by God, speaking directly to me. And thereby, to you."

What follows are lightly edited excerpts from Brailsford's "God stories," which represent the words of God. I've placed them in a loose narrative.

## EIGHT PASSAGES FROM SACRED LANDSCAPES OF THE SOUL

1. Lately, it appears that the world is spiraling into chaos. Rest assured—everything is in divine order. When you choose to rest within the shade of my love, to seek comfort in me, you will be relieved of all worry and will go forward in love.

2. Love stands at the door and knocks. It will be there when you are ready, awaiting your acceptance. Love is who and what I am. Therefore, it is who and what you are.

3. The highest intention you can set is to reveal me. Let me be the only thing you desire. Let me be that which causes you to leap from bed every morning filled to overflowing with unparalleled joy. And here is what you can expect in return, every minute of every hour: I am going to be with you.

4. You get to determine where you are going. That's right! You get to choose—how quickly, how slowly, how painfully, how fretfully, even how soon. You get to make it all up.

5. Own your mysticism. Know that you are your own greatest teacher. Look within. Find me there. Surrender. Shine your light. Soar. Be the spark for others.

6. You are drawing unto you the people, the situations, the inspiration and the insights necessary for realizing your purpose. That purpose is to come into full alignment with why you are here and how to best deliver your gifts to the world.

7. It's time to take a stand. Are you for you—or against you? Can you see yourself as I see you—lightness and loveliness, poetic possibility and greatness always on the verge of something even more expansive? You are perfect exactly as you are. You know it all and possess it all. You are all of it.

8. Remember that in between each inhalation and exhalation, I am there. In between the doubt and the certainty, I am there. In between longing and manifestation, I am there. In between the singing of the note and the hearing of the note, I am there. There is no place else I would rather be because there is no other place to be. I am with you.

# Can Kindness Make You a Happier Person?

For those who say it is hard to find good news these days, let me tell you the story of Jon Potter of Pittsburgh, Pennsylvania. He may be the kindest person in the world.

I learned of Jon in a story published in *The Washington Post* titled: "'I have $1500 that I'm giving away': Man becomes legend for extreme acts of kindness toward strangers." Potter has used his limited financial resources and skills as a handyman to say yes to essentially everyone who asks him for help. He does everything from giving people rides in the middle of the night to doing home improvement jobs, from buying groceries to finding housing for those in need. Oh, and he also donated a kidney to a total stranger. All for no monetary gain.

Here's an excerpt from the story that will give you a good idea of just how generous Potter is and how this generosity has inspired others:

> When a local group awarded him $500 for being an exemplary community member, he posted about it on Reddit and asked who needed the money. Several people responded that they needed help, and others contacted him to donate more money. In the end, 'I have $1500 that I'm giving away,' he wrote in an update. He used the funds to help two people get bus passes for work transportation, buy groceries for several other people, pay a gas bill for another, fund new shoes for a struggling nurse with foot troubles, contribute to a service trip in Costa Rica — and for many other causes.

According to the story, Potter himself has struggled in the past with his own personal issues. But he says that "helping others has brought on a big turn for the better in my own life," especially by keeping his depression and anxiety at bay. He highly recommends his unusual lifestyle and likes encouraging others to help people when they can."

### IS KINDNESS AND GENEROSITY THE KEY TO YOUR OWN PERSONAL HAPPINESS?

Jon Potter may have tapped into an idea that is as old as humankind. It's the idea that when we help others, we also help ourselves. It's the Golden Rule, as found in Matthew 7:12, and in a nutshell it reads "Treat others the same way you would like them to treat you." But this sentiment is not exclusive to Christianity; it is found in other religions as follows:

- **Hinduism:** The true role of life is to guard and do things for others as they do on their own.
- **Islam:** No one of you is a believer until you desire for your brother what you desire for yourself.

- **Taoism**: Regard your neighbor's gain as your own gain and your neighbor's loss as your own loss.

This idea is expanded on in this passage from Siddhartha Gautama, aka The Buddha:

> Giving brings happiness at every stage of its expression. We experience joy in forming the intention to be generous; we experience joy in the actual act of giving something; and we experience joy in remembering the fact that we have given.

John Templeton, writing in *Worldwide Laws of Life*, calls kindness and generosity "love in action." Yet he points out that we are often so overly concerned with our own life situation, which is often far superior to those in true need, that we "fail to see blessed opportunities to be love in action." He asks you and me: "Do you rush so fast from one thing to another, perhaps from one appointment or meeting to another, that you fail to notice how others are feeling or what may be happening in their lives?"

What's the key to being kinder and more generous in our own lives? According to Templeton, "shifting your awareness outside of yourself to others." Let's stop and do that right now. Who will you encounter in the next few minutes, hours or days, that can use your gift of kindness? Might offering these gifts become a regular practice?

It's a small ask and it does not require the almost superhuman efforts of Jon Potter. All you need to do is shift your awareness to those around you and ask yourself the question: "Who can I help today?" Then repeat that question tomorrow and the days after that. You might be surprised to find that your small acts of kindness make you happier, as well.

WEEK FIFTEEN/ DAY 4: CALLING

# Why Let Others Set Your Course? Do It Yourself

In her book *The Benevolent Universe, The Story of Your Unique Genius*, Dana Drake puts forward a unique and powerful theory: Any problems we have, any issues or big life questions we face, can all be solved by ourselves. In her words, "We are designed to know everything we wish to know," including our purpose in life.

It's Drake's assertion that we've been given all the life tools we need by a Universe that "is not only kind, it is generous, forgiving and staggeringly compassionate." Which raises several questions, including: If the Universe has given us these tools, why don't we intuitively know about them? And why do we struggle so mightily to navigate the many choices life presents us?

### THE PROBLEM FOR MANY OF US: WE PUT OUR EGO IN CHARGE.

Drake writes that one reason we may perceive the Universe as being silent is our own human ego, "the ugly, hard shell of stories and behaviors we embody to protect our culture, our ideas, our beliefs." She goes on to identify the ego as "the false, lesser self," one that represses our soul's connection to the higher, universal self.

As a result, we miss out on the guidance the Universe has to offer and "our lives become exercises in wake-up calls, where environmental factors such as divorce, accidents, or bankruptcy begin the self-reflection and awakening." But ideally, we want to be able to bypass the more troubling "wake-up calls" of life. We want to be in a place where we make smart decisions from the get-go, where our actions are aligned with our purpose in life.

**WE NEED TO FUNCTION FROM A PLACE OF**
***KNOWING* BEFORE DOING.**

How do we do this? By tapping into a state of consciousness that Drake refers to as "genius." While we often use this phrase to describe brilliant minds like Albert Einstein or Marie Curie, she believes we all have the ability to access the genius within. That's because it's a trait given not just to a select few, but to everyone—a gift from the Universe. In Drake's words: "Genius is simply our purest, most genuine self, manifesting that which comes effortlessly for each of us."

**THE KEY TO ACCESSING THIS INNER KNOWLEDGE**
**MAY BE GETTING INTO A "ZERO STATE."**

Drake uses the phrase "the zero state" to describe the state of mind that puts us in touch with the universal consciousness. Think of the moments in life when you're feeling totally calm and at ease. For me, this state can be induced through physical activities like running or a morning meditation session. Drake calls it "the state of the mind-body in oneness with the Universe ... where we align ourselves with the true nature of our being." She continues:

> When you achieve Zero, you will know you're "there" and will redesign your entire existence to find more of it. This is the state in which you know your unique purpose on the earth. From Zero state, you will be guided step-by-step into an authenticity and abundance you've only glimpsed before.

It's at these moments, when we immerse ourselves in "the boundless love and guidance of the Universe," that we are best able to make difficult decisions and take a clear-eyed look at our lives. We can then determine if we're on the right path or need to map out a detour to get back on course.

**DRAKE BELIEVES THAT WE ALL HAVE OUR OWN
UNIQUE PATH IN LIFE.**

It is a sentiment shared by the spiritual teacher and author Caroline Myss who, in a conversation with Oprah Winfrey, once said that we all have a path—even if we are currently unaware of it. Myss suggests that we know when we are on that path because life just feels right. We know in our hearts that we're not betraying or compromising ourselves.

Similarly, Drake writes that "the Universe is always conspiring to help us become conscious while on our path" and that "… we all have destinies. All of us. We are designed to know what we came here to do." When we're not on that path, we can sense that something is wrong. We might even feel ashamed of our past and present actions.

**NOT SURE OF YOUR LIFE PATH? THE BEST WAY
TO FIND IT MAY BE TO DO NOTHING.**

Drake advises that "doing nothing—literally and spiritually—is the highest choice when we don't know what to do." When we have the time (and we usually do), it's best not to create an artificial deadline to make important decisions or attempt course corrections. We need to wait and do the right thing rather than to try and force the action. That means:

> No speaking, no acting out, no eating, smoking, texting. Simply witness your stories and pain until it softens into wisdom of the mind-body. The energetic block releases, compassion awakens. Do nothing, change everything.

**WE MUST LIVE OUR LIVES WITH COMPASSION— ESPECIALLY TOWARD OURSELVES.**

No beating ourselves up for past mistakes or blaming ourselves if the answers we seek don't come instantly. As a wise acquaintance once said, "Always give yourself the same love, compassion and acceptance that you seek from others." In closing, Drake gives us the following reminder, one that encapsulates her philosophy:

> We are designed for happiness and bliss every moment. If we are looking for others to fix us, we are disconnected from the place that knows we fix ourselves. When we are ready to seek true understanding and health and happiness, it will come.

## WEEK FIFTEEN/ DAY 5: PRACTICE

# Are You Listening to the Still Small Voice Within?

If you read enough books about the soul, you'll come across a reoccurring theme. It's the idea that we all have a small, still voice within us that is there to guide us as we make our way through life. The voice represents the deepest, truest part of us, our soul, and it knows what we want and need from life—if only we would listen to it.

*The Voice*
*There is a voice inside of you*
*That whispers all day long,*
*"I feel this is right for me,*
*I know that this is wrong."*
*No teacher, preacher, parent, friend*
*Or wise man can decide*

> *What's right for you--just listen to*
> *The voice that speaks inside.*
> — *Shel Silverstein*

The late American spiritual philosopher Ram Dass also discussed the power of the inner voice to help guide us through life. In this passage from his book *Paths to God: Living the Bhagavad Gita*, he advises us to use this voice to our advantage, as it represents the equivalent of an inner sixth-sense:

> Begin paying more attention to the inner voice of our intuition, because that's the clue to what we should be doing. We start to listen to the tiny, intuitive whisper that the Quakers call "the still small voice within."

## THERE'S JUST ONE ISSUE WITH THE STILL SMALL VOICE. WE DON'T ALWAYS HEAR IT.

Sometimes we find it's easier to ignore it or brush it aside. The reason: What the soul wants does not always jibe with what the people around us want or what society expects from us. Richard Bode, writing in *Beachcombing at Miramar: The Quest for an Authentic Life*, explains it this way:

> The world is full of those who would keep us from singing the songs we want to sing and painting the pictures we want to paint. Some are bosses, some are officials of oppressive regimes—and some are our mothers, fathers, teachers, husbands, or wives, who, for whatever their reasons, try to stifle the life force that makes us who we are. But we have the choice: We can empower them, or we can empower ourselves.

Some say that when we don't listen, the voice quiets, until it becomes just a whisper, eventually disappearing altogether. According to spirituality author Shakti Gawain, when we squash the voice and its message, we pay a price for it: "Every time you don't follow your inner guidance, you feel a loss of energy, loss of power, a sense of spiritual deadness."

Richard Bode amplifies this point, warning of us something that no one wants:

> The deep, driving hunger of the soul is there; it will not go away—and we pay an awesome price each time we push it down into the pit of our being. Little by little the colors fade and the sound of music goes out of our lives.

## HAS THE STILL SMALL VOICE QUIETED IN YOUR LIFE?

If you look inside and hear only the faintest of whispers or even silence, there are other ways that the inner voice makes itself known. There are signals that tell us we are on the right path. On her blog, Gail Brenner gives us a few clues as to how to know "when truth is talking." She writes:

- It moves us toward love – for ourselves and others.
- It ultimately brings enjoyment.
- There is no sinking feeling that something is wrong.
- The body unclenches.
- There is a sense of clarity, excitement, or relief, an undeniable knowing.

To hear this voice is one thing, but there's more to it than that. We also need the courage to act. As Bode says, "It astounds me when I think of the courage it takes to live, to behave as we want to behave, to be who we want to be." But if we are being true to ourselves and want to live the life we were meant to live, we have no other choice but to listen—and act.

WEEK FIFTEEN/ DAY 6: INNER WORK

# Nine Very Short Prayers for People Who "Maybe" Believe

Have you ever occasionally wondered if prayer isn't just a big frigging waste of time? Donna Schaper hears you and she is no religious skeptic. She is, in fact, the senior minister at Judson Memorial Church in New York City.

Schaper tends to a diverse flock in Greenwich Village that includes undocumented migrants and members of the LGBTQ+ community, as well as what she calls "doubters." She has written several books on religion and spirituality and one that recently caught my eye is titled *Prayers for People Who Say They Can't Pray*.

While we all may sometimes question the value of prayer, Schaper says that for most of us, prayer satisfies a deep yearning that comes from within our souls. She writes that prayer can provide us with "a pause that refreshes, a clarity that battles confusion, a peace that passes immediate understanding."

In her words, "prayer is awareness that there is more to life than itself" and serves as a conduit to the great unknown force of life that you, like me, may call God. Shaper tells us that prayer takes us out of our thinking minds and that's a good thing:

> When prayer is genuine, we pray from our guts and not just
> from our heads. Our heads don't go away. Instead, our hearts
> and heads join together. Sometimes our heart has a wisdom
> that our head does not.

Schaper believes we are way too busy with our jobs and to-do lists and need to devote more time to addressing our "inner space." Prayer is a way to do that. She advises us that we need to take the occasional break from our everyday worries and "instead pray our way awake or pray our way to sleep."

She is aware that many of us "are tentative about God," hence prayers for people who "maybe" believe. She views these prayers as "momentary stays against confusion, as poems, as pictures of what we might say if we were to speak our heart's deepest longings, and if we were to find a way to trust the universe and its partnership with you and me."

The prayers that Schaper has written are simple, disarming, and, well, unorthodox. They are unlike prayers that I, and probably you, have ever used. They beseech and question God, they bring to light our own personal imperfections, and they make small asks, requesting tiny mercies in ourselves and the way we view the world.

Below are several of my favorites, with a few minor tweaks. I think you'll find that they change the way you view the meaning of prayer.

## NINE PRAYERS FOR PEOPLE WHO "MAYBE" BELIEVE

1. When I go to sleep at night, let me name those I love, even if they are far away or no longer close in spirit, and say thank you to them again for being alive. *Amen.*

2. Let my goings out and comings in have a bit of pizzazz, O God. Let my stopping and starting aim somewhere. And keep chaos at bay. *Amen.*

3. Henry David Thoreau wanted to live deliberately the way that I want to be fully awake. Deliberately awake. That is my goal. Is it all right if I meet that goal slightly, every few days? Or is something more complete demanded of me? *Amen.*

4. William Butler Yeats argued that we can "live with a clearer, perhaps even with a fiercer life because of our quiet." Grant me ferocity, clarity, and quiet. *Amen.*

5. When I ask for transformation from monkey mind, one that jumps from tree to tree and subject to subject, I am asking for a discipline, not from the outside, but from the inside. Let me be a person who can focus on one thing at a time and is in charge of myself. *Amen.*

6. Send me a wake-up call about my mortality. Let it ring every day at 6 or 7 or 8 so that when I go to sleep at 10 or 11 or 12, I am aware that I too will pass. *Amen.*

7. When I am afraid that I can't "get it all done," remind me that I never will. Let me rejoice in the great unfinishedness and remember that there is nothing to be frightened of. *Amen.*

8. From haste and its waste, rescue me, O God. Slow me down long enough to enjoy my time, here, now. Make me ask the question of where it is I think I am going in such a big hurry. *Amen.*

9. Let little things mean a lot today, O God. Coffee breaks, convenient parking spaces, exact change: Let each permit me an ounce of joy and gratitude. *Amen.*

**WEEK FIFTEEN/ DAY 7: CONTEMPLATION**

# Were Jesus and Mary Magdalene Lovers?

In the book *Jesus Behaving Badly*, Mark L. Strauss reminds us that the Jesus of the New Testament exhibited more than a few human traits. He calls them "the puzzling paradoxes." They include Jesus losing his temper (Matthew 23:33), Jesus railing against families (Mark 10:29-30), and Jesus taking his vengeance out on a fig tree (Mark 11:13-14).

This got me thinking—if Jesus occasionally showed flashes of anger or spite, didn't he also experience the whole spectrum of human emotions—including joy, wonder, and dare I say it, lust and romantic love?

I bring this up, in part, because of the recurring stories I come across on Jesus and his relationship with Mary Magdalene. For instance, a few years ago, an ancient papyrus fragment was discovered called "The Gospel of Jesus's Wife." While its authenticity has been questioned, in the worn fragment Jesus refers to Mary as his wife. It's not the only evidence that a special relationship existed between Jesus and Mary.

While most of us are familiar with the four gospels found in the Bible, in the first few centuries of Christianity there were dozens of gospels in wide circulation about the life and teachings of Jesus. These gospels were passed around fledgling churches throughout the Mideast and beyond and show the rich diversity of early Christian beliefs.

Unfortunately, in the fourth century, these gospels were banned by the church and an edict was passed to destroy all gospels not named Matthew, Mark, Luke, or John. What we lost with this purge of competing gospels was a richer, more fully developed picture of Jesus the man, especially as it relates to his close relationship with Mary.

What follows are three passages from the Gnostic texts that speak directly to Mary and Jesus, the first is from the *Gospel of Philip*, the second and third are from the *Gospel of Mary*:

**Passage 1:**

The companion of the Son is Miriam of Magdala.

The teacher loved her more than all the disciples;

He often kissed her on the mouth.

**Passage 2:**

Peter said to Mary, "Sister, we know the savior loved you more than any other woman. Tell us the words of the savior that you remember, which you know but we do not, because we have not heard them."

**Passage 3:**

Levi said to the other disciples: "Surely the Lord knew her very well. That is why he loved her more than us'"

In his book *Writing in the Sand,* Thomas Moore tells us that Mary Magdalene was at one time confused with a prostitute by the same name in the Bible, perhaps intentionally by those in the church who sought to downplay her importance. She is now recognized as "the beloved disciple to whom the Gospels never refer by name." In fact, in 2016 Pope Francis designated her as "the apostle of the apostles," deeming her the most important of Jesus's early followers.

Over the years, the legend of Mary Magdalene has grown and there have been several books that make the case that she and Jesus were husband and wife. They include *Holy Blood Holy Grail,* which lays out evidence that after the death of Jesus, a pregnant Mary traveled to France, gave birth, and began a long line of Jesus's descendants.

But to me, what is most intriguing is the relationship Jesus and Mary Magdalene had in life. In her book *Wild Mercy,* Mirabai Starr adds to the notion that Mary was more than the closest disciple to Jesus, writing that she may have also been his spiritual equal. "After all, she was present at the foot of the cross as Jesus suffered and died, present at his burial, present to anoint his body."

Perhaps we should acknowledge that the obvious love between Jesus and Mary Magdalene may have crossed cross over into real romance. To that point, Starr opines that "it seems unlikely that a young Jewish man in first-century Palestine would have been unmarried, no matter how counter-cultural his lifestyle may have been." Thomas Moore goes a step further, stating that:

> What is shocking about the new view of Mary Magdalene and Jesus, of course, is the implication that Jesus was not celibate. People who see Jesus in an entirely spiritual light may have trouble considering the possibility that he was a sexual being as well. Yet … if you're going to acknowledge Jesus' humanity, you have to include his sexuality.

### DOES IT MATTER IF JESUS HAD A ROMANTIC RELATIONSHIP WITH MARY MAGDALENE?

For some in the church it poses a problem, who I suppose see Jesus as above the earthly desire for romance and sex. But I believe that seeing Jesus as having had a romantic relationship makes him easier to relate to. He is a savior who knows first-hand not just the pain and foibles of our flesh and blood experience, but also its pleasures. Moore writes:

> How you imagine Jesus' sexuality may depend on how you feel about sex. If you think it's contemptible or at least a low part of human nature, you may not want a sexual picture of Jesus. If you see the beauty and full significance of sexuality, you may understand how important it is to allow Jesus his sexuality. Anything less acknowledges his incarnation except for sexuality—and that makes no sense.

# WEEK SIXTEEN

## Insights from Two "Dudes" on Love and Marriage

Sometimes wisdom comes from places you don't expect to find it. In this case, from a movie star, a guy nicknamed "The Dude," aka Jeff Bridges. Several years ago, Bridges published a book titled *The Dude and the Zen Master* that contained many keen insights.

"The Dude" is a role Bridges once played in the movie *The Big Lebowski*. And while he may have received an Academy Award as Best Actor for *Crazy Heart*, his performance as the chillaxed stoner in *The Big Lebowski* really struck a chord with a lot of people. The character seemed to be an extension of Bridges himself and may be the role he is most closely associated with.

*The Dude and the Zen Master* shows that, in reality, Bridges is a great deal wiser than the Dude, with astute views on subjects like living in the moment and trusting one's gut. But perhaps most compelling are his views on the nature of love and marriage. You see, Jeff Bridges has been married to his wife Sue Geston for well over forty years, a notable feat for any marriage, but especially impressive for a "Hollywood" couple.

Bridges has sage advice to offer on the winding road that is marriage, and if you've been married a long time like I have, you can probably relate to them. I've taken the liberty of organizing his thoughts into a progression of five key moments of realization, because I think they accurately represent the arc of marriage, at least from my own personal perspective. Bridges's exact words appear in "quotes."

**#1. It starts with finding your true love.** Bridges met his wife on a movie set in Montana in 1975. The first few times he asked her out, she turned him down, until one night he saw her in town and *"we danced and I fell in love."* The very next day, Bridges had an appointment to look at a house that was for sale and he invited Sue to come along on what was officially their first "date."

> "I hear a voice in my head say: You are now looking at this house with your future wife. I thought, 'what the fu-k, what are you talking about?' And the voice continues, This is your wife."

**#2. Next, you have to overcome commitment phobia.** Things progress, but like a lot of us guys, Bridges became frightened by the thought of marriage and a life-long commitment. In his words, *"You begin to wonder: Is this really the one? What if I fall out of love?"* He also wondered if he might miss out on someone he loved even more.

> "I felt cornered, not by Sue but by myself. I couldn't bear to let the love of my life slip through my fingers, but at the same time I was afraid of declaring: This is the one! To make a long story short, I finally got the courage to ask Sue to marry me, with the secret caveat that I could always get a divorce."

Bridges eventually reached one of those "Oh no, what have I done?" states of mind during their first year of marriage. Sue picked up on it and offered to annul the marriage if he didn't want it. Bridges response was "No, no." In his words, it took a couple of years but "I finally got with the program."

**#3. In time, you see the depth and beauty of married life.** Once you get past the first few shaky years, you find your relationship growing stronger, the roots growing deeper. You have a perception shift where you no longer see what you're missing but see the beauty in all that you have. (This was especially true in my case when our first child came along.)

> "You close one door, the door to all other women, but you open a door that leads to a long hallway lined with doors. Incredible doors like children, grandchildren, deeper intimacy with the woman you love, and so many other things that would not be available to you without marriage, without the water under the bridge ... thank God I went for it."

**#4. You engage in epic battles—and the marriage endures.** Like all of us who have been married for a while, you know that it's not always bliss, especially if you both have strong personalities and opinions. Arguments and disagreements are bound to happen. The real test is in how you handle them.

> "We do have one ancient war that comes up again and again, which basically runs like this: 'You don't get it; you just don't get me; you don't understand.' And that's true. I don't entirely know Sue or her perspective, I never will. And she won't know me or where I'm coming from, really, entirely ... but as this ancient war rages, with each battle it becomes more apparent that this inability to truly know the other's perspective is what we have in common."

**#5. Come hell or high water, you're in it for the long haul.** With time, you know that even the "ancient wars" can't give you a big enough reason to split. You have an unbreakable bond. An occasional storm may hit, it may even cause damage to the figurative home that is your relationship, but the foundation stays rock-solid. And you become expert at repairing the home, each time making it a little stronger.

"We're going to experience all our stuff, I'm going to get pissed at you and you'll get pissed back, but we'll be in a marriage. We know we'll have tough times, but we're doing it all together."

## WHICH BRINGS ME TO THE ONE AND ONLY WEDDING SPEECH I EVER GAVE.

Right after I celebrated my own twenty-fifth wedding anniversary with my wife Laney, I was asked to speak at my nephew's wedding. I thought the longevity of our marriage might make a good topic—which got me thinking: How had our marriage endured through good times and bad? What kind of advice or tips could I pass on?

My wife and I are yin and yang in many respects, different personalities that somehow fit together, with a healthy cross-section of interests and opinions that intertwine. Yet, I don't think this adequately explains to a newly married couple how it leads to a relationship that endures. So where to begin?

*"How we spend our days is how we spend our lives. What we do with this hour, and that one, is what we are doing." — Annie Dillard*

As I grow older, I become more and more aware that to get the most out of life, you need to be present. You need to pay attention to the small things, the details of life, because they add up to something greater than their parts. They are the ingredients of a live well-lived.

This awareness means you cannot sleepwalk through life, you need to *engage* with life. And there's no place where this engagement is more vital, than with the regular, daily interactions you have with your spouse. In the edited text below, you'll see how I tried to explain this to the newlyweds Natasha and Ryan.

"As we're gathered here today, I'm sure you can feel it ... the sense of love in the air. Love for this beautiful day and setting. Love for the friends and family around you. Love for this beautiful couple.

In marriage ... and I speak from 25 years of experience...the key is to keep this love alive not just today, but tomorrow, and the day after that and the day after that. But how?

It's all about giving love.

Here's what I mean by that. It's about being the first one to touch ... the first one to hug ... the first one to kiss ... the first one to say I love you. It's about taking the initiative and expecting nothing in return.

Give love. Not with the expectation of getting love, but for the sheer joy of giving the love that is inside you as a gift. It is a limitless resource that can be given again and again.

Give love when you rise in the morning. When you come home from work. Before you go to sleep at night. Give love in the spaces in-between, whenever and wherever it feels appropriate.

I know, sometimes giving love can be hard. This is especially true when your spouse has had a bad day at work ... or is in a sour mood. At these moments, they may seem unlovable ... and feel unlovable themselves.

But that's when your wife or husband needs your support the most. That's when they need your love the most.

When we make giving love our focus, it somehow all works out. And we wind up getting the love we need in return.

When we remember to give love ... each day ... day after day_... the rest just takes care of itself."

## WEEK SIXTEEN / DAY 2: AWARENESS

# Are You Already Holding the Key to Happiness?

It's a given in life: We all want to be happy, all the time. Yet, the challenges that occur in our lives, whether it's issues at our job, with our finances, or with our spouse or kids, can often get in the way. But what if that isn't really the case?

What if the key to happiness is this simple: Do you want to be happy or not? Answer yes, and you have a life of happiness. Answer no and you don't.

The idea that our personal happiness is a choice made by us is put forth by Michael Singer in his book *The Untethered Soul*. He proposes that our happiness is based not on our external circumstances but on our state-of-mind.

Singer points out that when everything is going well in our lives, it's easy to be happy. But the moment something difficult happens, it's not so easy. When an unpleasant or problematic event upsets our personal apple cart, we get agitated, we worry, we grow melancholy. That's a tough way to live and this popular bumper-sticker line calls out the reason why:

SH*T HAPPENS

The guy behind the deli counter is rude to you. Someone cuts you off in traffic. Your water heater springs a leak. You come down with a nasty cold, don't get the promotion at work, have a fight with a significant other. All these things may happen and worse.

## THAT'S WHY YOU HAVE TO COMMIT TO HAPPINESS, REGARDLESS OF YOUR EXTERNAL CONDITIONS.

We are all born and we all die. What happens during the in-between time is up to us. We can choose to ride the peaks and valleys, the ups and downs, and let our level of happiness be determined by the roller coaster of life—or we can commit to living a happy life all the time. Again, it's easy to do this when things are going well. We need to keep this same commitment to happiness when things go south.

This means when something "bad" happens, we need to just let it go. It's there, it happened, deal with it and move on. Let it go.

*Time for a quick reality check.* By no means do I believe this is easy. In fact, it may only be possible if you have a defense mechanism in place for when bad things do happen. For some people, this involves repeating a positive affirmation. For others, it's remembering to breathe. It can also help if you engage in a regular meditative practice and have a mantra that can bring you back to a contented place.

According to Singer, the key to letting go is keeping your heart open to life. When we are stressed or upset, we often shut down to life. He reminds us that just like the body needs oxygen, the heart must remain open to let positive energy in. When your heart is closed, no energy can come in. You wallow in your own toxic stew. Singer offers the following advice:

> When you start to close, just question whether you're really willing to give up your happiness. If you learn to stay open all the time, great things will happen to you. You simply have to learn not to close.

The key is to take action the moment you feel like you want to close, when you feel yourself falling into the "woe is me" mode. That's the time to "just pick yourself up and affirm inwardly that you don't want to close, no matter what happens." You don't want your happiness to be conditional on other people or outside events. Again, from Singer:

> Things are going to happen to you, and you're going to feel the tendency to close. But you have the choice to either go with it or let it go. Your mind will tell you that it's not reasonable to stay open when these things happen. But you have limited time left in your life, and what's really not reasonable is to not enjoy life.

### YOU MIGHT THINK THIS IS EASIER SAID THAN DONE. I HEAR YOU.

But I think much of what Singer says dovetails with the philosophy of Viktor Frankl and his classic book *Man's Search for Meaning*. As a Jewish prisoner in a Nazi death camp, Frankl faced the harshest living conditions imaginable. Yet, while others around him deteriorated spiritually, Frankl persevered, somehow finding the good in the most deplorable of situations. In his words: "Everything can be taken from a man but one thing: the last of the human freedoms—to choose one's attitude in any given set of circumstances, to choose one's own way."

He repeats that sentiment here: "Our greatest freedom is the freedom to choose our attitude."

While imprisoned, Frankl came to this conclusion: "It did not really matter what we expected from life, but rather what life expected from us." It raises the question: *What does life expect from you?* Will you live this one precious life careening from one emotion to another—or with a commitment to happiness? The choice is yours.

# The Importance of Sharing the Wisdom You've Learned

What have you learned during your time here on earth? And who will you pass these lessons on to? The wisdom you've obtained becomes even more valuable when you pass it on to a young adult in your life, be it a son or daughter, niece or nephew, granddaughter or grandson. Scholar and author Arthur C. Brooks recommends you:

> Devote the back half of your life to serving others with your wisdom. Get old sharing the things you believe are most important. Excellence is always its own reward, and this is how you can be most excellent as you age.

While my daughter was still in college, I came to realize that the best way to communicate the life lessons I learned was not via long-winded, preachy speeches, but by sharing my hard-earned wisdom little by little, bit by bit. My source for these lessons: a personal journal I keep, where I jot down insights and "aha" moments as they come to me.

To this day, while I'll still cover the basics like "how is work?" and "is your car still running?", I'll sneak in a life lesson or two. Looking through several years of journal entries earmarked for my daughter, I saw that many of my conversation points return to familiar themes, often dealing with issues of character and being a better person. What follows are twelve of my favorites. Feel free to pass them on— or consider starting your own list.

**Twelve Life Lessons I Passed on to My Daughter.**

1. **Learn to trust your instincts.** It's the feeling you have in your gut that some call "the second brain." It can help guide you in making the right decisions and even steer you away from danger. Unless your head can come up with a very good reason to overrule your gut, learn to trust it.

2. **Don't force things to happen, let them happen naturally.** You can be ambitious but also be aware that the best opportunities are often right in front of you. Life has a funny way of bringing you the things you need. Keep your eyes open for them.

3. **Be fully present to the moments of your life.** In other words, put down your phone. Many life experiences only happen once—don't miss out on them.

4. **Give as much as you take.** Someone smile at you? Smile back. Receive a compliment? Give one in return. It's an unwritten law that the more you give to those around you, the more you will receive.

5. **"Build pockets of stillness into your life."** —Maria Popova. Don't rush through life without taking breaks. Learn to say no to some social events and schedule regular periods of "me time" to meditate, contemplate, or just be.

6. **"If you want to improve, be content to be thought foolish and stupid."** —Epictetus. Never pretend to know something when you don't. Ask questions. And when an uncomfortable situation arises, lean into it, don't shy away. It's when you'll often learn valuable lessons you can use another day.

7. **Be less reactionary.** When you find yourself in a situation that leaves you feeling stressed or hot under the collar, remember to take a breath. This momentary pause will allow you to

think before you act and can be the difference between saying something you'll regret and being a calm voice of reason.

8. **Sometimes you have to go with the flow.** Be flexible, things may not always work out exactly as you planned. That's okay. Reset yourself and move on.

9. **"Make peace with the fact saying 'no' often means trading popularity for respect."** —G McKeown. Learn to say no to any situation or activity that doesn't feel right and may put you, or others, in harm's way. If your intuition tells you it's not a good idea, it's probably not a good idea.

10. **"People will not remember what you said. They will always remember how you made them feel."** —Maya Angelou. In every conversation, be fully present. And make it about the other person, not about you. If they ask about you, ask about them. If they don't ask about you, ask about them.

11. **"Don't trip over what's behind you. Move ahead."** —Mika Brzezinski. Did you mess up something? No problem, as long as you learn from the experience. Failure is a necessary part of becoming wiser.

12. **Try to be better than you were the day before.** As musician Steve Earle once said, "each day is a new opportunity to get it right." Take stock at the end of each day, determining what went well and where you might be a little better tomorrow.

One thing I didn't mention: I consistently remind the young adult in my life to take care of their physical, emotional, and spiritual well-being. That means making time for exercise, getting enough sleep and eating right. Plus, unplugging from time to time to engage in the spiritual practice of their choice, like reading, yoga, or taking a hike in the woods.

## Not Sure of Your Path? Try This Prayer from Thomas Merton

Thomas Merton is perhaps the most influential Catholic author of our time, writing more than sixty books, including his best-selling autobiography, *The Seven Storey Mountain*. Yet, his spiritual path was a crooked one.

A graduate of Columbia University, Merton spent much of his early post-collegiate life partying in New York City. While he liked to spend his evenings drinking beer and hanging out at jazz clubs, a spiritual side began to emerge as well. He began reading religious texts, attending church, and after a late night out carousing with friends, he made the surprise announcement he was going to become a priest.

Merton's path was not that of an ordinary parish priest. In 1941, he decided to become a monk at the Abbey of Gethsemani, a Trappist monastery in the backwoods of Kentucky. He had just published his first book, but instead of this being the end of his writing career, Merton was encouraged by the monastery's abbot to continue writing, which he did prolifically.

Several years into his life as a monk, Merton tired of the communal life and, perhaps due to his celebrity, was allowed to spend part of his days in solitude in a wooded area on the monastery's grounds. He converted a garden shed, the size of a studio apartment, into his living quarters, and this space would become his home.

One might think that a man like Merton had his sh*t together, that as the years passed his belief in God and his conviction that he was on the right path would only strengthen. Yet in 1955, while spending time in seclusion at the abbey, Merton wrote a prayer (later published in the book *Thoughts in Solitude)*, that conveyed the thoughts of a man humble enough to know that he knew nothing for certain. It went like this:

> My Lord God,
>
> I have no idea where I am going.
>
> I do not see the road ahead of me.
>
> I cannot know for certain where it will end.
>
> Nor do I really know myself, and the fact that I think I am following your will does not mean that I am actually doing so.
>
> But I believe that the desire to please you does in fact please you.
>
> And I hope I have that desire in all that I am doing.
>
> I hope I will never do anything apart from that desire.
>
> And I know that if I do this you will lead me by the right road, though I may know nothing about it.
>
> Therefore I will trust you always though I may seem to be lost and in the shadow of death.
>
> I will not fear, for you are ever with me, and you will never leave me to face my perils alone.

It's the same kind of humility we might try to bring to our own lives, instead of allowing our ever-striving ego or societal norms inform us that our personal path is the right one. As the philanthropist and philosopher John Templeton wrote: "Our outlook is tremendously broadened when we approach life from an awareness of how little we yet know."

Templeton advised us against trying to solve problems through our own human efforts, without seeking spiritual guidance. He also made it clear that we shouldn't equate the humility of relying on a higher power to being passive or withdrawing from the world. It is a thought echoed by journalist David Brooks in his 2015 book *The Road to Character*: "As people become more dependent on God, their capacity for ambition and action increases. Dependency doesn't heed passivity, it breeds energy and accomplishment."

Might Merton's prayer of humility apply to our own lives? Might we be better served by asking for life guidance from a Divine source? Might this also be a better way to evaluate whether our current course is the right one? I can't say for sure, but will leave you with the thoughts of John Templeton:

> Prayer helps bring us in tune with the infinite. There is a real mystical power in prayer and it works. Through our times of prayer and conscious attachment with spiritual energy, we are increasing our own spiritual light.

**WEEK SIXTEEN / DAY 5: PRACTICE**

# Are You Giving Your Soul What It Wants?

Do you live life in touch with your innermost feelings? Or do you live strictly through your head, letting your mind call the shots? If you've been feeling a bit adrift lately—empty, down or direction-less—you may have lost touch with a vital part of yourself: the soul.

**THE FIRST THING TO DO IS RECOGNIZE THE SOUL, WHAT IT IS, AND THE ROLE IT PLAYS IN YOUR LIFE.**

I like to think of the body as a figurative home. Our spirits, the fanciful part of ourselves that dreams, imagines, and creates, lives in the well-lit attic. But our soul, the deepest part of our inner being, resides in the dimly lit basement. Like any basement, it also includes the foundation, the one on which our lives are built.

In an issue of the *New York Times Magazine*, the spiritual leader Ram Dass pointed out that we often ignore the soul, because we are entranced by the nonstop stream of thoughts entering our head. These thoughts engage the ego and until we stop long enough to break away from them, we don't recognize the soul. That's important, because it keeps us from the better part of ourselves. In his words: "The soul contains love, compassion, wisdom, peace and joy, but most people identify with the mind. You're not an ego. You're a soul."

We ignore the soul to our own detriment. David Brooks, writing in the *The Second Mountain*, reminds us that while powerful, the soul "is also reclusive. You can go years without really feeling the force of its yearning. But eventually the soul hunts you down."

Your life may be full and active with a never quite finished to-do list, but this busyness is not what the soul wants. If you are not satisfying the needs of the soul, Brooks tells us "there are spare moments when you vaguely or even urgently feel her presence." It can happen during a sleepless night, or even on a crowded street, when a vast hole in the center of your being makes itself known.

What does your soul want from you? Our souls are all different so the answer varies from person to person. But in general, Brooks says that:

> The soul yearns for righteousness, for fusion with the good.
> Socrates said that the purpose of life is the perfection of our

souls—to realize the goodness that the soul longs for. The soul demands your justification. What good have you served? For what did you come? What sort of person have you become?

Brooks says that in our modern world, we are too often caught up in the wants of the ego, the desire to "be in control" or to "impress the world." This is not what the soul, "the deeper self underneath," wants from us. He writes:

> Achievement, intelligence, the need for recognition, are wants of the ego. They do not fulfill the needs of the soul, which is aligned with the deepest yearnings of the heart and the pursuit of fulfillment and joy.

Writing in *Original Self, Living with Paradox and Originality*, Thomas Moore digs a little deeper into the wants of the soul. As he has shown in a dozen books on the subject, Moore has seemingly intuited the inner workings of the soul and what makes us tick. He points out:

> The soul has its own set of rules, which are not the same as those of life. Unlike the steady progress of history, the events of the soul are cyclic and repetitive. Familiar themes come round and round. The past is more important than the future. The living and dead have equal roles. Emotions and the sense of meaning are paramount. Pleasures are deep, and pain can reach the very foundations of our existence.

In a sentiment echoed by both Ram Dass and David Brooks, Moore also fears that we have lost touch with our souls, our lives "getting lost in the busyness of the world." When the soul cries out for attention, we misdiagnose what we are feeling:

> Today many people live the external life exclusively, and when the inner world erupts or stirs, they rush to a therapist or druggist for help. Often they have no idea what is happening, because they have been so cut off by the deep self. Their

own soul is so alien to them that they are unaware of what is going on outside the known realm of fact.

How do we find and connect with the soul? Moore points out that in the past, before technology came to dominate our waking lives, we had ways to connect:

> Former methods of keeping in touch with the inner life have gone out of mode. Diaries, letters, and deep conversation help focus attention on developments and materials that lie beneath the surface. Only 100 years ago, people kept elaborate and detailed diaries and notebooks. We seem to have left behind these methods of reflection.

## WHAT CAN WE DO TODAY TO ENGAGE THE SOUL AND HEAR ITS YEARNINGS?

Moore advises us that the key to cultivating a rich internal life is to "simplify the externals." In his words:

> For many, turning off the TV would be an act of simplifying that might have magical results. Staying home, instead of going out, can work magic. Not buying something, not going somewhere, and not endlessly watching our phones can each be an effective application of the simplicity rule.

There's a phrase we use in my home called "hunkering down," as in "we're hunkering down this weekend." That means avoiding social engagements, dimming the lights, enjoying a home-cooked meal and bottle of wine, limiting the use of our phones. Hunkering down can also mean spending time in nature, walking a beach or a tree-lined neighborhood. These quiet moments, breaks from the busyness of life, give us the time needed for contemplation and reflection. We might ask ourselves:

- Where is my life headed?

- Am I following my passions?
- What am I yearning for?
- Do I need to make any course corrections to put my life on a different path?

Moore says that if we have not always been smart about the decisions we've made in the past, solely using our intellect to make important life choices, it may make sense to follow the lead of our souls:

> We may allow our decisions to rise from a deeper place, a place lower than rationale intelligence ... using our interests, intuition and even divination. Doing the prudent thing may prevent us from following our passions. It may overrun our intuitions and may give us the illusion of being virtuous when life is asking us to explore territory lying beneath the horizon.

Ask yourself: What is the soul asking of me?

## WEEK SIXTEEN / DAY 6: INNER WORK

# Six Steps to Realizing the "Christ Consciousness" Within You

Are you familiar with the term "Christ consciousness"? It's also known as higher consciousness and plays into the idea that you actually have two types of consciousness. There's the ordinary consciousness or awareness that's part of our everyday lives—and a more profound type of awareness, or a higher consciousness, that has the power to put you in touch with God.

While the idea of higher consciousness dates back to the Bhagavad Vita, which was written about the time Jesus of Nazareth walked on this earth, Christ consciousness is more a product of modern-day spirituality. It was a major theme of the book *I Am the Word* by Paul Selig. In a nutshell, Selig explained it like this:

> While most people operate at a lower energy, guided by their ego, others are able to tap into a higher energy or their higher self. This energy is known as Christ consciousness. When you engage with life at this level, you resonate at a higher frequency. You realize that God is the frequency of every cell in your being. You know that God is in everything and everyone.

Similarly, the American clairvoyant Edgar Cayce referred to Christ consciousness as "the Christ pattern" and described it as "the awareness within each soul, imprinted in pattern on the mind and waiting to be awakened, of the soul's oneness with God."

It's important to note that Christ consciousness is not purely a Christian thing. Its name is merely the recognition that Jesus achieved this state in his lifetime—and that you and I can achieve this same kind of spiritual maturity, a feeling we are at one with God, regardless of our religious or spiritual affiliation. Anyone can be "a conduit with the divine."

I would sum up (and greatly simplify) Selig's core teaching in *I Am the Word* like this: People function at different frequencies or energies. Most people operate at a lower energy, guided by their ego or false self, while others are able to tap into a higher frequency or energy. This energy is known as Christ consciousness. Here are a few other key points Selig mentions:

- When you set the intention to vibrate at a higher frequency, your frequency changes and the feeling in your energy field will shift.
- Each time you progress in the higher frequency, you retain the information and the consciousness that you have come to.
- Once this change has been made, your feelings in your body will begin to shift as you begin to exist in a higher frequency.

Now it's one thing to read a description of Christ consciousness and imagine what this state of mind must feel like—it's quite another to have the experience for yourself. To me, it sounds a lot like the runner's high I sometimes get after a vigorous run. It might be the feeling you get after a long meditation session or an invigorating hot yoga class. But is this the same as Christ consciousness?

Fortunately, Selig provides an easy visualization exercise that can help "activate" the Christ consciousness within us. I've broken down a passage from the book into six steps and have made some revisions for clarity. (Note that Selig does not take credit for his work. His book is a channeled text and comes from an unnamed universal source of wisdom that he is able to tap into.)

Ready to start? Before you begin the exercise, stop for a moment. I believe that to do this right, you've got to be in the proper state-of-mind. Calm, relaxed and sitting in a comfortable chair, as far away from the noise and distractions of the outside world as possible. Read the six steps a few times so you're aware of what they are and can move freely from step to step.

## Six Steps to Realizing Christ Consciousness

1. Turn your attention to the center of your heart. Imagine that in the very center there is a light, a burning. This aspect of the self, living between your breasts, is alive.
2. In your heart, begin to activate this spark, this piece of light. Feel it begin to flicker and glow.
3. Feel the radiating heat coming from the light at your center. When you feel this, acknowledge it, give thanks for it. This heat in your heart is a sign of the Christ consciousness within you.

4. Allow the light to fill you and become you. Imagine it filling your entire body. There's no effort involved because the light does the work.

5. As the light fills your body, feel yourself becoming aligned to a higher frequency, the source of all that is good in this world. You may call this source God. Become one with this source.

6. Feel the expanded energy field around you and the vibration of the Christ consciousness within you. Know that this expansion of light is your light, available to you at all times.

———

*"God loves things by becoming them."*
*— Richard Rohr*

———

These words from the American author and Franciscan friar Richard Rohr really struck a chord with me. They describe what happens when we achieve Christ consciousness. In his 2019 book *The Universal Christ*, Rohr says that the life of "Jesus was meant to declare that humanity has never been separate from God." We have always been one.

Rohr goes on to say, "When we recover this fundamental truth, faith becomes less about proving Jesus was God and more about learning to recognize the Creator's presence all around us and in everyone we meet." There is no separation between us and God because, like Jesus, we are one and the same. God is in us. We are in God.

## WEEK SIXTEEN / DAY 7: CONTEMPLATION

# A Crash Course in the Language of God

From the story of Moses to passages found in the gospels of John and Luke, the Bible is filled with stories of people claiming to hear the voice of God. Yet today, most of us would be suspicious of anyone who claimed that God had audibly talked to them. We might believe they were lying or mistaken, perhaps even cuckoo. Which got me thinking:

### DOES GOD STILL TALK TO US? IF YES, HOW DO WE TALK TO GOD?

If you're like me, you may occasionally feel the presence of God. It's the suspicion that there's a powerful essence beyond ourselves, that exists both in us and around us. But the feeling can be fleeting. It's easy to forget, especially at our lowest points, that God is always with us. Thomas V. Morris, writing in *The Hidden God*, explains God's presence this way:

> God is omnipresent, pervasive of all reality, and infinite. There are no divine boundaries. What seems to be a total absence of the divine is only an illusion produced by the reality of his all-encompassing presence.

So how do we communicate with this "all-encompassing" presence? First, we would need to know God's language. And as it turns out, we do. The language is universal because it is not made up of words but is the universal language of the heart. This language cannot be spoken but can be sensed within us. It is the language of silence.

**A CRASH COURSE IN THE LANGUAGE OF GOD.**

In the book *Finding God in the Body*, Ben Riggs tells us that God is always talking to us, but it is a silent conversation. He goes on to say we should not mistake this silence for proof of God's absence. Riggs backs up this idea with the following quote from Trappist monk Father Thomas Keating: "God's first language is silence. God still speaks, but people do not know how to hear the sound of silence."

Riggs expands on this with an anecdote involving Mother Teresa. She once said that "When I pray, I just listen." A puzzled reporter queried her about this statement, asking "What does God say, Mother? What do you hear from God?" Mother Teresa's response: "God says nothing. He just listens."

**BUT HOW DO WE HEAR THE SOUND OF SILENCE?**

Toward the beginning of his book *The Silence of God, Meditations on Prayer*, James P. Carse writes of his initial dismay at discovering that God was silent. This silence did not sit well with the author and for years he looked for proof of God's existence. In his words:

> What I experienced, and experienced repeatedly, is the silence of God. For many years, this was a distressing matter for me. I did not consider it an experience, but the absence of an experience.

Yet, in time, Carse came to see the positive spiritual value of God's silence. He writes "… in an encounter with divine reality we do not hear a voice but acquire a voice, and the voice we acquire is our own." In other words, when God speaks, God speaks through us.

There are several passages in *The Silence of God* that explain this process and I share Carse's wisdom below, strung together in a loose narrative.

- The silence of God is everywhere.

- It is not a silence into which God has disappeared, but a silence in which God is remarkably present.
- God comes to us first as a listener, not a speaker. There is not a conceivable human setting in which God is not present, listening.
- God does not come when you call. God is there, then you call.
- You must move toward God from the heart, then God will respond. God will first wait until you do what it is possible for you to do within yourself, even if that action is exceedingly modest.
- If you speak from the heart, God listens.
- God does not respond to us; we respond to God. God is already silent and does not become silent when we speak.
- To speak from the heart is to ask and to receive at the same time. Whomever you speak to from your heart you receive in your heart. You will have God in your heart—in the very act of asking.
- It is not theology or philosophy, but only your heart that will lead you to God.

To summarize:

1. In silence, we sense the presence of God.
2. When we sense this presence, we can speak to God.
3. God listens.
4. God responds through our own voice and actions.

# Acknowledgments

Almost all my writing is a solo project. I hole up and write in my office, a comfy chair on the porch, or seated at the back of a bus. But this process doesn't happen in a vacuum, and I am forever indebted to many others for their ideas, inspiration, and support. This book would not have been possible without the guidance of my editor and friend Kate Sheehan Roach. She helped convince me that my weekly Patheos columns had the makings of a book, brainstormed the format with me, and connected me with my publisher—Wildhouse Publishing, where thanks go to Wesley Wildman, Molly Silverstein, and Melody Stanford Martin who created the beautiful cover and interior design. Thanks also to the team at Patheos, especially Alan Crandall and Travis Henry, for their ongoing support.

A huge thanks to my friends Sue Hetzel and Peter Meade for giving the book an eagle-eyed read as we approached deadline. To Laney and Jade, who continue to teach me daily about the importance of love, patience, and kindness. I am also tremendously grateful for the wisdom and generosity of my fellow authors, including Philip Goldberg, Karen Brailsford, Matthew Fox, Eiman Al Zaabi, Dana Drake, and Tom Stella. Last but not least, I extend my deep gratitude to Thomas Moore, whose ground-breaking work on the soul continues to inspire me, as it will inspire others for generations to come.